T0281836

Luftwaffe Bomber to Nightfighter

The Memoirs of a Knight's Cross Pilot

Volume I

Edited and annotated by Thomas Baumert

Foreword by James Holland

Greenhill Books

Luftwaffe Nightfighter: The Memoirs of a Knight's Cross Pilot, Volume I

Greenhill Books

First published by Greenhill Books, 2024
Greenhill Books, c/o Pen & Sword Books Ltd,
47 Church Street, Barnsley, S. Yorkshire, S70 2AS
For more information on our books, please visit
www.greenhillbooks.com, email contact@greenhillbooks.com
or write to us at the above address.

Publishing History
German-language edition published in 2024 by
VDM Heinz Nickel, Flechsig Verlag,
Kasernenstraße 6–10, D-66462 Zweibrücken, Germany
www.VDMedien24.com

CIP data records for this title are available from the British Library

ISBN 978-1-78438-816-4

Typeset by JCS Publishing Services Ltd
Typeset in 12/15pt Minion Pro
Printed and bound in Great Britain by CPI Group (UK) Ltd,
Croydon, CRO 4YY

Contents

Foreword

Saturday, 27 November 1941. Leutnant Arnold Döring and his four other crew are flying their Heinkel 111 bomber towards the Soviet city of Kashira, some 120 kilometres south of Moscow. It's been just over five months since the Germans invaded the Soviet Union, which means the campaign has already been going on two months longer than had been planned. Even so, the Germans are closing in towards the capital city; the weather is against the attackers but they're so close now. Since early morning on 21 June, the start of Operation 'Barbarossa', they've advanced more than 1,400 kilometres, captured over two million Red Army troops and captured among the most important cities in the Soviet Union.

And the Luftwaffe, the German air force, have supported this enormous campaign on the ground, every step of the way. Today, Döring, and the rest of the 9th Staffel of Kampfgeschwader 53, are carrying out yet another mission in support of the troops below. The crews have been briefed that their lead army units are nearing Kashira and their task is to help secure the flanks to the south of the city and also carry out reconnaissance. It's filthy weather – there's snow on the ground, the temperature is plummeting and there's plenty of cloud about so visibility is poor. These are far from ideal flying conditions, but the Luftwaffe has a firm press-on attitude and the crews know and accept this. Tighten the straps and fly on, come what may, is the order of the day.

They've also learned to take off and fly individually in such conditions rather than operate in formation. This makes sense as there's no point risking crashing into one another for lack of decent vision, but it does mean Döring and his crew are very much on their own. He's used to it by now, however, and trusts implicitly his crew, especially his navigator and bomb-aimer, Richard Wawarek.

They see flak bursts off their starboard wing but aren't bothered by this; it's a way away and no danger to them. Instead, they follow the road that links Serpukhov, a little way to the west, with Kashira. There's not much going on until south of Kashira they spot a melee of fighters over the battlefront to their south. They're flying low and can see their own panzers on the move so turn and head northwards back towards the town. The cockpit of the Heinkel is a large Perspex cone with the navigator–bomb-aimer sat right up front ahead of the pilot. The visibility this offers is excellent and suddenly Wawarek spies Red Army vehicles below, grouped together, but well camouflaged near a number of houses. Not a soul seems to be stirring but Döring swings the Heinkel around and decides to drop a few bombs on this peaceful little scene and see whether they can stir up the hornet's nest.

Down their bombs whistle and no sooner have they detonated than a furious anthill of activity is disturbed down amidst the snow below. Döring loops round again. Trucks are frantically driving off, but he drops more bombs while his gunners, Wawarek included, pound targets with the combination of machine-guns and cannons the Heinkel carries; that they can do so is testimony to just how low they're flying. The Heinkel might be a twin-engine bomber, but over the Eastern Front it's being used as a ground-attack fighter as well. In moments, houses are on fire, then soon the entire village, it seems, becomes engulfed in flames. Only once they've dropped all their 'eggs' and hosed the area thoroughly, do they turned for home, although they soon fly into heavy flak. Tracers are also hurtling past them. A fragment of an exploding shell hits the fuselage with a dull thud and so Döring makes for the clouds and a cloak of invisibility. Once clear, they dip below the cloud bank again so they can mark up any further features on the map then eventually they set course for their base. 'Once we've crossed over the front line Richard extends his congratulations to me,' notes Döring. 'I look at him in surprise when it dawns on me that I've just completed my hundredth enemy operation.'

British bomber crews in RAF Bomber Command were expected to complete one thirty-mission tour, then, after a stint instructing, a second of twenty, then no more. American bomber crews flew different numbers depending on what stage they were flying in the war and which theatre, but for most in the Eighth Air Force, for example, the standard was twenty-five and later thirty missions. Admittedly, German bomber crews were not generally flying long-distance operations, but even so, a hundred missions in five months was a huge amount. Much was expected of all aircrew during the war, but there's no denying the Luftwaffe expected more than almost any other combatant nation.

The Luftwaffe also developed and was constructed in a different way to the Allied air forces, and bomber crews were expected to carry out a far greater variety of missions. Sometimes it might be strategic operations to hit a specific city – such as Moscow – but more often than not, over the Soviet Union, at any rate, they might be flying ground-attack missions and armed reconnaissance, directly supporting the troops on the ground. Döring's extraordinary diary reflects this varied and incredibly intense combat flying, laying bare, with graphic detail, the relentless nature of operations. Day after day, he finds himself sent out to bomb Red Army troops, or bridges, or villages and towns and even shipping, which, in July 1942, he attacked on the mighty Rover Volga – sinking two vessels in the process.

And it is these operations with which he is primarily concerned in his daily jottings, each recording innumerable close shaves. Twice he is forced to crash-land in circumstances where severe maiming, if not death, appear likely, and yet he and his crew somehow seem to emerge unscathed. There are hair-raising night operations, landings in thickening snow, repeated encounters with enemy aircraft and intense flak. An engine gets hit, the fuselage is peppered, a hole is blown in a wing, and yet every time he manages to nurse his repeatedly stricken Heinkel back to base. Many others are not so lucky and Döring charts most of those who are shot down – sometimes in vivid detail – or who fail to return.

The diary starts on the eve of Barbarossa in June 1941, the German invasion of the Soviet Union and, at the time, the largest military operation ever mounted in history. Döring was twenty-three years old at the time and although he had passed through flying school the previous autumn, the launch of the invasion sees him flying his first operational sortie. This is something very eagerly anticipated by Döring, who is itching to get into action – and curiously, his enthusiasm for flying barely seems to diminish as the diary progresses. He's clearly an exceptional and instinctive pilot, and fearless too. Many in the war kept diaries as a means of unburdening internal fears, stresses and anxieties, but there is no such evidence of this with Döring, who remains undaunted by all that is flung at him. Occasionally, he admits the action is a little intense and suggests it is time to get out of the fray and head home but there is no sense of him suffering from combat fatigue or any obvious dampening of spirits. Rather, he appears utterly imperturbable and, if anything, revels in the excitement and intense drama.

Nor is there much pause for introspection. We get only fleeing glimpses of life on the ground – there is a scene in which he is awoken with a bucket of icy water and much tomfoolery follows, and a touching scene when one of the aircrew hears he has become a father, but otherwise the diary focuses almost entirely on the experience of flying. That he and his crew are responsible for killing many Red Army troops and civilians alike, destroying numerous buildings, villages and towns, prompts no regret; rather, these episodes are recounted with immense relish. Once, whilst forced to ditch an aircraft en route back to Warsaw, he meets a Jewish lad who helps them, but he makes no further comment about this. There is no sense that he is politically motivated, although he is contemptuous of Bolsheviks and clearly has an innate belief in the superiority of the Luftwaffe over the Red Army air force. Photos show a remarkably good-looking and fresh-faced young man.

Because Döring writes about his flying experiences with so little regard to his own safety or well-being – physical or mental – it is easy to think the Luftwaffe were in the driving seat throughout the year and a bit featured in this first volume of his diaries. In fact, the Luftwaffe's planners had seriously under-estimated the huge numbers of Soviet aircraft or their ability to produce more. It was certainly true the Luftwaffe secured total mastery of the air over the front line in the opening weeks of Barbarossa, destroying a staggering 3,176 Soviet aircraft on the ground by the end of June 1941, so after only nine days of fighting. Most of these, however, were obsolescent aircraft and the losses amongst experienced Red Army pilots and aircrew was comparatively low. Even with the move of much of Soviet industry to the Urals, more than 650 kilometres east of Moscow, and the disruption this caused to productivity, the Russians was still substantially out-producing Germany in aircraft in 1941 – all the while with newer, more modern aircraft which were correspondingly tougher opposition for the Luftwaffe.

By contrast, the Luftwaffe began Barbarossa with only 2,995 aircraft, of which just 2,225 were combat ready. This might sound like a lot, but to support a 2,000-kilometre front it was nothing like enough and meant that they had fewer aircraft than when they invaded France and the Low Countries in May 1940. The shortage of aircraft is not something Döring makes much comment about, but by the end of 1941 and into the following year, he and his colleagues are regularly flying three operational sorties a day. This amount of flying would be unthinkable within the Allied air forces and was ultimately counter-productive because of the wear and tear on both aircraft and aircrew alike. At one point, the Staffel is reduced to just four aircraft and it the best and most experienced pilots who get to fly these; but in doing so, those higher up the chain were risking over-flying their most precious jewels: the aircrew themselves. Few were as phlegmatic and seemingly impervious to the stresses and strains of combat flying as Döring.

At the same time, the repeated moves, ever closer to the front, placed these Luftwaffe units in great danger from being attacked in turn by Red Army air forces and put a greater strain on logistics. Again, Döring never really complains about this except for occasional comments about making a bed of straw rather than face an assault by bed-bugs in the cots they are given. Inevitably, though, these moves put further strain on the overused German air force. 'The constant movement of flying formations,' noted one Luftwaffe fighter pilot of this period, 'usually without adequate ground personnel, resulted in such bad servicing that a Luftflotte [air fleet] had often on a sector of about 400 km only 10–12 serviceable fighter aircraft.' It was a similar picture for the bomber formations, which required even more servicing. This picture of a Luftwaffe increasingly battling too many expectations and demands is there in Döring's diary but implied rather than explicit.

This volume ends in the summer of 1942, by which time he and his trusty crew have been transferred from KG53 to the famous KG55 'Kondor Legion'. It's a remarkable contribution to our understanding of the air war over the Eastern Front, and for all the gung-ho and occasional savagery of Döring's daily scribblings, it is hard not to admire his irrepressible spirit and obvious courage. Clearly, he was a truly remarkable young man and his diaries are all the more fascinating for the extraordinary extent of the relentless combat he witnesses and to which he contributes with such relish.

James Holland

Translator's Note

Unlike memoirs by many other former Wehrmacht soldiers which are often written retrospectively, in hindsight and with the passage of time invariably changing memories to suit contemporary thinking, *Luftwaffe Nightfighter* (published in German as *Meine Erlebnisse*) is an unembellished, honest and meticulous record in real-time. Moving swiftly from one geographic location to another, from one operation to the next, the diarist mainly uses the present tense and short sentences, placing the reader in the midst of the air battle raging on the Eastern Front during the Second World War.

Luftwaffe Nightfighter, therefore, reads not so much as a carefully crafted narrative but rather as a log-book, with Döring making no pretences to be reflective. He offers us a collection of thrilling action-packed snapshots, not introspective musings. The language echoes this, with Döring reporting on the weather, engineering and pilot skills and sorties – all conveying a detached professionalism instead of a description of emotions, moral scruples, fear or indeed political belief.

While the reader might be able to hear at the beginning of Volume I the lieutenant's wry humour, understatements and facetious comments about the enemy, his boisterous language changes with the decline of the Luftwaffe's success and Nazi Germany slipping into disastrous defeat. With the Luftwaffe's changing fate, it is the brevity of Döring's sentences, rather than actual language which make us listen up. Short sentences which previously might have reflected the pilot simply following orders now may point to perhaps Döring suppressing or omitting something. Perhaps it was fear or hidden doubts?

Aircraft in the sky create distance, of course, and have us see the war and the world below literally from a bird's eye view. This holds true for the crew, the pilot and, by extension, the reader. Finding ourselves high above the ground, we miss the atrocities committed down below. With that, we also fail to hear the language of famine, torture, death, destruction and human tragedy – we do not hear the screams, see the blood, smell the stench or feel the pain. Instead, we learn the vocabulary pertaining to aircraft engineering, the state-of-the art armaments, strategy and individual prowess applied in manoeuvring machinery and bombs.

This distance, therefore, creates the impression of Döring as an emotionally detached, professional pilot of the Luftwaffe rather than a man of considered political beliefs, emotional depth or indeed conscience.

Aiming to retain the informality of the diarist's personal entries and the colloquial style in which he often omits pronouns or only jots down abbreviated sentences without adhering to grammatical rules, I decided to convey this in the English translation by contractions and the spoken form – after all, Döring speaks directly to his diary: 'Nichts wie weg von hier' ('We've got no choice but clear out'), 'Kann mir nur recht sein' ('as far as I'm concerned').

For German and cities then under Soviet rule, I have maintained Döring's spelling, e.g. Orsha, unless the city is particularly well known by its English equivalent, e.g. Munich.

My notes or additions to the German edition's notes are prefaced by *TN*. Simple explanations of terms or abbreviations are inserted in the text in square brackets.

Editor's Foreword

With nearly eighty years having passed since the end of the Second World War, one would not expect a new eye-witness account to surface, and certainly not one that would prove a relevant and enriching addition to the current body of literature on military history. And yet occasionally it does happen – and the war diaries penned by Arnold Döring are a case in point. Not only have these not been published before today, but they represent one of the most significant memoirs ever written by a military pilot and will, without doubt, make for fascinating reading for all those interested in this type of warfare. No other first-hand report presents both an exhaustive account including detailed technical data and vivid, even poignant, snapshots of events[1] and, by the same token and much to the delight of non-technical readers, offers a well-crafted story. This is all thanks to Döring, who turns out to be just as gifted a diarist during lulls in the fighting as he was talented a pilot during times of action. The latter is probably the single most important reason why this book stands out from most other memoirs covering active service during the war. Additionally, the palpable tension felt during the air attacks retains its immediacy throughout the diary, from the entries dating from Döring's first sorties as a fighter pilot to his last ones as a nightfighter. This holds true of both *Wilde Sau* sorties on single-engine aircraft and *Zahme Sau* sorties on twin-engine nightfighters.[2] These plus the occasional day and bombing missions made up Döring's impressive total of 392 aerial attacks,[3] earning him as early as March 1943 the Front Flying Clasp of the

Luftwaffe in Gold with Pennant. It is fair to say that no other memoir covers such a broad spectrum of missions across such a wide range of aircraft types apart from the one by Hajo Herrmann[4] of the Jagdgeschwader 300, who was Döring's superior and with whom our diarist would remain in close contact well after the war had ended.

Döring's biography is remarkable not only because of the high number of his achievements but also because of their sheer significance, borne out by the fact that on 17 April 1945 he was decorated with the prestigious Knight's Cross of the Iron Cross. Because confirmation of this award was held up due to the turmoil reigning at the time, news of this honour never reached the squadron and Döring would only come across the information two decades later when he was serving in the Bundeswehr.[5] In summary, Döring's wartime memories are a veritable treat for all those fascinated by military history in general and more specifically by aviation history.

Döring wrote his reports using a fountain pen and traditional notebooks which he had properly bound after the war. The first volume, based on his longer manuscript and depicting his years as a fighter pilot is entitled *Meine Erlebnisse im Kampf gegen den Bolschewismus* (My Experiences Fighting Bolshevism). The second volume, a shorter text containing his memories of his training and sorties as a nightfighter, were kept in a plain black card-bound booklet. His personally signed *ex libris* sticker features on the inside cover of both the first and the second volume. Döring dedicated his diary to his crew, three of whom did not survive the war.[6] Their names were:

Unteroffizier Richard Wawere[c]k (observer)[7]
Feldwebel Richard Brösing (aerial gunner)[8]
Feldwebel Karl Krupitza (aerial mechanic)[9]
Feldwebel Anton ('Toni') Grimmer (aerial radio operator)[10]
Oberfeldwebel Georg Eberhardt (aerial radio operator)[11]

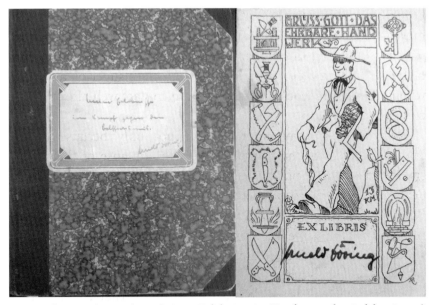

Cover of Döring's war diary (*Meine Erlebnisse im Kapf gegen den Bolshweismus*) and his hand-signed *ex libris* sticker.

In listing each sortie while elaborating on all aspects of the missions, Döring apparently intended to go into as much minute detail as possible. Supporting this assertion is his habit of not only dating each entry, which is customary for most diarists, but also consecutively, diligently numbering the missions he had been tasked with. As the number steadily grew, in tandem with the advance by Nazi Germany, it eventually became impossible for Döring to keep this up on a daily basis. He thus occasionally resorts to summarising several flights in a single entry and sometimes even skips one mission or another, focusing instead on how they happened, why, and what the results were. This, in his mind, deserved special attention, not a perhaps cumbersome report of exactly how many sorties had actually been undertaken. At times he would seamlessly pick up from where he had broken off the report and list the subsequent attacks by enumerating them sequentially.[12]

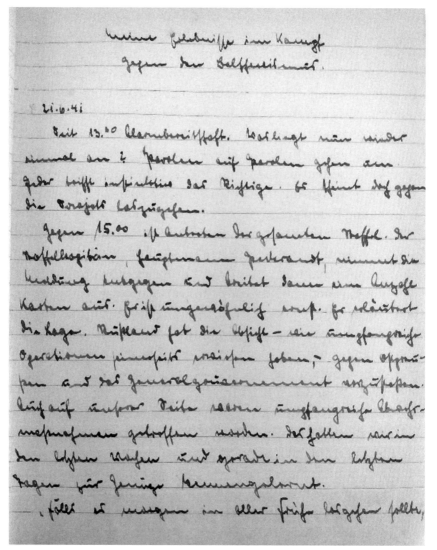

First page of Döring's war diary.

By editing or tightening the text with respect to redundant or routine missions, Döring allows the reader to gain a clearer understanding of the events. What he offers us is a precise, extensive war diary filled with suspense and excitement, and as such it distinguishes itself from other war memoirs by German pilots. Furthermore, Döring writes from the perspective of a bomber pilot – a different ilk from aviators flying Stukas or fighter planes – a breed that are underrepresented in the military history literature.

The diaries open with the start of the battles on the Eastern Front – his first entry is repeatedly and extensively quoted in specialist books on the subject[13] – and end with an entry on 14 August 1942, with the first part of Volume 1 covering the period from 21 June to 7 October 1941 and the second part covering the period from 8 October to 16 December 1941. During that time Döring was part of the Luftwaffe bomber wing Kampfgeschwader 53 'Legion Condor'. After a break of six months, with the unit being recalled to Ansbach for rest and refit, followed by Döring attending a bomber training course in Anklam, he then transferred to Kampfgeschwader 55; he returns to his diary on 10 June 1942 and continues with his entries until 14 August.

The originally planned fourth part starting with 15 August apparently did not materialise, or I simply have not been able to get my hands on it yet.[14] However, I would venture the guess that my first assumption might be the correct one as there are several pointers to support this. For example, even during Döring's lifetime extensive references were made by other historians to missions flown by Döring and his squad, all mentioned in the first three parts of Volume 1 as well as to events referenced in the diary entries in Volume 2 – his missions with Jagdgeschwader 300 and Nachtjagdgeschwader 2 and 3. No references can be found, however, to any entries which would have belonged to the fourth part, and surely Döring's missions during the battle of Stalingrad (especially the three nightfighter operations flying a modified He 111[15]) would have warranted a quotation. Yet another clue is Döring's handwritten structure for his war diary (see image on the following page), which omits the end date. Furthermore, there is the question of why, if he had the booklets comprising that fourth section available, Döring did not have these bound along with the other manuscripts, unless perhaps they were too bulky.

Döring's handwritten Index of Part I of his war diary without a final date inserted for Part IV.

However, the amount of material in our possession proves to be more than enough to make for a complete and honest account of the two offensives against the Soviet Union. Narrated by a German fighter pilot who lived through them, the text does not shy away from the facts – the attack on civilians using aircraft armaments is referred to explicitly – but at the same time it does not delve into critical reflections with respect to any military issues; certainly this holds true with regard to political questions, probably intentionally. In Döring's second volume we read his request that it 'should exclusively be a memory of nightfighters', with the term encompassing all types of fighter planes, and the reader is advised to keep this appeal in mind when reading this first volume as well. Respect for the author and his principles governed my editorial work on the two volumes and I inserted only the occasional annotation, explanation or literature reference, primarily intended to clarify for the reader the strategic and military circumstances within which Döring and his crewmembers carried out the operations. Juxtaposed with Döring's own prevailing optimism concerning the outcome of the campaign, these comments are, of course, written with the benefit of hindsight and they will inevitably put a damper on Döring's enthusiastic entries.

Finally, I would like to thank the Döring family for their permission to publish the manuscripts of their father or, respectively, grandfather, and for their support, patience and generosity in sharing their story. My thanks also go to my publishers Flechsig and Greenhill for printing these two volumes. I also want to thank my wife Laura who graciously accepted that I spend so many hours in the company of Döring's manuscripts. I dedicate this first volume to Frenz Tomasko in dear friendship; and to the memory of my father who in 1956 helped build up a new, democratic Luftwaffe.

Madrid, 20 November 2023
Thomas Baumert

Introduction

Arnold Ulrich Fritz Döring was born on 29 January 1918 in Heilsberg, East Prussia, which today is Polish Lizbark Warmiňsli. He was the second eldest of four children of Anton Döring, a schoolmaster, and Hertha (née Dost).[1] In that year the county which belonged to Warmia was celebrating its centenary, though the town's history actually goes back several hundred years. One would assume that, with the world war still raging, celebrations must have been muted.

Arnold Döring with his two brothers, Hans-Werner and Klaus. Later, a sister by the name of Ilse completed the family (Source: Döring).

City view of Heilsberg
(Source: https://commons.wikimedia.org/wiki/File:Heilsberg,_
Ostpreu%C3%9Fen_-_Stadtansicht_(Zeno_Ansichtskarten).jpg).

The hussar monument located in the market square of Heilsberg (Source:
https://commons.wikimedia.org/wiki/File:Heilsberg_Hussarendenkmal.jpg).

Aerial photograph of Heilsberg, 1932
(Source: https://ansichtskarten-lexikon.de/ak-183070.html).

Nestled within a loop of the Alle river, Heilsberg was until 1945 famous for being one of the most beautiful cities in East Prussia.² Its Gothic church of Saints Peter and Paul with its 66-metre steeple rising high above the rest of the town's buildings was noted as one of the major architectural landmarks of the area, along with a castle built in 1350 as the other grand historical sight. This fortress belonged to the Teutonic Order and was the seat of the Warmian bishops until 1795; one of the bishops, Lukas Watzenrode, was looked after there by Nicolaus Kopernicus, his nephew and private physician from 1504 to 1510.

The Langstrasse was the principal axis, with the city hall at its far end leading into the marketplace. After several fires had practically reduced the city hall to ashes, it was decided to replace it with an equestrian statue as a war monument and thus the Husarendenkmal was inaugurated on 18 August 1913 by the general of the cavalry, August von Mackensen, an honorary citizen of the town and erstwhile captain of the 1. Leib-Husaren-Regiment. The occasion marked the centenary of the German campaign, with the monument gracing the marketplace until it was destroyed during the Second World War.³

It is entirely possible that Döring was particularly drawn to aviation activities and flight operations because of his background, in particular his great-uncle on his mother's side, Hermann Ganswindt, the well-known German spaceflight scientist.⁴ There was an even earlier connection too – one wonders if Döring had a hereditary inclination towards a career as a fighter and bomber pilot: he was also a relative of Lieutenant Otto Parschau,⁵ an Ace, one of the 'Alter Adler'⁶ as they are known in German airflight history, the holder of pilot licence No. 455.

While still a student at the Heilsberger Gymnasium, Döring took part in glider training programmes held in Rossitten and Sensburg and obtained the A, B and C glider licences. After graduating from the Oberschule für Junge, the young flier volunteered with the 4. Fliegerersatzabteilung 10 in Neukuhren – the Aviator

3

Hermann Ganswindt (Source: https://en.wikipedia.org/wiki/Hermann_
Ganswindt#/media/File:Johann_Hermann_Ganswindt.jpg).

Otto Parschau's 'green' machine, armed with a synchronised Parabellum
MG 14, the precursor of the Fokker EI/EII monoplane (Source: https://
en.wikipedia.org/wiki/Otto_Parschau#The_Green_Machine_(A.16/15).

Two related and highly decorated fighter aces of the two world wars:
Pour le Mérite Lieutenant Otto Parschau and Lieutenant Arnold Döring,
recipient of the Knight's Cross of the Iron Cross.

Replacement Department 10 – where he was first trained to become
ground crew, then moved on to military pilot training with an
attachment to 3. Staffel, Jagdgeschwader 1 (a special fighter wing
operating primarily on the Western Front) from 23 March to 11 June
1939 and to the Schulstaffel I/Jagdgeschwader 1 (another Luftwaffe
group) in Jesau from 12 June to 17 July, and thereafter to the
Fliegerausbildungsregiment 10 in Neukuhren,[7] an aviator training
regiment, where he remained until 15 January 1940.

Döring completed the last leg of his education at the pilot training
school of the 2. Kompanie in Wiener Neustadt from 16 January
to 15 July,[8] to then specialise as a fighter pilot in the 8. Gruppe
der Kampffliegerschule 2 in Hörsching near Linz, after which he

completed a one-month special training course in blind-flying at the Blindflugschule in Vienna-Asper (15 September to 15 October), where he was instructed on a Bf 109, the He 111, the Ju 52 and the Ju 88.[9]

The very next day, Döring was ordered to report to 2. Ergänzungskampfgruppe 3 in Cracow, to be moved on 3 December 1940 to 9. Gruppe des Kampfgeschwader 53, with whom he fought against Britain in the position of corporal.[10] Between 11 February and 7 May 1941 Döring was deployed in home territory, was promoted to sergeant on 1 April and fought in occupied Poland[11] between 8 May and 8 July 1941. From there, along with his comrades of Kampfgeschwader 53, Döring took off to fly his first strafing attack against the Soviet Union; he was informed about this mission only on the day before departure. This is the day on which he starts writing his diary.

The young Arnold Döring in Tilsit, 1937 (Source: Döring).

The twenty-one-year-old
Arnold Döring during his pilot
training in Jesau/Königsberg
(photo taken on 1.7.1939)
(Source: Döring).

Döring during his training to
become a fighter pilot
(Source: Döring).

Dedicated To My Crew

Uffz. Richard Wawere[c]k
Fw. Richard Brösing
Fw. Karl Krupitza
Fw. Toni Grimmer
Ofw. Georg Eberhardt

PART I

With Kampfgeschwader 53

[21 June to 6 October 1941]

21.6.41[1]

On standby since 1330 hours. What's going to happen? Rumours are going round. Everyone's instinct is spot-on. The attack on the Soviets seems imminent.

On 21.6.1941 towards 1500 hours the entire squadron reports for duty. Its captain, Hauptmann [Fritz] Pockrandt[2] receives the message and proceeds to unfold several maps. He's unusually serious and briefs us on the situation. Russia intends – and our in-depth reconnaissance has confirmed this – to push forward against East Prussia and the Generalgouvernement.[3,4] Extensive provisions have been made on the German side as well. We had become well aware of that over the last few days.[5]

Insignia of Kampfgeschwader 55 – named after the 'Legion Condor' but not to be confused with it.

'If it all starts tomorrow morning, we're to attack the airfield Biels-Piliki[6] south of Bialystok, some 80 km behind the front line. The area is swarming with fighter planes. Here's how we'll distribute: we, the 9th Squadron, will attack the ammunition bunker and the runway, the 7th Squadron targets the barracks and the 8th Squadron the machines placed on the eastern edge. I hope that you, the young new crews, will prove as feisty and successful in this your first enemy attack, and in those that follow, as the old ones did before you. Pilots and observers will receive maps and images, and above all: make sure you do a proper job tomorrow – hit your targets!'

Initially, his words are met with dead silence. Everyone is deeply impressed. This is followed shortly afterwards by loud jubilation drowning out anything anyone tries to say. All crewmembers were overjoyed to finally see some action, finally be able to prove themselves to the enemy and at long last be allowed to show what they had been learning during so many years of training.[7]

All crews gather and try to figure out what are the optimal targets to engage with, from the images provided to us. Our crew seems to have been given the off-cuts – the bunker, it looks like, and the runway. But bunkers certainly needed to be cracked.

That evening at 2300 we have to report a second time. The flying personnel immediately report in the long corridor of the barracks. The captain announces the start time: tomorrow, at 03.30. We make our last preparations and go to bed. But then again, who can sleep before their very first operation?

22.6.41
First Operation

Night 01.00. Reveille. We're dressed in no time, and we wait for the trucks in front of our barracks. A few minutes later we've boarded and approach the yard at full pelt. Far away we see fires burning, and a slim sliver of skylight indicates dawn. Standing in the middle of the HQ courtyard the Gruppenkommandeur [Major Richard Fabian] explains the situation once again, allocates the targets we are to engage with and wishes everyone good luck. He'll take the lead.

Once again we find ourselves on the truck. Each crew is being driven to their machine. An 'all-clear' is reported from the first control room.

On the left: Fritz Pockrandt, captain of the 9th Staffel. On the right: Major Richard Fabian, group commander (photo 1944).

There's quite a bit going through my mind. Will my He 111 cope with its cargo? Will my bird manage to take off with it being pitch dark outside and having to make do with the miserable small airfield which we've only had a few days to get familiar with? If everything just goes to plan and doesn't … No, it doesn't even bear thinking about! Everyone will be cruising up there in the sky, except for you – you'll crash. Just clench your teeth – it simply must work!

In you go! Get yourself into the good old crate! Let's do one last check, but frankly the work done by the control room never disappoints, it's 100 per cent. The engines of the old guy ahead of me start revving up and a moment later I too roll along, positioning myself to his left, as I am allocated to his section. I can see Rudi Schwarze grinning over to us from the right.[8] That guy with his big gob cannot be made to shut up. The old guy lifts his hand. We're set. The next minute our section rolls forwards, rumbles along the uneven runway and our bird lifts off easily despite its heavy cargo. Bang on the dot, at 0330 we take off.[9]

Our squadron whips into a sharp left turn and zooms up in a corkscrew climb, and in tight formation targets the Sielce airfield[10] to chase the intruders. And guess who doesn't turn up? The good old fighter planes.[11] Didn't much bother us, mind you, as we didn't carry ammunition with us just for fun and games![12]

Single-mindedly our squadron flies towards its target after changing course only slightly. At 0415 we cross over the Bug, the border. In quite a few places below us the spectacle has started. Artillery advances into Russian territory. Can't make out any enemy guns or cannons.[13]

A thick bank of clouds bars our path. We press down and fly just below the cloud ceiling at some 2,000 metres and before we know it we've reached our destination. Banking sharply, the commander steers us towards the optimal course of attack.

Two He 111s posted to KG55 – to which Döring was due to switch – at take-off at dawn on 26 June 1942, on course to attack the Soviet Union.

'Open bays!' Richard [Wawerek] quickly cranks up the lever, then pores over the bombsight: 'List to port – more! Stop – pull it back – good, that's good … again, list to port … Full throttle! *Achtung*! Bombs dropping!'

Calmly I've been observing the needle indicating the small changes in course. I then look outside. It's still quite hazy below, but I can make out the targets. No air resistance as of yet, which slightly puzzles me. Have we really succeeded in our surprise attack and are the guys down below still asleep? Looks like they're in for a rude awakening.

We drop our eggs, fire clouds rise up, great masses of dirt fountains spurt into the air mixed with all kinds of debris, and flames of fire come belching out from all directions. Pity, but our bombs have hit the area to the right of the ammunition depots. Nonetheless, another wave sweeps across the entire field and rips through the runway with two deafening explosions at the top end. No chance for a fighter to take off for quite a while, as the bombs jettisoned by the other crews come whistling down, carpeting the rest of the runway.

Peering down during our sharp turn, I catch a momentary glimpse of several parked fighters with fifteen of them ablaze and flames pouring from most of the barracks. 'Flak!' exclaims Rudi, but all we can make out is a single shot which missed its target by a good kilometre. By then, we're well beyond the range of fire. But then comes the alarming call: 'Fighters at the rear!'

Blazing away until the barrels are hot, our formation packs up tight – easy target for the Russians but our defence is in shape. A fire trail from twenty-seven machines streaks across the sky, near-blinding the Russians, who prefer to dive off immediately.

Ahead of us the protruding nose appears in our sights. Some artillery exchanges – not much else as far as we can tell.

In front of us the airfield and within a short time our entire task force has landed. No losses – we return and fly home. Such was our success that a further sortie which had initially been scheduled to take place was not flown.

Towards the evening a second sortie was flown to the Bialystok airfield,[14] which had already been under attack during the day by other units. But just before crossing the border we are forced to turn round due to rapidly falling darkness and when we land on our small Polish airbase it is pitch black.

23.6.41
Second Operation

Attacked and hit tanks and motorised units heading north-east of Brest-Litovsk, passing Koboyn towards Bereza-Kartuska. These, more or less, were our orders.[15] Some ten minutes later our team is in the air, calmly gliding towards our target crossing over Brest-Litovsk at 800 m. Parts of the city were burning, with large columns

Werner Mölders after being awarded the Knight's Cross of the Iron Cross with Swords (Source: https://en.wikipedia.org/wiki/Werner_M%C3%B6lders#/media/File:Bundesarchiv_Bild_183-B12003,_Werner_M%C3%B6lders.jpg).

of bright red flames lighting up the night. Ferocious fighting on a grand scale around the citadel. We carry out escort patrols and Mölders[16] personally heads up Jagdgeschwader 51.

Lots of traffic on the road to Koboyn. Everything down below is stuffed with troops. Vehicles drive long stretches off-road. Our advance pushes forward inland, our tanks are at the front. Ahead of them some 2 km of no man's land. Then column after column stack up in disarray. Hurrah! These are Russians. Clunky Russian tanks of all sizes, motorised troops, military vehicles, artillery sandwiched in between, throngs of people fleeing by the hundreds, charging east. We've reached our objective. Our Staffel dived from our higher altitude and pelted the road with our machine guns. Boy, oh boy – we sure hit our targets. The first bombs hail down in quick succession. We fly in a line alongside the road and carefully take aim. Our bombs explode among tanks, armaments and vehicles, spraying panicked Russians with a rain of fire. All hell breaks loose down below and nobody even considers defensive fire. All over the sky the flash of tracers illuminates the targets like beads of a necklace. To safeguard the road for our own advance we avoid full-scale action, giving a few bursts into the ditches alongside instead. Our shells crashing and bombs exploding in all directions create a sea of flame. Actually hard to miss targets that are presented so neatly. Overturned tanks are swiftly engulfed by fire, with pillars of smoke and dust billowing into the air. Armoured vehicles obstruct the road and horses rearing up and thrashing around add to the fear and frenzy.

Gradually some of those down below manage to gather themselves. Searchlights went on, pointing their thin fingers of death against our bombers. In pairs these tracers swoop over us. In between, red balls zoom past, barely missing us. Escaping light flak shells and bursts of MG fire, we climb higher and though it looks rather harmless we certainly don't want to be hit. Singling out their batteries, we drop a few fire salvos and with that their posts are silenced.

We are in hot pursuit. Right in front of me a truck explodes, smoke spiralling up into the air. It was probably loaded with ammunition, causing the air pressure to fling me a good distance higher. Quickly I test the rudders and check the engines and the rest of the instruments, but all seems well. At practically the same time Karl and Toni experience something of a mental block when the realise that they aren't managing to fire at some really juicy targets and they start swearing as only Landsers know how, but moments later tracers from all sides converge on Bolshevik targets, with bullets lashing and slamming into the enemy.

In front of us: Bereza-Kartuska, our turning point. A few tanks give us quite a spectacular welcome from the entrance of the village. We have a close shave with the tracers that come up in orange-coloured smoke chains streaking away over our heads. At times we hear a hollow tin sound of crashing metal. A hit.

A quick check of the instruments and controls while briefly glancing at the visible parts of the machine; I feel reassured about the fine state my crate is in.

Tanks enveloped in the dense web of our tracers while we remain unscathed. Pity that we've dropped all our bombs.

The old guy in front of us peels away in a sharp left turn and it's only then that we commence on our dive to then follow up with strafing the road while heading home, shooting at everything in our sights. Weaving back and forth across it, sometimes zooming straight ahead, at an altitude of very nearly treetop height we spray death and confusion into the red columns. There! I've spotted one seeking cover behind a thick tree trunk, someone else flits across the road like a madman, he's shot and a moment later crumbles into a heap like a blazing torch. All we see are his legs. Bang! A bomb explodes, probably the last of the old guy's supply, and clean overturned a tank, sending it hurtling down a small embankment – I never expected such a small device to have such an impact. Richard sits huddled up in the cabin, continually banging away at ground targets with empty capsules swishing in the air.

Gently pushing the throttle back, gradually slowing the machine down, I straighten myself out and keep shooting. Edging up close alongside me, a machine overtakes and flies some 100 metres ahead of me. Then, suddenly, four bombs are dropped. With the engine at full throttle I wing over into a steep dive, then engage in an abrupt climb when there's a thunderous crash, another one and a third. Pressure rises sharply, pieces of shrapnel fly through the cabin, mixed with splinters and shards and the next second the cabin is choked with smoke, dirt and dust. Fighting to get this tricky beast under control, I grapple with the instrument panel but fail. Instinctively Richard and I hunch over, burying our heads.

Before long Richard changes tack, launching into a barrage of not so flattering comments about the poor chap in front. I actually can't help but laugh as his litany of insults breaks the tension. I ask whether all is all right in the rear, but that isn't so necessary as they too are happily engaged in foul-mouthing our enemy. Thankfully, our engines seem to be holding up and no one's hurt. The bomb thrower better beware – we'll give him a piece of our mind sooner or later. Not everything seems to be going smoothly as the aileron can only be lifted with a lot of effort, but I sort of manage, level the bird and continue low-level flying until all my drums are empty. Pulling the aircraft up to get a better general view, the leader of our tank convoy comes into sight and Landsers wave their hands at us. Looping down, unfortunately, is out of the question.

Gradually our Staffel comes together, flying towards our base. But, hey? What's that? Two machines are missing … surely not …?

Scanning the area for the squadrons attached to First Lieutenant Lehmann and Lieutenant Hubenthal, we draw a blank – they're missing. [Rudolf] Nietzsche totters with one engine towards base and two fighter planes accompany him.

A few moments later the field comes into view and my bird too lurches forward onto the apron. Our team, which is waiting for us, won't stop asking us questions which we try to answer to the best of our ability while not missing a beat and at the same time properly inspect our machine. Looks like we've been hit by quite a few

MG bullets, with our fuselage and wings slashed by a good dozen splinters and a maelstrom of shards. One splinter, must have been as big as a handball, has punctured the aileron. Bullets have scraped past the radio operator's seat and even penetrated the dashboard. Two tanks have been shattered. Unfortunately, our bird is out of commission for several days – but should be up and flying in some three days.

A truck drives past on its way to the command post. Above us a one-engine crate hovers in the air then lands smoothly on the tarmac, reducing speed as it taxis towards the edge of the field. Nietzsche. After his radio message, he'd been hit with MG shelling damaging his left engine and forcing him to shut it down as he couldn't sustain a good margin of height. A few treetops were clean shaved off, which would explain the damaged elevator. But eventually the crate managed to gain some height, make a wide sweep and then land properly. The fellow certainly lucked out.

Gradually we're able to gather more details about the whereabouts of Hubenthal and Lehmann. Hubenthal attempted an emergency landing in open countryside between the lines. One team claims to have watched several men bail out – running towards territory behind their front line. Lehmann's machine had crash-landed on its belly. The crew was nowhere in sight, but having come down over our own land, we know they're in German hands.

A Fieseler Storch landed that afternoon with Wieser on board, Hubenthal's radio operator, who brings us sad news: Hubenthal and his gunner were killed by the Russians on their march to reach their front line. My namesake, Paulchen Döring, was injured in his calf and as for his observer, a bullet had grazed his right elbow. While all that happened, Wieser was tucked underneath the crate, pistol at the ready, waiting for the Russians to move away. Pity – they were all good mates of ours.

First Lieutenant Lehmann reappears the following day. Poor fellow had been taken down by a tank, fierce shelling had pierced through his engine, the cockpit was practically wrecked and flying

Flight above Russia, 1941.

shards embedded themselves in the second engine. Crossing the Bug, he approached land and then, like a flaming torch, he crash-lands. They'd all bailed out and everyone was back safely.

25.6.41

We were ordered to attack the Luminec rail junction located in the Pripet marshes.[17] The route takes us from Piasov via Brest along the train track which runs across Kobryn–Pinsk direction east. We're to disconnect the lines running both northwards and eastwards.

We're cruising at an altitude of some 1,200 metres, tightly below stacked blobs of cumulus clouds which are slowly and ominously gathering in on us and keeping me terribly busy while I attempt an accurate approach – phenomenally difficult.

21

Finally, I pinpoint our target. Across the train tracks, in close squadron formations, we draw wide loops making directly towards the tracks to put them out of use wherever possible. Then the bombs are dropped. It is sheer impossible to get away, what with the high winds. A stick of bombs explode right across the train tracks with thick banners of black smoke and stabbing jets of flame shooting into the air. Tracks are ripped apart and large craters dug into the embankment. Looks like we've disabled that stretch of steel for some time to come and managed seriously to disrupt reinforcement efforts. Not such an easy feat to crack a junction like that – some 4 to 6 metres wide, it was.

After a few turns and wide loops, we get away and fly across the town and its train station, where several trains are lined up. Shame that we've completely run out of bombs by now. Tracer flares come whizzing in streams out of everywhere, framing the puffing train carriages – but we're unable actually to confirm what impact they have.

Diving down, we get out of the glinting sunlight to then climb up and across the town. This is our first time confronting solid black clouds of concentrated flak fire exploding at perfect altitude, but fortunately not adequately angled, and with us drawing wide sweeping curves to get into position, the Russians are forced continually to adjust their position – which in turn sends our needles jumping around wildly. Some targets we've identified are strafed with precision and despite the powerful noise of our radial engine we could still hear the dull thuds following the explosions. Damn close to us, bombs begin raining down. As if on cue, we fan out and whatever else is dropped into the sky, now obstinately empty, may or may not be a winner.

On our return we seize the opportunity to make good use of our hard-hitting and effective aircraft armament, launching ourselves into targeting enemy troops and tent lines the minute we catch sight of them. Needless to say, in our low-level attacks we aim with absolute precision. Long trails of smoke and jets of flame rise and encircle the first squadron, flooding the sky in a ghostly light. The boys are real pros. Here and there we can hear hammer-blows to the crates – sure hits. Glancing briefly at the wings, I can attest to a number of bullet holes. Our left fuel tank also got its fair share, steadily losing fuel, but after some vigorous pumping we manage to maintain some formation and remain on course. The leaking fuel stank to high heaven – literally.

We continue on our course, beneath us airfields still partly under construction. With no sign of any personnel, the fields look abandoned. As we roar over wide expanses of marshy ground interspersed with dark open water, ink-coloured ditches and basins grin up at us as if with a smirk. I hold my stick with a tight grip – the thought of going down is not a pleasant one. Only a single road winds its way through the wetland.

The Soviet air force suffers significant losses during the first weeks of the attack (Source: Werner Haupt, *Sturm auf Moskau: Der Angriff, Die Schlacht, Der Rückschlag, 1941* (Friedberg, 1986), p. 44).

A few moments after landing we attend a special briefing. Looks like we've taken down over 2,300 Russian aircraft within three days.[18] Good news indeed.

That's the reason why, so far, we've only had a few of the fighter planes turn up. But no doubt they will prove challenging further back in the hinterland.

Our orders state that we are to interrupt the train line heading east and attack at low level deep down in the hinterland. Two machines return from that mission, with the squadron leader First Lieutenant Lehmann shot down. Engulfed by flames, he was forced to make an emergency landing. Looks like an armoured train tank platoon had shot him down. Jonas, right-hand squadron leader flying alongside him, attempts a landing but is forced last minute to yank up the machine as he realises that the meadow is just vast and treacherous – nothing but marshy ground. Out of the corner of his eye he catches a glimpse of the entire crew making a run for it towards the forest. Well, with any luck they'll muddle through somehow, though marching a distance of 450 km is nothing to sneeze at. Looks like within a short time span we've already lost a second crew.

26.6.41

Heavy fighting going on around Bialystok.[19] Twenty-two Russian divisions are encircled, staring square into the face of annihilation. The majority of the Russians are stuck in the dense woods, trying to find break-out routes on all sides.

Our team was deployed to this huge pocket. Our mission was to keep watch for break-out attempts and prevent them. This was one way for us to participate in wiping out the enemy in battle. A dream come true for us bomber pilots.

Start time was towards 1700 hours. Our Staffel takes the lead with our commander at the head. We fly direction Bialystok and then follow the road east. The road is fairly empty. There're only a few vehicles en route and they immediately disappear to take cover in the woodland. Russians open fire on us from within – the fingers of death reaching out for us. While these comrades sure have good aim, we're nonetheless able to identify the hiding spots where they're located. We do a low dive towards our objective and let our eggs drop with our blessings. Terrible fireballs! Long columns of smoke and dirt whirl up from trenches, fields and edges of woods where the Russians have dug themselves in, and slowly trail upwards. Dull thuds of heavy bombs detonating reverberate.

Searchlights, like spiders, point their thin fingers at us. Despite bombs hailing down, these guys below continue to pick on us with their MGs bolted together two by two or even four.

Bombs drop sporadically and strike their targets. Some tanks are hit severely, causing extensive damage or total destruction; several gun positions and a great number of vehicles are blown apart.

Richard still has an especially heavy bundle up his sleeve and intends it for a special target – but nothing comes his way. But then, just ahead of us, the small town of Volkovysk appears. Surely this place has some goodies tucked away for us. The train station is heavily guarded. One has to be particularly careful! Troops have apparently massed on the eastern edge of the town. Our aim is to focus on the large storage sheds. So, let's get a move on and drop our gorgeous egg. Sure enough, we see fire erupting and rubble flung into the air, twirling around with a huge black cloud of smoke fanning out. Dark red flames continue to spread and the cloud rises above 1,500 metres. Must have been a pretty awesome collection of flammable stuff stored in there.

In the meantime, our Staffel is heading home – barely visible against the darkening sky. Anyway, let's get this old cart back – and just short of Bialystok, now in flames, I reach base and place my bird where it belongs. In my rear mirror I catch sight of the city disintegrating and monstrous juggernauts of flames drawing black clouds into the skyline. We must have unloaded practically all our smackeroos in one fell swoop, but were mindful to retain a certain amount for special occasions.

Once again we swoop down onto Bialystok. Looks like all exit routes are firmly closed off and any breakthrough attempts have so far failed. What's even better is that the Russians are now crammed into an even tighter space than before.

Our first attack takes place early, at 0600 hours. This time we fly in close squadron formation and are dispatched on a rotating basis. There's a real rhythm to this, with a constant number of aircraft hovering above the target while others are about to be reloaded or refuelled at top speed, or take off.

Criss-crossing above forests and fields, we see empty roads beneath us and must assume that everyone is hidden away in the large dense woods. Eyes peeled, we're keeping a close watch but cannot spot a soul or a sausage – the Russians are well camouflaged. Hard to believe that there are as many as twenty-two divisions down there … somewhere, and yet … we see nothing. The Russians appear to have taken cover and remain still, letting us continue in our search. At long last we catch sight of a few vehicles winding their way along a field path. Our balls do their job – they don't fall short. Richard is an expert.

In front of and behind us other aircraft are targeting the forest, but not us. We can't see a thing and don't want to risk squandering our load, thus return with half of our ammunition intact, and this obviously gets us into trouble.

On our second mission we make sure to take our binoculars as we're keen to drop our bombs as accurately as possible. Richard realises that the woods are practically teeming with army men and now there's heavy traffic on the roads. Fire has broken out in some parts of the forest with Russians spilling out into the open fields where, naturally, we receive them with a warm welcome. We work over the area feverishly, systematically firing at every target that presents itself while emptying our magazines. We attack, successfully bombing and strafing vast areas, with our heavy artillery doing its bit. That's one hell of a battlefield. Once in a while the Russians make a feeble attempt at breaking out, but pretty much immediately get caught in a hail of fire. Our artillery knows its stuff, instantly recognises the Russians' intention of escaping and doesn't lose a second in wiping them out. During those sorties us lot often help out others in the nick of time. Pity we can't simply continue circling over the target. There comes a time when one just runs out of fuel, bombs and ammunition – so we've got no choice but to return home and leave it to other units – still on their approach route – to do what needs to be done: achieve the total annihilation of the Russians. We draw another few loops above battle scenes which scream out acts of atrocity and slaughter the like of which the world has never seen before. We then fly home in compact formation.

29.6.41

We're forced to move our living quarters, made necessary because it turns out that our approach flights are taking too long, considering the rapid advance of our ground troops.[20] We inspect a new airfield; it's very large, flat as a pancake and meticulously kept. The only disadvantage is the forest embankment reaching far into the grounds of the airbase. Radzyn is still part of Poland.[21]

Barracks are available but are occupied by other units. Nothing for us to do except resort to sheds and tents at the edge of the forest, and seeing as we actually have no choice in the matter we make ourselves at home. We have to be grateful that at least we have a roof over our heads, as that night a torrential downpour comes down on us. Wouldn't you know it but of all people it is me who gets drenched as it is the bit of the roof just above my head which is leaking and has me lying soaked through in a puddle of water in the early hours of the morning. The others don't fare much better and eventually the encampment is teeming with men cursing and desperately trying to find a dry spot. Stupid Pollaks, can't even build a watertight roof. But before too long everyone is asleep again.

30.6.41

Training takes place throughout the morning. Finally, we're all done and ready to go. It's 1300 hours, a truck arrives and we pilots are driving to the command post where we assemble for the commander's instructions for the operation: 7th Staffel to attack Orsha train station – that's our main priority. 8th Staffel to attack the Orsha airfield; 9th Staffel is assigned to the Mogilev airfield situated some twenty minutes' flight south of Orsha. The weather conditions allow us to go solo and the all-clear for take-off follows, one by one with ten-minute gaps in between. We're ordered to cut short our mission once the cloud ceiling is down below 7/10, as otherwise this would most certainly result in heavy batteries of enemy flak defence. Ground situation: our own troops are positioned east of Minsk. No accurate data on where the front line runs so we'll need to be careful. Pilots are being left to map out their own course. Minsk is the navigation point for all crews and, depending on weather conditions and cloud cover, it will be up to them to decide on their flight path. 'Any questions …? Good luck!'

A brief glance at the maps and while the captain gives out various tips on how to manage tricky situations, he insists that we return to base immediately should weather conditions prove not to be as predicted. We simply cannot afford to risk losing men just on account of some missing clouds.

Then we spend time calculating various options with respect to which routes to take, at what speed and so forth and conclude that it'll be a long flight. Over four hours. I'm the second to take off, at 1420 hours.

Laboriously my bird climbs to 3,200 m. Above me there were gaps in the cloud ceiling with clouds beginning to thin and then, according to my estimation, vanish completely. Short of Minsk I decided to do some low-level flying in order to be able to make a quick escape should it come to that. Eventually the clouds disappeared and at the height of Beresina, that fateful river where

Napoleon suffered the loss of so many of his men,[22] I continue under a bright blue sky. Now what? Should I change course and return or do I carry on flying? Certainly I have the order to reverse and perhaps, who knows, I might soon hit storm clouds. Should the Russians swoop down with too many of their fighter planes, I have no problem in turning my cart upside down, fly low level and clear out.

Looking down below after several moments, I notice a thick layer of haze and dense fog with the ground completely invisible. Breaking away in a steep dive, I continue flying just above the blanket, always on the ready to seek protection in the veil of fog should hostile aircraft make an appearance. Keeping our eyes fixed on the sky, we carefully scan each white scrap in the sky. Further on, towards the end of the bank of fog, we spot some single cumulus clouds gradually forming stretched-out banks but unfortunately criss-crossing our flight path. Below us, the fog slightly thinning, we note some heavy troop movement which we mark onto our maps,

Polikarpov I-16 (known as 'rats') flying in formation (Source: https://science. howstuffworks.com/polikarpov-i-16.htm).

ordering them according to strength, march direction and timing. Based on our calculations, we should have reached our destination.

A bright band of light flickers on the horizon and we figure it must be the Dnieper, which means that we've still got another ten minutes to reach our destination. The river lies smack below us – we make a sharp left and zoom towards our target. The bank of clouds has suddenly been sliced apart as if cut with a knife. Ahead of us we make out Mogilev and behind it to the right appears the square bounded by impressive buildings. A thick layer of cumulus covers the city. On the outskirts of the city a fire envelops a hamlet – who was the culprit, we wonder? Suddenly I notice three tiny dots approaching us at lightning speed and before we know it they're close up – three 'rats'[23] in perfect flight formation swoop down and have the cheek to obstruct our path to the base. Long streaks of dark smoke rise upwards. Whipping around, they tip sharply and approach. Their shell-shaped fuselage forms a stark contrast against the clear horizon in the background. Clearly visible on the fuselage and wings are the bright stars – with the one on the far left painted a blood-red colour.

And then they swing in a steep spiral upwards – a long trail of black smoke streaks past our crate and our MGs start rattling like mad. One by one they peel off, dive down, making space for the next one to attack. Hanging from their loosened safety-belt, they fire, then drop down in a nosedive, gather speed to then swoop up – but these bastards have blocked our flight path to base. There's no way for us to attack. More fighter planes swarming around down below. It would be great if clouds came our way – but Petrus seems to be in cahoots with the Reds.

'Get those bombs out!' I scream. 'But make sure to aim well!'

'No worries, let me take care of that. I'm concentrating on that dump over there – it seems to be crawling with those guys.'

Behind me they're shooting like nobody's business. Our tracers flash into and around the machines, but those fat beasts won't turn off. They probably think they've ground us down.

At long last the bombs drop. Richard swiftly retracts the flap and we catch up in speed, keeping one eye on the rear mirror to watch the bombs plummeting but the other on the fighters who continue attacking strongly.

'Fire! Perfect hit! Hurray!'

'What's on fire? That dump or one of those blasted fighter planes?'

'The dump, of course. Three buildings and some ten to fifteen vehicles!'

Richard seems perfectly composed, the epitome of calmness itself, while I was feeling quite anxious. He, of course, was a person who'd participated in the Poland campaign and served as infantry in the Winter War, so it's little wonder that it'd take quite a lot to rattle him. But now is different, as his Upper Silesian temperament gets the better of him and he swears like nobody's business when he realises that all he can manage is one measly shot against an attacking 'rat'. Something then went wrong – seemed that he was having a mental block or something and he couldn't manage the loading.

I put the cart on its head and zoom full throttle into the next thick cloud which luckily seemed to have appeared out of nowhere and it sure wasn't a moment too soon, as our three Russians had become increasingly cheeky and pushy. The cloud is actually massive and forces me to change course and head eastwards to deceive the Russians. Hidden by the next cloud, I steer towards base, whipping from one cloud bank to the next. Toni screams that the three Russians are continuing like madmen to whirl round and round the thick cloud I first disappeared in and it pleases me no end how we have fooled them. Heavy flak blasts some pretty impressive holes into the air. Are they actually targeting us? There's no denying that we're breathing a sigh of relief when after some ten minutes still no fighter plane appears in the sky. Would not have been a pretty sight if instead of the Russians we'd been caught out by the Tommies. Not sure we'd have scraped through in one piece.

'Has our machine suffered any holes?' I ask.

All of us inspect our bird but can't find any spot where we'd been shot at. Could it be that these guys actually didn't manage a single hit during the ten-minute shoot-out? Barely believable.

Finally, we've reached our own lines and Karl moves into the cockpit. Slapping me on my shoulder, he then grins broadly. Below us we make out our own reinforcements – which has me turn our crate on its head to allow me a closer look while flying low. Wobbling, tossed up and down, we wave at them, and the Landsers wave back.

After an hour the airfield comes into view. Flying low over the fields, I direct the plane towards its landing place, briefly climbing up sharply. I then make a flat turn and, lowering my undercarriage, I get into position to land; a few minutes later, rolling smoothly towards the garage to fill my bird up with petrol, I switch off the engines and we clamber to the ground. Giving our machine a thorough once-over, we can't detect major damage except for one hit in her right wing.

'These guys sure are lousy shooters,' comments Richard, practically spitting with outrage. A cigarette wedged between our lips, we proceed to regale the ground personnel with our antics against the rats up above and, in turn, are informed that the old guy had returned due to the weather conditions.

That'll end up with us being given a tongue-lashing for certain … Richard and I drive to the command post to deliver our report. We're not exactly praised to the skies, but contrary to our fears, the commander doesn't tell us off and instead congratulates us for the mission's good outcome. Our reconnaissance is immediately transmitted to the upper echelons. Taking a swig which puts an end to the meeting, the old man admits that it could all have ended up far worse.

'Listen up guys, in future,' he warned, 'don't be so pig-headed and push ahead. It's important to keep the entire picture in mind and it is by far preferable to cut short an operation – even if it's damn hard to do so – than be taken down on the other side. An order is an order!'

Orsha train station after the attack.

Gradually, in dribs and drabs, one crew after another hands in their report. There's only one of the crews who doesn't arrive and that's Lieutenant Bauer's lot.[24] He must have run out of fuel ages ago and everyone fell silent, fearing the worst but not daring actually to spell it out. Eventually, however, the realisation that this crew will not return sinks in when Sergeant [Wilhelm] Haster[25] is the last one to return with his crew and reports that he had sighted an He attacked by five 'rats' with a long trail of smoke rising to the sky, indicating that they had been shot down. That was the third crew.

We found their burial site later on in Orsha, where comrades from the army had laid them to rest.

1.7.41

Attack on the Mogilev airfield, yesterday's target. This time in tight-line-astern formation – yesterday only two machines were able to pelt down their ammunition. Take-off is 0420 in the morning. It had rained throughout the night. It is humid and warm like in a hothouse, with steam coming out of the ground soon developing into a sort of ground fog. Visibility still fine, though the cockpit windows are getting misted up. We wipe them down from the outside, from the inside – nothing helps … they just keep misting up – we can only hope that we'll have no problems with take-off.

… but we do! It all goes wrong. I'm practically blind-flying and with a heavily loaded machine to boot. At take-off the aircraft swerves sharply round to the left as the left engine won't fill up with fuel but I manage to get control of the beast, and to get better visibility I stick my head out of the side window, keeping an eye on the crescent-shaped forest with its protruding tip – but what I couldn't see was that I was approaching the massive building of a gas station, and I come dangerously close.

Suddenly there is a violent jolt and with my right undercarriage slumping down I pull the stick hard into my belly. The machine is in full throttle, obeys and I manage to scrape through just above the treetops which flash past underneath. Several more jolts and judders as I sweep across the area, touching the branches from time to time, but quickly regaining control.

Richard's head appears in the cockpit, informing us that the right undercarriage is broken but then I see him managing to retract the left one. Looks like two struts have been ripped apart in the right one and the wheel is bent perpendicular to our flying direction. I fear this noodle is not going to go much beyond 240 klicks despite the engines running at full throttle. Eventually the windows are clear of the annoying mist and I can make out the machines in front of me, which allows me to catch up with them. At long last I'm flying alongside the captain, who spots the damaged undercarriage and immediately waves me away. Much to my regret, I have to drop out of the operation as it makes no sense to continue at this slow pace – all I would have achieved is keeping the rest of the unit from doing their job.

I make a sharp turn direction airfield but bad luck has it that the mist had turned into a thick blanket of ground fog and we're left with no choice but to draw several loops while waiting for the sun to penetrate and dissolve the fog. Liaising by radio with the airfield, we get our bearings and circle the field. Slowly visibility improves with the filthy mist moving away. Fire tenders and ambulances have been alerted and are on standby. Soon the sun appears and with a fresh gust of wind the fog has all but disappeared.

Richard shoots a red signal cartridge as a warning for the ground crew and we drop our bombs – with dectivated detonators – beside the airfield. We take good note of the place where they have fallen.

Forced to make a one-wheel landing, I prepare for touch-down. Ground conditions are damp and wet, making my crate slide something awful, but I desperately want to avoid a belly-landing which would demolish my dear machine. My left undercarriage is lowered. Our safety belts are fastened. Short of the base, I cut the ignition and fuel while Richard closes the radiator cooling flaps. We approach land. With my feet clamped on the rudder pedals, I make a sharp turn and, touching down, I do my best to keep the machine upright – but with the reducing speed she turns on her side. There's a heavy jolt, the bird is violently flung to the right with its right wing whirling up great masses of dirt into the air. After skidding along some 50 metres on the left wheel, it finally comes to a stop. Fortunately, the left undercarriage held out for just the right amount of time. I fling open the window but that same moment the pressure line of the hydraulic system bursts and fluid gushes into my face. Shit, the stuff tastes awful. Let's just get the hell out of here. Slowly we clamber out to take stock of the extent of the damage.

The fire engine comes to a stop right in front of the machine, but their services are no longer needed. Same with the ambulances, seeing as nobody is injured.

The sustained damage doesn't seem to be terribly extensive. The right undercarriage is gone, the right beam is bent and the right wing is dented. Whether the engine was hit remains to be seen. The machine should be up and running within thirteen days.

One-wheel landing of another aircraft operating for the III/KG53 (in this case the right wheel) (Source: https://reibert.info/thread/kg53-legion-condor-kampfgeschwader%20-53-legion-condor.233139/brandt).

The Staffel returns after three hours, without having dropped any of their load as dense fog completely obscured the target. No other worthwhile targets could be engaged as they too were shrouded in ground mist.

That afternoon the Staffel takes off again on a mission direction Minsk–Orsha. Doesn't really concern me and I have a rest. They all return except for Lance Corporal Nitzsche's crew.[26] Nobody seemed to have seen where and how they'd been shot down by the Russians, as once again these were solo flights. This makes them the fourth crew of the Staffel downed within just a few days.

2.7.41
Eighth Operation against the Enemy

Operations taking place in three airfields near Gomel. I fly solo as the weather conditions seem perfect. Long stretches of cumulus clouds at an altitude between 800 and 2,000 metres up to 9/10 allowing us a seamless run across the clouds.

Soon I'm cruising at 2,000, gliding towards my objective. Lots of forest areas below us – hardly any villages.

Crossing the Dnieper. I make out some trenches and must admit that I had had a completely different picture in my mind of what the Stalin Line would look like.[27]

Just before 1100 hours we sight the city of Gomel. Targeted by anti-aircraft guns, our MGs respond vociferously. Flying close underneath the cloud cover, dipping in and out, I avoid the worst of the shelling.

The first airbase is located at the southern tip of the city. Despite circling around several times, we still can't quite confirm its configuration or staffing level and can't make out what's in the hangars either. Although the gates are wide open, it's not possible for Richard to see any planes, even with his binoculars.

The Stalin Line: this shows a destroyed tank (a bunker with armaments and machine guns) above the Dnjestr near Bronila and underneath the Mogilev (Source: Zu Bundesarchiv_B-145_Bild-FO16204-06_Russland_Panzerwerk_ über_dem-Dnjestr.jpg).

Our orders specifically state to attack stationary machines and not the hangars, sheds or runways and we swiftly move on to the next airbase. About time that we leave the wild anti-air gun barrages behind us. The boys eventually close in and get within firing range, while I'm surprised not to spot a single enemy fighter plane. The first machine flying over the target to observe weather conditions reports heavy defence.

No machines visible on the second airbase either. Here too we circle the field several times – but other than some burned-out four-engine bombers, we can't see anything. For good measure we whip across the field, streaking it with a few bursts and then we fly on to the next airbase, seeing as nothing was happening. Not quite sure whether this is actually an airfield or just a decoy – but in any event, we're not ones to fall into a trap. We spend quite some time looking for signs of an actual base but can only find marshy forest clearings – looks as if our reconnaissance was wrong.

In the meantime, a train engine is bombed. Long trails of white smoke streak across the sky – one can safely assume that this old boy won't be travelling anywhere in a hurry.

We circle the airbases one last time and wonder where the hell the fifty to sixty fighter planes are hiding – the ones that had not only been reported by the reconnaissance aircraft but also confirmed on the aerial photographs? Has Ivan cleared out, or had they got wind of our visit and quickly relocated?

Quite disgruntled at this point, we draw one more loop – but can't detect anything. We have to turn round, having wasted some 1,000 litres of fuel for absolutely zilch. Sadly, we're not permitted to drop our bombs onto the troops below us. An order is an order. But they can't escape our MG firing with everyone banging away like crazy into the moving vehicle columns. Weird that they all seem to be heading east, concentrically to Gomel. Richard, meanwhile, makes notes on his map, giving this outing at least a modicum of purpose. You can imagine the swearing that went on about this mission!

Our bombs have been taken on this ridiculous excursion lasting an interminable four and a half hours for absolutely nothing – hugely annoying. So once we finally land it's hardly surprising that we're in a foul mood. We report our findings and it turns out that my machine is not the only one to return with a stack of bombs on board. However, we're told that our reconnaissance is considered important, that it is being compared against others' reports, adjusted accordingly and then forwarded to the upper echelons.

Sadly, yet another crew of the Staffel doesn't return from this mission. It's Sergeant Niggemann's plane, including his four crewmembers.[28] Caught out by anti-aircraft attack over Gomel. Several other machines return some hours later having put the entire route behind them single-engined. Sergeant Haster's plane suffered a second hit to his engine at standstill just above Luminec – he's one incredibly lucky man.

7.7.41
Ninth Enemy Operation

This is certainly a weird operation! No defensive air or indeed ground fire despite flying for three and a half hours over enemy terrain, taking off and landing from the Karanovitski railway junction.

Richard has reported sick for several days already, so it's Pitt who's dropping the bombs. Pitt is also trained as an observer and acts as my air gunner.

We reach our target at about 2000 hours. Split up into carefully separated groups, we cross the railway station, which is occupied by a large number of trains – which we immediately take care of, and in a spectacular manner. One bull's eye after another. Then we set about the train lines with our heavy load, tearing huge craters in the ground and inflicting destruction on a large scale. Several train carriages are on fire, as well as a large number of storage sheds

Bombs hailing down on a Russian airbase.

and houses around the station area. There's no doubt about it: this rather important railway junction will be out of commission for the foreseeable future.

One and a half weeks later we take both the train station and the city by storm. Such was the devastation caused by our bombs that the Russians were slow even to get started with clearing up the rubble, the debris, the shattered buildings and roads, something which they usually wouldn't hesitate to embark on immediately.

8.7.1941

Once again we're ordered to relocate to the front. This time round it's deep into Russian territory. We occupy the Minsk [Dubinsky] airfield – a desolate area with woodland and steppe as far as the eye can see. Bare expanses of the open steppe and marshes cover huge stretches of land. Minsk still alight in various places, three-quarters of the city's been totally destroyed by us, by the artillery and by the Russians. What's surprising is that dotted around the city are several modern high-rises built in the American style and unharmed by the onslaught.

No lodgings available in the airbase situated close to the forest, so we're forced to pitch some tents, but not before having to clear the rock-hard ground of rubble and roots. The many mosquitoes are a huge bother ... in fact they turn life into hell.

Scorching heat. We have to make several flights in order to transport all the personnel and equipment of the Staffel. But nothing will stand in the way of us taking off for an operation that same evening. Along with another crew, I am given the task of reconnoitring the infamous Orsha anti-aircraft bases and open fire on enemy tanks.

In the meantime, with our aircraft loaded, the engines begin to vibrate and quiver. The small base resembles a moonscape due to its many craters. At the very edge of the so-called runway, I manage to pull my bird off the ground, but my wheels touch the field several times before I can finally take off fully. It very nearly all went haywire – with the base being so tiny, it was a close shave.

I gingerly climb up to an acceptable altitude – it's simply awfully hot and the cart is certainly not in peak form. The engines too have clocked up a fair number of operations.

Finally, I've reached the acceptable altitude and, at 2,000 metres, I'm on the lookout for tanks, but heavy ground mist seeping across the land makes it difficult. Before we even know it, however, we're above Orsha and welcoming us is anti-aircraft fire which literally takes our breath away. In front of us, located next to an area occupied by a battery of flak guns, is a large factory. Just you wait, you dirty lot! In a few moments you'll get your comeuppance! Richard opens fire, aiming accurately at identified targets, and plasters the enemy with a stream of shells. Bombs detonate close to the battery, hitting also the largest of the halls.

German soldiers marching in front of a Minsk building (Source: https://commons.wikimedia.org/wiki/File:Bundesarchiv_Bild_101I-137-1010-37A,_Minsk,_deutsche_Truppen_vor_modernen_Geb%C3%A4uden.jpg).

The modern Soviet party buildings show a level of modernisation and
development which was not shared by the majority of the population
(Source: Werner Held, *Die deutschen Jagdgeschwader im Russlandfeldzug*
(Friedberg, 1986)).

The battery stops its attacks, but all hell breaks loose at the city
outskirts. Shells detonate close by and the relentless pounding
and ensuing explosions can be heard clearly. Within just one brief
moment the Russians had locked themselves in. In steep corkscrew
climbs, abruptly changing course and altitude, I try my best to put
an end to this annoying shooting.

We can make out a few vehicles below but there's no telling
whether they are tanks or not: the ground mist sweeping along the
dispersal area is too dense. Stüder's fixation with flying straight
ahead allows the Reds to improve their shooting, making it barely
possible for me to keep the aircraft under control. The detonations
and intense air pressure are such that my crate bounces and jolts
violently. Nonetheless, much to my surprise, we're not hit. Looks
like the Russians' ammunition is poor and the impact of their shell
splinters even more so.

At long last bombs are jettisoned once more and everything starts to move again.

Our eggs pound the ground close to the road, but don't cause much damage. Richard cranks shut the flaps to the bomb bay while remaining rested on his pad – he's still not fully recovered.

I turn my crate upside down and manage to leave the firing behind me.

10.7.41
Attacks on the Stalin Line

The Staffel is ordered to blast the fortifications of the Stalin Line in order to clear the way for our infantry who are lined up to storm ahead at 0700 hours. That means that all bombs would have to be dropped by 0655 hours.

We start early. Each section takes off until all squadrons are in the air flying towards their targets. Before too long Beresina lies below us and then it continues east. Above Slobin[29] and neighbouring Stagatschev, the only bridgeheads along the middle of the Stalin Line west of the Dnieper currently still under Russian control, we're met by heavy anti-aircraft fire – but given their aim is poor, we're quite happy with them squandering ammunition.

Unperturbed by these attacks, we cross the Dnieper, which measures some 150 m wide at this location. No sign of any dugouts, my guess is that they are well camouflaged – something for which the Russian has a knack. We can see a trench system broken up by a wide tank ditch.

There and then a bright flame flashes into the sky, followed by large masses of dirt fountains spurting up, most likely from flak batteries hidden behind the forest boundaries. The moment they've caught sight of us, they cease firing. But this doesn't help them a great deal as we now know their positions despite their camouflage. The result is a series of attacks, one after another, with each

A Ju 88 jettisoning bombs (Source: Klaus Häberlen, Klaus, *Erzählungen eines Lebens in drei Epochen* (Ulm, 1998), p. 84).

A Ju 87 flying across the Soviet Union (https://www.asisbiz.com/il2/ Ju-87/StG2.2/pages/Junkers-Ju-87B2-Stuka-7.StG2-(T6+IR)-WNr-6006- Barbarossa-1941-01.html).

machine individually hailing down its bombs. Our eggs don't miss their target and, honestly, a Stuka couldn't have been more spot-on.[30] Only four of our bombs miss – the rest are sure hits. The air is still allowing me to make a clean approach. Today, Richard really goes above and beyond. Stukas too are hovering above the Stalin Line, as well as other He 111 and Ju 88 units. They're all focused on the Russian posts. No ground defence to speak of, just occasionally blazing tracer rounds, like corpses' fingers, eerily slide past us – but we barely take any notice of them. An aircraft flying alongside me dives and picks a flak post as his target, which is barely able to fire off a single shot before being ripped apart by two massive bombs. Unfortunately we're actually running low on bombs and eventually we're forced to consider a return to base.

We've barely touched down when once again our machines are being loaded up. Orders to go on the attack have been given, which means that nothing stands in our way to start all over again. This time round it is the troops along the Stalin Line who get the worst of our excursion as we promptly blast them a few kilometres south of our target.

Before too long we are cruising above the area we devastated just this morning, spotting in various places some of our infantry which had crossed the Dnieper and was now forging ahead. No sign of any Russian infantry on this particular section of the front.

Heavy fighting between the positions. Dark vapour trails rise from above the treetops just where we'd dropped our babies. Can't be a bad thing, I think that this is just about right and we'll have fumigated the woods and got rid of the Russians.

Making a wide turn to the right, we're bound for our target. The forests we're meant to hammer are teeming with Russians. Clouds of smoke envelop us, we fly strung out in open formation across the strips of forest with row after row of the heavy bombers dropping their deadly charge into the dense masses of people and spreading a chain of bloodshed. We then follow the flight path along the road toward Gomel, taking note of how choked it is in both directions with trucks and other vehicles. Great – our bombs are doing their bit. Firing in all directions, we swiftly move along, make a sharp turn and go on the attack again, releasing several rounds of ammunition, which results in a good number of trucks burning fiercely, others being turned upside down and a few blocking the road. Others still drive into a ditch. Shells detonate, tearing large craters in the ground, panic breaks out among the Russians, who escape the onslaught by dispersing into the landscape – away from the road. We don't let up, pounding the area with a systematic barrage of fire. Our ammunition has run low by the time we cross the front line but we're well pleased with what we've achieved. We could have done with an aircraft capable of storing an amount of ammunition sufficient to allow several hours of uninterrupted bombing. Well, here's hoping that such a machine will soon be invented!

11.7.41
Thirteenth Operation

We're deployed to different troop assembly points along the Stalin Line with our ground units having pushed far inside already. Russians are heavily attacking the southern tip of this enclave, which leads to us being ordered to advance and crush those guys. The head of our squad on the attack has reached just short of the essential road connecting Orsha–Gomel and is meant to block any reinforcement. We had received reports that heavily armed Russian units are moving fast, approaching from the south, meaning that it was now up to us to protect the right-hand flank of our troops. We attack throughout the day in continuous waves, not letting up.

Taking off, my engine rumbles ominously but fortunately doesn't die altogether, with my aircraft waddling along until it finally lifts off just short of the tent encampment. My captain is far ahead of me, but gradually I catch up with him. My baby is sure the slowest of the lot and the old man has a hard time throttling back so I can keep up. Slowly but surely we bounce through the air towards our target. Fuel is still leaking out with the engine losing power. Very worrying and it's about time that it's replaced.

Finally we've crossed the Dnieper. With the motor stuttering on, we're flying on, determined not to turn round before all bombs have been dropped.

The targets down below – on roads and fields – were clearly visible – one couldn't hope for better, really. We're advancing deep into enemy territory, some 40 kilometres, when we note the Bolshevik front progressing from the east. At different sections they're already badly bruised by our V-formations of attacking aircraft.

Our target is a wide field path crammed with vehicles entangled with infantry troops in one huge morass. Let's liven the place up with our goodies … and down come our blessings. All hell breaks loose down below, with blasts from massive explosions reaching us far above the blazing inferno. Between trucks wildly zooming ahead to then all of a sudden brake to abrupt stops, and Russians thrusting in all directions and firing flat, we bash them with our cluster bombs. Thirty to forty trucks lie abandoned, glowing wrecks, and the road is ripped apart at various points. The ammunition we have on board comes into its own and we're firing relentlessly. We keep diving down, doing our thing, until we have run out of ammunition and the engine, quite poorly, calls on me to turn round. Slowly I climb up, steeply breaking away from the Russians, thus avoiding becoming a clean target for them.

Crossing the Dnieper, I shut down the engine, report this to the old man and then gradually continue on my way by following him. We barely need to check our maps, seeing as we now know only too well which flight path to take. Eventually Karl, positioned in the ventral gondola, curtly informs us that this is our thirteenth mission. Not surprising.

My crate – the 'Anton' – gradually loses altitude but it's not long until we reach home. Keeping to the highway towards Minsk, we notice heavy transport of reinforcements. There's an advantage in that the highway, or runway, is smooth and concreted, which means our trucks make good headway while previously they could only do some 20 km/h. Even then, our truck drivers aren't to be envied.

In front of us Minsk looms out of the haze. Gently dipping my left wing, I try to take some photographs of the city now three-quarters destroyed. Then south in a wide turn, crossing over two airfields with our home airbase in front now. One machine lies flat on its belly and by its red engine flap we realise that the 8th Staffel must have been involved. Because of this wreckage blocking the base, I restart the engine and prepare for landing, but it doesn't go smoothly at all, with the engine spluttering and spewing big-time and making everyone below concerned. Drawing a wide right-hand turn, I once again attempt landing and this time I manage to touch down on the bumpy runway. All are assembled to receive me, with the black corps exclaiming how anxious they had been about me and my aircraft, seeing as I hadn't turned back. Immediately a few engineers busy themselves with my sick patient and have soon identified the sustained damage. The valve had snapped. Given that prior to take-off the engine had been working perfectly well, the valve must have fallen apart during take-off. The line chief gives the order to throw out the engine because after five more flight-hours it would have to be replaced anyway.

During the subsequent operations the Stalin Line and the hinterland once again become our target and the onslaught is on. We focus on assembly points while our comrades hack bunkers and fortified buildings. The large motorised columns give us special pleasure and we strafe and attack them with a continuous barrage of fire. Leaving destruction and devastation in our wake. Gradually we're approaching the city of Gomel with its three airbases.

14.7.41

Today we're the first up in a wave of operations. Our line is the furthest south. Fifty kilometres short of Gomel and just in front of us a huge cloud of dust rises, leaving what is beneath it to our imagination! Flying above, we spot a large column of transport vehicles and instantly we're met by fire. Christ Almighty, there sure must be valuable stuff rolling along those roads, we say to ourselves, as until now we'd never come across quite this number of flak guns mounted on trucks. Well, what can one say: another little surprise, and Orsha, still to come, didn't lie far beyond.

A moment later we were hovering in the air prepared for attack, right above the column, which by that time had thinned out as groups were trying to escape our bombs by rolling forwards and backwards. Our first attack comes to nothing. Yes, a few bombs drop just alongside the trucks and several Russians are seen scrambling off their vehicles, seeking cover somewhere in the fields, but, honestly, the impact is far from noteworthy.

Suddenly we hear a shrill alarm cry: three fighters attacking in the back! We immediately join up and fly in close formation, but Russians are already targeting us – three I-17 monoplanes,[31] clearly identified by their long and pointed noses. We immediately notice that these fellows are deploying different attack strategies from the

The Polikarpov I-17 (Source: https://en.wikipedia.org/wiki/Polikarpov_ITP#/media/File:PolikarpovITP.jpg).

'rats', by targeting us not from above, but from left behind and right above us. Rascals, the lot of them! But they haven't figured out that we're onto them and they will be getting a bloody nose from us, seeing as they're neatly positioned right in our bull's eye. And, boy, are they ever getting it over their heads, quite literally. Tracers come whizzing in a stream close up to their aircraft, leaving the guys no option but to turn round – only to come at us again. Now they approach from above left, I instantly dive low, allowing the old man and his companion to swing up in a steep spiral – he gets a clear field of fire. Bullets slam their aircraft like a hailstorm and those poor sods, now aiming far too low, are severely hit. Looks like it was 30 to 40 metres too low, according to the trail of smoke. What do you know, but they're forced to make yet another escape and for a while they bank downwards, obviously in an effort to keep a respectful distance from us.

One or another enemy aircraft are still making half-hearted attempts at attacking us, but true to our established tradition, we force them to back off at each attempt. Looks like it has finally sunk in and they are in fear of our perfectly aimed fire. Defending against such an onslaught is not really everybody's thing, especially not when tracers come whooshing towards you.

We proceed to attack the truck convoys a second and a third time, all under the watchful eye of Ivan. Were they in any way happy seeing our bombs blow the vehicles into pieces and hurling clouds of debris and smoke into the air? Looks like they're knackered and have given up attacking us. Maybe they're too busy watching their comrades being ripped apart below on the ground. Even once we dive away to fly back to base, they seem to be at a loss for what to do.

There's quite a racket in my crate due to Toni swearing like a sailor because of some obstruction in the pump. Meanwhile Karl is killing himself laughing, watching the Russians draw circles above the flaming wreckage left by the cowardly bunch of soldiers. Pitt feels obliged to fire off one last round of ammunition onto the congested roads with me watching this entire spectacle in my rear mirror. Richard, stuck in the cockpit, only gets the stench of gunpowder without having the benefit of launching some of his own concentrated bombs. He is pretty furious.

Happily enriched by this further adventure, we're heading home. These Russian fighter planes certainly didn't impress us in the least, with our ground personnel barely able to believe their ears when we relate our experience to them. What a difference it would have been to fight Tommy or Frog up there; they sure would've had a tale or two about sleepless nights having to repair wrecked planes, ready for action the following morning.

That evening roll call took place in celebratory style. For the first time in a long while the pilots engaged at the Eastern Front are awarded the Iron Cross Second Class and these were indeed well deserved. Nearly all of us won this insignia. The memorable occasion where we all lined up proudly wearing the ribbon with the medal on our uniforms in front of the reporter from the PK [Propaganda Department] is engraved on the photographer's photo plate for posterity. My entire crew displayed the ribbons with the crosses.

15.7.41

We have traversed the Dnieper at multiple points along the front line. The only bridgeheads left in Russian hands are Slobin and Rogachev and they are clinging onto them tooth and nail.[32] Their reinforcements come via a bridge and some sort of gangplank – which we're ordered to blow up.

That afternoon, heading east, we fly the now well-known route, reaching our destination after three-quarters of an hour. We passed three crossings, where one of them, the railway bridge, is destroyed with its debris floating in the water. Diving down in echelon, we swoop upon the two crossings still intact, but the old man then does some crazy turns, with the result that all his bombs splash into the water and us lot aren't given a chance to drop our bombs. Then the old man decides to do some reconnoitring by flying crisscross above the forests surrounding Slobin. At that point, flying one behind the other, I'm expecting the old man to come down on the bridges for a second time, but there's none of that and he simply loops and rolls above the woods – while flak scores direct hits on our planes. You just wait, you beasts, we'll soon show you who's master of the skies. 'Fire – fire! Now!'

We fire ferociously, unabated, into the enemy positions below us. They immediately react by putting a stop to their firing, but before too long pick up again, chasing us with heavy barrages of bullets. The old man insists on circling over the same area and I have no idea what it could possibly be that so fascinates him down there. We continue flying over flak sectors, Richard lets some bombs drop from his bay and the journey continues, slicing straight through heavy barrages of fire. At various spots we notice bright red flashes lighting up the sky, scores of Russians dive into the nearby wood for safety, but our good selves keep spraying fire indiscriminately. Only one of the enemy batteries continues after our bomb drop – but we're not letting this go by unpunished. The old man is still cruising above the positions and once again we jettison some of our precious eggs … these are our last ones. They practically fall into the same craters the previous bombs had ripped in the ground, but cause extensive damage to the two batteries – not to the third, unfortunately. Instead, bullets whip across from all three of our machine guns, it's total mayhem and makes the Russians think twice about firing back.

Looks like the old man has finally had his fill and presumably must have seen everything there was to see as he turns round. He isn't at all pleased that the bridges have remained intact, but has to console himself with the fact that six anti-aircraft guns have bitten the dust. Once again Richard proved that he's master of the trade.

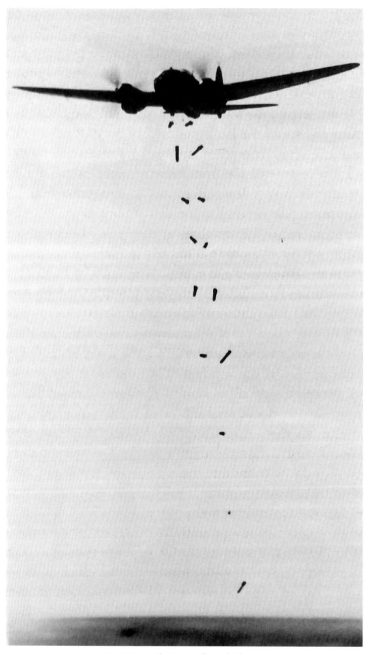

An He 111 during a bomb drop
(Source: Ron Mackay, *Heinkel He 111* (Ramsbury, 2003)).

16.7.41

The ring of a shrill alarm. Orders barked out while on the double heading towards our planes. Heavily armed columns are lining up at the far end of Kritschev. A brief glance at the maps and we've got the full picture. Before too long we're up in the air. Streaking after the enemy at full speed, we bank sharply and Richard tries to identify the objective yet again on the map for me to take a closer look.

Soon we've crossed the front line and we're hot on the heels of convoy after convoy of fleeing Russians. An enormous pillar of smoke rises up, practically enveloping the road leading east. God Almighty, what a traffic jam! Russians three abreast, sometimes four, convoys of vehicles of all sorts, some spilling into the field bordering the road, and many a Russian trying to escape on foot. For us it's as if Ivan has been served up on a platter. Without much dilly-dallying we zoom down, our machine guns rattling – it's a fanfare of missiles with every shot, every bomb precise and lethal. Nothing else will do, what with these crucial targets we're ordered to destroy. These fellows leap off their vehicles, which are demolished, wrecked, wedged between trucks, burned out or still in flames. A dark mass of scorched metal. We push further down, level off just above the roadway, drop one bomb after another, while liberally emptying our cartridge drums into this hellish chaos. Mud and smoke fountains spray in all directions, hurling debris into the air. There must be some forty fires alight dotted around the place … What can you say: bull's eye hits are precisely that. Our tracer bullets and incendiary ammunition unleash a hurricane of fire, turning countless vehicles into distorted, burning wreckage. We fly all the way to the far end, then lean into a controlled semi-circle turn and then swoop low for one last check to see whether the area has been swept clean of opposition. Looks like the comrades have come to their senses. Nonetheless, there're still a few four-barrelled machine guns spraying their fire around our machines. It has to be said that despite the confusion we've caused, they're aiming pretty accurately, with the net tightening uncomfortably around our aircraft. Unperturbed, we drop some more bombs, wreak more havoc, and the only pity is that we've now run out of bombs. We could have continued for hours on end! We then circle above the target like birds of prey, carpeting it with a hailstorm of fire. Not a single blockage, not a single obstacle prevents us from literally slamming salvos of shots into the enemy. The weapons we deploy work like a miracle. It's pure joy to be able to target with such precision. Bit of a shame that I myself don't get to press the trigger – I'd really have loved to be part of it. But there you go.

Finally, with our magazines totally empty, we break off, gather ourselves, circle the sites of ruin and devastation for a final review – and are satisfied with the destruction that has been wrought: around fifty vehicles have been destroyed or are burning. Unfortunately we can't quite assess how many machines, vehicles or armaments have been put out of working order thanks to our bombardment and gun attacks, but it must amount to quite a bit and they are certain to be out of commission for some time to come.

Humming and whistling to ourselves, we return home and are so cocky about our success that we triumphantly embark on several sharp dives to alert our comrades and technicians who had been left behind at the airbase of the good news. The minute we touch down the whole lot crowd around us, and we have to give them a detailed account of our mission while the old man makes the official report in our stead. Lots of shoving each other in the ribs, lots of shoulder thumping – it was glorious. It's been ages since we've been able to celebrate such a magnificent achievement. If only we could find such targets again soon.

24.7.41
Twenty-Second Mission

We've been waiting for some time to be charged with a mission of a different kind and then it happened: attack the city of Roslavl.[33]

This time around, our unit is headed up by Lieutenant Beckmann, who's been seconded to us by the 7th Staffel, seeing as we've been reduced to only two officers – that is, the old man and Hauptmann Haster.

It started mid-morning, around 1100. Weather: clear blue sky up until the front line, clouding over towards the target and above it, a thick blanket of cloud to an altitude of 1,500 metres. We follow a highway leading to the city, straight as an arrow, like so many roads are in Russia. I've got to admit, deploying us for an outing of this kind is pure madness, seeing as it sort of advertises our presence long before we've even reached our target. But those are the orders and we're sure as hell going to follow them. You could navigate by the rule: left wing over right roadside ditch. We see the vehicles passing by – there aren't many of them. Isolated Russians seek protection in the ditches along the road. Crossing over an airbase, we can make out three fighter planes down below – demolished the lot of them.

Ahead of us emerges the target. White high-rises are clearly visible even at a 30-km distance. Gritting our teeth, we glide along, Richard fondly scanning the tall buildings which literally stare us in the eyes. Doing him a favour, I zoom towards them while the leading aircraft is bound for the railway station.

Though still a few kilometres short of the city, a cacophony of exploding ammunition and bursts of machine-gun fire already fills the air. Concentrated flak is coming up at us fast and furious, making it hard to keep the aircraft under control. Curiously, it's only heavy flak – not a single one of their harmless tomatoes swooshing past us. At some 10–20 metres away, shells detonate and within seconds a dark smoke-pall drifts up, which we immediately sweep through. Thrust back and forth as during choppy weather – makes me wonder whether we'll make it through in one piece.

At the border of the city a barrage of flak closes in on us tightly, Richard urges me to drop away below and hold the bird steady, but what with it violently shaking the whole time, this is simply impossible. At long last it looks like those tall, white buildings –

Roslavl after being bombed (Source: Atlantik Pressedienst).

surely they are administrative tower blocks – are in our crosshairs and after what seemed like an age, but must have been mere seconds, we finally drop our explosives and firebombs.

Took a crazy zigzag course right behind the captain who, obstinate as a mule, keeps flying dead ahead. For me the moments leading up to diving down to the target and keeping the machine as steady and level as possible were probably the worst, and my heart nearly stopped beating. I was prepared to be hit, set on fire the next moment and disintegrate in the air. Much to my relief, I'm able to sheer away from flames coming belching out at me. Lieutenant Beckmann doggedly flies on, unflinching, much like a tank, probably because he hates like a pest everything that even approximates a curve or spiral, and he dislikes turning the crank. Far behind the city, we finally make a wide sweep to the left. In reverse course this allows me to observe the impact of the bombs. Reddish-brown mushroom-shaped clouds blown aloft into the air at several spots. A sure sign that the bombs had exploded right then and there. The bright, white glow of our explosives bathing our air route signposts our lethal flight path above the city, spelling doom and disaster.

The minute our contraptions, packed with high explosives, release their charge, we see hundreds of locations erupt in bright flames, naturally setting the buildings – flimsy constructions, obviously – and other ramshackle houses on fire. Flak is blazing away at us like mad once we're up close to the city, but nothing deters us from steering our machines towards base. I glance down and realise that I've just flown over the area where not long ago stood the blocks of high-rises, now largely destroyed thanks to our bombs – they folded literally like a house of cards. And this was achieved by no more than 50-kg bombs. The Russians don't seem to have a clue about construction!

Once again we run into heavy flak, which comes at us from a ludicrously tiny railway station. Karl and Pitt bang away vigorously with their MGs, targeting the clearly visible posts, but today we're presented with a different scenario from what we've hitherto encountered, showing us an Ivan who's determined to whack us. Small course adjustments allow us to leave the concentrated flak behind.

Even before this encounter I had examined my machine to establish whether it had suffered any direct hits. But neither I nor my comrades could find even so much as a trace of a fracture. Hardly believable, I thought to myself – surely we would have sustained at least a few knocks, considering that literally hundreds of shells had exploded right next to us? But – there was nothing. We simply conclude that the flak ammunition must be total rubbish, which, admittedly, suits us just fine.

We cross an airbase. Looks like it isn't manned. Then another flak attack just short of reaching the front line. Karl efficiently silences them with a chain of orange-coloured tracers. Shooting from above seems to do the trick in practically all situations and, if nothing else, tracers whizzing past has an impact on morale.

Once we've traversed the front line we breathe a sigh of relief as this initially harmless mission was, truth be told, more than we'd bargained for. What follows seemed like child's play. With the unit flying a zigzag course direction home, we train ourselves to use the lowering cloud base as coverage to then zoom across the countryside. I must admit feeling totally elated zooming just above the fields like hedgehoppers then diving down to base and announcing our arrival in the traditional low-level whoosh over the runway.

Once again we look the crate up and down, but still, much to our amazement, not even the tiniest of marks. A fluke, really. The captain and his right-hand officer had suffered a series of small hits but they too are quite surprised to find that they've got off relatively scot-free. Hard to imagine what impact the Russians' heavy flak might be scoring, if what's been demonstrated so far is all they're capable of. Pitiful, really.

25.7.41

Today there should be another attack on Roslavl, we're told. The weather is miserable, with one ferocious thunderstorm after another, throughout the day. But the attack is to go ahead nevertheless.

With our heavily loaded bays we stay down low, streaming head-on for the front line where, according to reports, weather conditions should improve. The visibility is low. Parts of the countryside are totally flooded due to the heavy downpours – Mother Earth remains completely invisible. Good fortune has it that the 'landscape' around here is entirely flat. We aren't able to make out much more than the shadowy contours of our captain's aircraft. Rudi Schwarze, on his right, our backstop, all but disappears into the masses of dirt and dust. The rain is simply too heavy.

After some time we're forced into violent manoeuvres trying to keep to a set course despite the turbulent weather. Tossed and buffeted by thunderstorms, there is no huge pleasure up here. Along with this comes dangerously reduced visibility, the knowledge that two aircraft are flying close by, that we're heavily armoured and consequently respond sluggishly due to the massive load, and that it is paramount to negotiate the geography. We've completely lost sight of the captain, but knowing that he's one to fly dead straight ahead, I am confident that I'll catch up with him at some point, which we do after crossing the front line, which measures some 20–30 kilometres wide. No. 3 also joins us but it's still a few kilometres until we reach the front line. That's where, all of a sudden, the cloud bank tears apart and we catch glimpses of the earth below, holding our speed while cruising in a clear blue sky with beautiful sunshine. High above us some stray white cumuli as we gradually climb higher. Except for watching eagerly as the odd shell smashes a huge hole into the ground, there's not much left to look at down below as we've now left the battles behind. That's all. No traffic on the roads.

At an altitude of some 2,500 metres clouds stretch across the sky in a continuous band. Passing straight through the middle of the cumulus, the aircraft heads towards its target. Our Staffel sticks together and we quite enjoy the feeling of zooming through this washhouse in a single cohesive unit. Though frequently slammed against the side of the aircraft quite violently, one never lets go of the good old He and she fortunately responds to the slightest flexing of the rudder. Just short of our target I lose sight of our captain swooping into a thick cumulus blob, he must have entered a curve and dived away. I, on the other hand, climb higher at full throttle soon to glide above the clouds.

As far as the eye can see, there's one towering mountain next to the other. There surely is nothing more beautiful to behold than flying in a cloudscape of fluffy, bizarrely shaped, bulging piles of cumulus clouds. This, at least, is how I feel.

After searching for the first hole in the clouds to pass through, we grab our opportunity, grit our teeth, dive down for a swift and precisely targeted approach. Just below us a bomb train explodes right across our flight path. Must be the captain. Looks like everything down below is ready for us – and our bombs come hailing down. The aircraft beneath mine is hit by a burst of flak. At times the light clouds are so closely stuck together that one can hardly make out what's what. Our lot is being shot at as well, looks like we've surprised them, and mindful of yesterday's hell, I yank my crate round to return, heading back the same way I'd come; hardly anybody is shooting at us now. I must offer a bad target, looks like. Behind me is the backstop. Once above the bank of clouds, he too went on the attack.

Toni radios me, instructing us to return solo to base. I chose the next best – straight path to the front line, to Smolensk. Why not make the most of our trip and take a closer look at this embattled city? Why not snap a few pictures? Let's see whether this time 'round us folks will be in the photo or the Russians. Within several days the place had degenerated into a wild tug-of-war.

Soon a gigantic column of black smoke appeared in front of us. Smolensk – our objective. The city is embroiled in bitter combat and street after street had gone up in flames. Keeping down low, we fly over it with our reinforcement planes touching down on the runway just short of the city, which by now is riddled with deep crater pits. Droning at low altitude above the helmets of our Landsers, we fly above the main motorway [Autobahn], only to end up once again engulfed in foul weather conditions.

Shortly before, we spot construction sites, blown-up bridges and huge craters being repaired by our pioneers and servicemen. Russian prisoners are toiling away, heaving crushing weights of heavy and unwieldy rocks and mounds of sand to the sites. They immediately lie flat on the ground as I pass low overhead.

The weather turns from bad to worse and visibility is appalling. Meanwhile I have to bend closely into the turns dictated by the roadway to retain the general direction to at least some degree. Short of Minsk, about 40 km away from our airbase, the ground station alerts us via radio to abandon the original route, dodge the fog and instead head for Orsha as the alternative landing field.

That meant turning round to make tracks to Orsha. We reach this dump in no time with the weather above quite acceptable. Steep dive and down we go. Landing with a few small bumps – and there we are back in the arms of Mother Earth. All hell has broken loose out here. As the airbase is enormous, it must have been considered the optimal assembly space for a larger number of combat groups.

Someone is waving at me and, taking a closer look, I realise it's the captain, who had landed shortly before us. Our backstop is here as well and it looks like he has once again been hit several times. Three other machines from a different squad have also arrived.

The group commandant from our II Group had food brought to us, and without missing a beat handed us his next order. Our crates are meanwhile loaded up and are ready to be refuelled for the next mission. And while haste is the order of the day, the entire process also turns out to be embarrassing and unprofessional, seeing as all the petrol trucks and personnel are busy with a group of Ju 88s. Hurriedly we wolf down some hefty bangers, inspect an I-17 that has been shot down, and gradually make preparations. The machines have been checked, equipment was working properly and nothing was found amiss.

After a terse briefing, we're off. Our destinations are troop positions in two forest areas south of Mogilev on the Dnieper. Being the last team, we take off just behind the other group, and we dive-bomb and strafe the area assigned to us, plastering it with shells and bombs like there's no tomorrow, while at the same time our ground troops had encircled it at a distance of 2 km, as we could tell from the white flares flooding the landscape. Mission accomplished, we return to base, flying low. Filthy weather just as before, but we plunge through and make a safe landing thanks to a slight improvement in conditions.

30.7.41

Once again our group is being transferred – this time to Orsha. The Russians flee in panic like scared sheep while the advances of our troops to the front line have become longer by the day. As far as I'm concerned, this rabbit-chasing is fine by me, as it means we can have a greater impact.

Our nomadic existence under canvas continues when we're posted to the outer edge of the woods bordering the field, with our machines well camouflaged so that they could not possibly be seen from the air. Once in a while, during daytime hours, we catch sight of Ivan – just as we'd been briefed by the reports. He'd bang away some ammunition but wouldn't cause significant damage, it said. Strange, that ... Here we are in Russia for quite some time already and so far, no sign of an enemy attack.

That same day we received the Front Flying Clasp in Bronze. We've got twenty-four missions under our belts and we've achieved quite a bit, causing a fair amount of destruction – but, at the same time, quite a few of our good mates have not returned from these missions.

31.7.41

The Russians at the front near Smolensk are receiving considerable reinforcements and equipment from Moscow. Hence, we're ordered to target the large railway station at Vyazma. Since weather conditions made flying in close formation impossible, each of us takes off solo in short intervals. The senior sergeant who's in charge of this mission along with the commander of the group allocates his aircraft to me.

Charged with bombs of heavy calibre – which makes it somewhat problematic – but without delay we pass over Smolensk, now firmly in our hands, and head eastwards. Keeping south of the Autobahn, our plan is to launch a surprise attack from the rear, as I'm determined not to go through another one of those Roslavl horrors ever again. I'm the last one to lift off, but just before I turn the ignition, the captain approaches my machine and alerts me to the fighters that have been reported swarming above the objective. 'Be cautious, comrade!' he warns, wishing me good luck. I give full throttle and was airborne.

Just behind Smolensk a thunderstorm breaks out and there's no way to turn away or avoid the bad weather by flying around it, so I slice through the middle. We tighten the safety belts and go into a merry spin. Violently jolted around, I fear the bird is going to fall apart any minute. Under the strain the wings of the aircraft bend, with the surfaces showing worrying waves in the metal. Gosh, how will this end? Sitting tight, Richard keeps his hand poised on the catapult release. The three behind us swear like navvies. And yet … we must make it!

Some long minutes tick by – but we've finally made it. My fingers are hurting, my shirt is clinging to my back bathed in sweat. Behind the front line terrific gusts of wind press my aircraft downwards, I sink some 100 metres as if in an elevator, but the engines then drag me up again to see me float at 3,500 metres.

There's always a cloud or two, behind which we can play hide-and-seek with the fighter planes, and we've got to keep our wits about us against the enemy who invariably appears out of nowhere and takes us by surprise. Further south it goes along the track, vast tree-covered expanses beneath us, and finally the cloud bank loosens, which makes it much easier to navigate. After several hours staying on course, we reach the railway lines leading south from Vyazma, where we turn sharply to the left, dive down and make for the railway station.

A gigantic cloud of black smoke rises before us, then hangs in the sky right at our height. I fly towards it, as this must be where the station – our objective – is located. With the thick clouds reducing visibility, I grit my teeth, plough my way through this muck, and at 2,000 metres finally see the ground. Before me, some 3–4 km away, lies Vyazma with its railway station ablaze.

Vyazma burning (Source: Werner Held, *Die deutschen Jagdgeschwader im Russlandfeldzug* (Friedberg, 1986)).

An enormous black bank of clouds rolls towards us. These are dangerous times. Bright flames spurt from three train engines, immediately enveloping this fantastic scene of devastation in smoke and dust. I slip past, heading to the station. As I level my bird off, Richard is now well placed to drop the bombs. Dull thuds, followed by deafening explosions down below, these are sure hits. The area close to the railway station is now on fire.

With the bombs now dropped, I climb up steeply and break away to the left.

'Enemy fighters approaching from directly above,' exclaim Karl, Pitt and Toni, practically all at once.

Off with us, into the deep end. But neither Ivan nor we have a chance to fire. What with this dense smoke, it is pitch black. The battered crate is tossed around, the back rearing up, I barely manage to press down and decide on trimming the machine. Though the tab is reset, the bird still climbs at an extraordinary speed of 12 m/sec – goodness me, a strong wind pushes me up! Inadvertently I think of how gliders must cope in these situations. Before I know it, I'm above the clouds and I immediately head to base.

After a while the Russian fighters have caught up. This time, there are three I-17s, who launch straight into the attack. Not a fair ratio: 3:1. This makes these guys unusually bold and has them drawing closer and closer to me, while I'm on my own. Banging away a salvo of fire-flashes, I then disappear behind the next cloud. I fly through the protective white haze, eventually sticking my nose out of the soup to get a sense of what those 'fast comrades of ours' are up to. Predictably, a few moments later two draw alongside of me at some 300 metres and, one keeping on my tail, they have their eyes trained on me. Responding with a further salvo, I swerve into another cloud. I poke my nose out of the muck again and bear down with tracers shooting from all guns. Ahh … they've resorted to a different strategy now. One is attacking while the others refrain. Alternating, they're literally hounding me and finally, exasperated, I dive for cover into the protective cloak of the grey fog. Let the Russians look for me until they're blue in the face – it'll be in vain.

Before too long we're above Smolensk. Losing height rapidly due to my phenomenal dive speed, we then continue in low flight back home.

After reporting on our successful operations at the command table, we return to our tents to rest. It was certainly a most eventful outing. My hands are still hurting from performing such wild manoeuvres in the air – indeed, I've got quite a few blisters.

4.8.41[34]

I've been on the alert since 1000 hours and Toni, the radio operator, is the only one who's with me. Am almost certain that we'll be deployed to one of those courier services – but then it turned out differently.

Towards lunchtime we're ordered to board the 'Maria' and head to Germany. We're landed with an old clanker of a machine! The weird 'M' had been converted to a transport aircraft with new engines, but that still doesn't mean that it can hold the cargo I am supposed to load. Three men are meant to fly along with us, one is headed for the field hospital, one is on leave and the third one is some official with the war chest – so all in all this is top brass!

Our 'company mother' hands me a long wish list, even specifying a barrel of beer! True, stuck in the Soviet Union we've sure missed a good pint – so, let's hope that we'll be able to scrounge one or two barrels of the stuff.

After about half an hour the aircraft is up to snuff and ready to go. Received the weather reports and we're off after our traditional farewell round. Conditions are filthy and it looks like flying won't be a great pleasure.

After a good hour or so, we pass Minsk on our right – a city completely in ruins now. With Baranovichi now also behind us, all of a sudden smoke billows out of the right engine. The coolant indicator flickers its warning signal and a long white vapour trail leaves the exhaust. Somewhere there must be a leak. That's all we need right now, is what I'm thinking, and I turn off the engine.

I'm rapidly losing height and it's barely possible to keep the machine in level flight with all that cargo on board. My variometer shows a steady loss of ¼ m[/s]. We set course for the next airfield, Bialystok, and can only hope that the other engine won't conk out as well.

Soon, however, we need to understand what's what and that there's no winning here. Flying at an altitude of barely 500 m, strong gusts of wind fling the machine about and I'm only just able to prevent a fatal crash. The needle on the speed indicator stalls at 170 km/h to 180 km/h – damn disappointing. Nothing seems to help – we've no option other than to start our descent. Using all the tricks in the book, I try lumbering my lame crate towards the next bigger village situated close to what I'm hoping will be a busy road.

We sink lower by the minute, below us a large dense forest. I don't fancy going down just yet and keep the engine going. What the hell – let it guzzle up all that's left. With great difficulty I manage to bring the bird below the clouds at 350 m. Below and in front of us vast meadows and fields, in part already harvested. Landing would not pose a significant risk. I am still deliberating when I spot, at a distance of some 15 km, two criss-crossing runways of an airfield. It's an absolute must to reach that. Gradually we sink lower, one last stress on the engine, pushed the throttle and climb down. Surely we will make it … my mind is racing… and though I could never rule out crashing, I manage to keep levelling the bird.

At long last the airfield is in full sight, and though minuscule and by all accounts quite bumpy, with the runways quite obviously still only half-constructed, I breathe a sigh of relief. I prepare for landing on the longer of the two runways. Our ailing engine creaks out the undercarriage but fails to extend the flaps. The hand-pump in this worn-out crate also malfunctions and my nerves are at breaking point. Obliged to land at great speed, touching down at some 190–200, I slam on the brake pedals with all my strength, but they too have had it and barely react! Damn this blasted bird, just when you depend on her – she fails you.

As the airbase was very small, my machine can't lose speed gradually, but does so abruptly, until the brakes finally do their thing and grip onto the smooth tarmac, with the aircraft then rolling to the far end of the field. Even if we're not able to come to a stop – worst comes to worst, beyond the field is nothing but farmland, I assume.

After some bumps and bounces the aircraft waddles up a slight incline – but we can't quite tell what lies behind. The 'M' is still going strong at 80 when we're approaching a mound of rocks. With full power, I tug the bird to the left, but she's got hardly any rotation in her, so just short of the mound I yank her up and away – well, I try my best … but seeing as there was barely any room for this to work, we bang hard into that heap of rocks. There's an almighty jolt, the crate sinks further down, thick rock splinters are flying in the air and come smashing down. Lying flat on our stomachs, we slide for some 50 m while rotating full circle around ourselves to finally come to a halt in the middle of a gigantic cloud of dust. That's it. Finished.

Swiftly I switch off the ignition, close the fuel shut-off valve, open the windows and scramble outside! Pale, knees shaking, the others come crawling after me. Thank the Lord – they are unscathed, it's only me who's injured, with blood dripping from my chin from when I hit the steering wheel.

First we light up a cigarette and after inhaling deeply we inspect the sustained damage.

The undercarriage has come off and landed in a high arc somewhere further away; it has left a gaping hole in the fuselage, and massively dented the tailplane. The slats are bent, the cooler punched in, the right-hand oil tank ruptured.

Barely upright, I circle the old bird, still feeling quite fuzzy as if I've been hit in the head.

Gradually I calm down. Two men try and get to a telephone while we clean up the debris, placing all cargo underneath the wings. This at least protects them from the rain.

People come running across the fields to us. Some young chappy speaks broken German and explains that we've come down on the Swizloozc airbase, constructed by the Russians. We check our map and yes, indeed, the location is marked. The next town is Volkovysk, albeit without an airbase and at some 40 km away, which is no big deal if flying with a machine that's intact, but on foot it's quite a distance.

The droning of a Ju 52 above us has Toni making a dash for the aircraft to fire several red flares into the sky which are spotted from up high, and, banking in a wide curve, they prepare to land, seeing as they too have flown the same path. They only just miss crashing into the same heap of rocks. Just a few metres short of it, the Ju comes to a stop.

A whole bunch of people descend and inspect the crash. The good Ju is packed to the rafters, leaving me wondering what might happen to us. Could they at least take a few of us on board, I ask, but they seem doubtful, just shaking their heads at the sight of our cargo. Explaining to them that my three passengers have nothing much themselves in terms of luggage, the pilot finally agrees and lets the three men on board. Meanwhile we'd wait for the Ju to return. No telephone.

Our guests happily climb into the machine which will carry them safely to another airbase from which they're able to return to the Reich. Meanwhile the Ju radio operator promises to contact the next airbase to inform them of our emergency situation and request help. That would be Baranovichi. I make my own attempts to contact the place.

The Ju turns and, directed into the winds, it takes off, disappearing eastwards after making a final farewell round.

From the flea-ridden boy who jabbers away in German I soon find out that the closest station headquarters is located 6 km from here, in Swizloozc. If it really exists, I say to myself, then surely there must be a telephone there. I organise a panje-cart for myself with the boy volunteering as my driver. En route we meet a Jewish lad who knows the area well and the way to the headquarters, and on he hops onto the back of the cart.

That decrepit old horse must have been born in the year dot as he stands still every few minutes with his whole body shuddering from weakness. That's no way to move ahead; I quickly decide to call a halt to this nonsense. Catching and haltering a new horse wasn't a problem and we let our old nag go. From then on our merry trip wasn't exactly something to write home about – but at least the beast moved.

After about one hour – during which I relieved a Polish man of his fully loaded MG that he claimed he had found somewhere in the field – we finally arrive at the headquarters. But wouldn't you know it – there's no telephone as in reality this place is nothing more than an outpost. Apparently, we would find one in Volkovysk. I have some food brought to me, pack up some sandwiches for Toni, board the cart along with two Landsers and drive back. The Landers are to help guard the machine.

Driving back, I decide to pick up the old horse as he had somewhat recovered in the interim, and we make good progress. Toni, not one to remain idle, had in the meantime organised some milk, bread and eggs. This should get us through for at least a few days.

The following morning I'm on the lookout for a vehicle which I could drive to Volkovysk, intending to contact a nearby airbase from there.

We've packed the rear of the fuselage with straw and once we curl up, the three of us have enough space to sleep tightly huddled next to each other. Toni prefers to kip in the cockpit; I myself use a coat which I found in one of the knapsacks as my duvet.

Towards evening the humming of an engine startles us and, looking up, we see two cars driving across the airfield. For good measure I fire a signal cartridge into the air. They approach, descend and much to our surprise it turns out to be none other than the district administrator with one of his employees. The area where we'd landed, so we're informed, had been included into East Prussia just the day before and he, the administrator, was on a surveillance trip but had lost his way. He's quite happy to take me in his car, and off we go, criss-crossing fields and roads, all lying in rubble and lined with debris. After a while, once we've reached the paved street leading into the city, driving becomes easier, though loads of potholes don't make it much more pleasant. At least we're not sitting in fear of breaking down.

After a journey of some three hours and with several stops on the way – necessary because every few kilometres we had to refill our leaking radiator with water – we finally reach Wolkoraysk. I take the map with me. I'm dropped off at the place housing the army switchboard and after about an hour they were able to put me through to the Baranovichi airbase. Busying himself with my luggage, an officious sergeant tells me that he'd already been messaged about the situation and that all is being arranged to get it sorted.

I spend the night on a heap of straw piled up in the switchboard office, though the constant ringing of the phone and the hundreds of flies don't make it a restful experience.

The following day I get myself to the army headquarters, only for them to direct me to an aviation supply depot. En route, I pass the railway station, which had been our objective not so long ago. Look at that – our big fat bomb had punched a huge hole into the storage shed which had been filled to the rafters with fuel and barrels of tar. The fires had spread unhindered, causing huge devastation in the surrounding area, but already people are seen busy clearing up the debris.

The city has been badly damaged. Looks like only one-third of it has remained intact and even in the relatively unscathed part several buildings have been utterly destroyed.

Finally I arrive at the company headquarters and report to the chief. He's a laidback man hailing from the Ostmark (Austria) and immediately puts at my disposal a vehicle which they had captured from the Russians. Once again I seem to revisit the past as, driving back, I recognise the road from having attacked it not so long ago. The losses the Russians had suffered in this devastating battle of Bialystok have been horrendous and what I see around me is horrific. I count over ninety shattered tanks lying in the ditch, among them some weighing over 50 t, streets reduced to rubble, hundreds of trucks overturned, equipment discarded and heaps of debris and ashes everywhere. They've put up collection points for looted goods – at a rough estimate there must be over 100 flak guns stacked up in a pile, and everywhere abandoned assault guns. As far as the eye can see, huge crater pits and holes wherever the shells had hit. Very many graves, some single, some freshly dug mass graves, are testimony to the severity of the battle that has ravaged this place. Friend and foe rest side by side, but the number of mass graves of the Russians by far outweigh those of the Germans. Once in a while we make a stop, inspect various pieces of weaponry strewn around, tanks and MGs. In some vehicles we still find the bodies of crewmembers caught in the wild firing. No matter how many litres of chlorinated lime we pour over their stiff remains, all entangled and hard for us to reach, there's no way of getting rid of the dreadful stench of decomposing bodies.

What catches my attention in all this mayhem is a four-barrelled machine gun mounted on a truck, where I find bundle after bundle of wiring harnesses – some hanging, some just discarded on the ground – all complete with their magazine holders. I fiddle around with one of them, pull at the release button and that's when all four start hammering like mad, though in a slower sequence – just like the solenoids in our aircraft MGs.

Everywhere Russian prisoners of war are toiling away – back-breaking drudgery; guarded by German Landsturmleute,[35] these Russians don't even think about how to get hold of arms and escape. They're an obstinate lot. I myself want to avail myself of a ten-shot carbine or a pistol, but there's nothing even close to be found in the piles of captured armaments. Much of what I come across can't be used or is badly damaged. Heading back, we make a stop at a nursery, pack up our truck with vegetables, and then continue to our machine.

When I arrive, I'm informed that an officer from Baranovichi has flown in earlier and picked up the safe box, and that's fine by me as at least I no longer bear responsibility for that thing. He, I'm told, has promised Toni that help would soon be on the way.

Though we wait for several days, nobody arrives. When we've just about had it, we flag down the first best Ju, load it up with our luggage and take off for Warsaw. Just before flying off, I put a note underneath the seat of our machine with our details and a brief summary of where we could be found should another aircraft land here some other day.

Once in Warsaw we telex the Staffel and hope for an answer. It is totally out of the question to fly eastwards as all aircraft are carrying heavy cargo with no space for any more passengers.

Finally, some lieutenant picks us up with a Me 108 and flies us to our Staffel, who welcome us with boisterous hellos as we had been assumed missing.

One of the three had contacted the Staffel from Borisov but the connection had been so awful, they couldn't hear anything beyond some snatches about some emergency landing and Borisov.

The chief mechanic of 'M' had gone by truck to remove any useful parts but turns out he couldn't locate the machine as nobody had any clue about anything in Borisov. What to do? The three guys had long ago boarded a different aircraft and were on their way to Germany. Eventually, there was a bit of a breakthrough, once extensive inquiries had been made, and finally information as to our coordinates had been received. My telex sent from Warsaw had never arrived.

The crates were transferred later on, and a barrel of beer also appeared.

Arnold Döring, late 1941 (Source: Döring).

At long last, after twelve long days have passed, I once again fly an operation against the enemy. Meanwhile, columns of motorised vehicles are intermittently attacked in the vicinity of Gomel. We're targeted by fighter planes but, as per usual, they disappear after being hit by some well-placed fire blasts from our side and subsequently turn round, removing themselves to a fair distance. By the same token, they never quite come close up enough for us to pick them out of the air. Most we achieve is that some diverge and then disappear. We've probably notched up some hits. This seems to work as a deterrent.

When at one point we cross over the Gomel airbase and drop a few bombs into parked machines, six fighter planes confront us – but, much as they tried, they too failed in registering any hits. Different story for our backstop, somewhat caught up in the explosions. He was forced into making an emergency landing just short of our own front line due to being on fire. Injured on his right arm, he nonetheless reported for duty the following day.

15.8.41

I'll never forget this thirtieth operation against the enemy – it'll forever be etched in my mind. The entire squadron is deployed to the troops embedded in Yelnya. At an altitude of 1,200 metres we attack in formation. Joined by the old captain, I lead the third flight. Facing heavy flak above Yelnya proper, it looks like the sky is filled with machines of all types. Everybody is targeting Russian divisions, which are concentrated within a perimeter of 4 to 5 kilometres. Below us, it's like an anthill. Every single one of our drops is a sure hit. Some 300 to 400 bombers of all kinds circle the objective. And everywhere our own fighter planes protecting us against Russian raids.

The formation thins out with Staffel peeling away and increasing their distances from each other with a view to carpeting the entire area with bombs. In short succession one round of bombs is released after another. The old captain is actually the one who drops them today. He has barely cranked open the flap of the bomb bay when the machine suddenly shakes violently. The machine tilts to the left and stalls. The rudder control is flung out of my hand and barely responds to pressure. A quick glance to the right wing reveals a gaping hole with the aileron shot. That, admittedly, was a fine hit by the 8.8 flak. Just before regaining control over my machine I spend some anxious moments unable to do anything. The unit flies high above our heads while we've plunged down by over 500 metres.

Carefully I try and adjust the aileron to bank – but it's awkward, to say the least. The loss of speed due to the ripped wing is considerable. But, would you believe it, the sun is shining through the many holes in the fuselage and tail unit – seems like all has remained intact in the back. The trimming wheels are turned up to the top. In order to somehow level the machine, I pump the petrol from the port to the starboard and that works, just about, the rudder is held at its maximum. The airstreams tear further into the armoured plate, already shredded to bits, and every time when the thin metal sheet cracks wider open, the aileron shudders under the terrific strain. We've all gone pale as I can barely control the aircraft.

The machine then tilts to the right but we're in luck: seeing as we're in an He 111, we can level her out with the aileron. But what's luckier still is that we're flying at night when the airmass is still – had it been choppy, we'd never have reached the airbase.

Beside us fly our wingmen. They've not remained unscathed. At low speed we return. After a few anxious minutes we reach the airbase. The landing cross is straight ahead of us. A short application of pressure on the hydraulic gear and down with the undercarriage, only seconds before touching the ground. I barely dare touch the flaps seeing as the good old crate is already tilting to the right, my right wheel has touched the ground and we then bob side to side like a drunkard. Slowly I roll to the far end of the airfield and come to a stop. The whole crew of the 'logistics', plus others from the camp, where they were living under canvas, have assembled as they have been alerted by two white flares fired by the old man. The ambulance has also arrived but doesn't need to attend to anyone. I turn off the engines and hoist myself up onto the wing to ascertain the extent of the damage from above. The old man follows me, shakes my hand in front of everyone gathered there and promises a fine bottle on the occasion of our 'birthday'.

The gap is so huge that it would be easy to drop through lengthwise. The armour plate has taken quite a beating and is riddled – the wings, the fuselage, the tail – all suffered fist-sized holes.

Hits are being photographed from all angles and when I slide down the wing, everyone wants to shake my hands. When it gets too much, I just slink away.

The chief technician taxis the machine to the hangar, where she will be fitted with a new wing and all cracks patched up. Within two days the bird is fit for flying.

That evening, the old man keeps his promise and treats me to a bottle of red wine and hands me the Iron Cross I. A further reason to celebrate, obviously, and I am over the moon with this simple cross on my jacket.

Ivan makes an appearance that night. Relentless, concentrated fire, and we're forced to dive for shelter in order not to be hit by shelling. Some tents have been destroyed. Bombs are dropped on the edge of the airfield but not causing too much damage. One bomb sets a barracks on fire, but fortunately those particular quarters had been cleared of personnel due to infestation. Burning down, it's eventually completely destroyed and along with it all those lovely animals.

Since it was the only machine that troubled us, we're off to sleep.

16.8.41

Reporting to the flight commander at the assembly point, we're informed that the Führer has ordered our squadron to annihilate the 5th Russian Army in and around Gomel and prevent it from escaping towards the south and south-east. At all costs we must stop this army, its reinforcements and equipment from concentrating in Kiev.

Something huge is afoot once again. This order by the Führer is a great honour, seeing as it was our squadron that has most successfully battled in Poland, France and against England, as well as here in the east, and whose oldest aircraft formations had proven themselves in Spain. We carry forward the 'Legion Condor'[36] – which makes it our duty to do everything in our power to live up to this order.

Our bomber streams would take off throughout the following days, alternating between splitting up in lines or in smaller pairs, all in strict coordination and scattered all over the sky above Gomel. In between attacks we would also carry out armed reconnaissance sweeps taking us deep into the hinterland. Every single troop movement, even a minor one, is recorded and once worthwhile objectives have been identified they are ploughed up by bombing and strafing. Of course reconnaissance is prioritised over attacks, as the operation of the entire squadron hinges on knowing the whereabouts of enemy positions and other details. Throughout the day, from early morning until it is completely dark, our reconnaissance machines fly sweeps over the battleground, communicating every single move by the Russians over radio. There is intense activity on the ground.

At lightning speed, messages are decoded at the signal services, then these pass the information on to the teams, who soon afterwards take off one after another to bring death and destruction to the enemy.

Gradually we seem to figure out a certain pattern in the movements of the Bolsheviks. During the night a large number of freight trains are being prepared, indicating to us that the Russians are minded to clear out. But we have no intention of making this easy for them. We're still here, still to be reckoned with, alongside other Stukas and bombers. Our armoured reconnaissance unit is airborne and for one hour busily scrutinises the battlefield. Once we know that the old man is leading, we know that we'll only return to base with a few drops of fuel, not more.

We cut across to Gomel and follow the line of the train tracks leading south and south-east. Gosh! What's all this? Two, four, ten, twenty – no, it's actually thirty to forty freight trains making their way south-east. Just you wait! One frantic message chases the next into the ether, Toni is kept extremely busy, desperately hammering the keys with his right hand. We count forty trains. Much ahead of the last train, Richard scores a direct hit and the train tracks are blown apart. Well, you mighty comrades – you're not getting any further than here in the next few hours. In the next forty-five minutes, you'll get the shock of your lives – just wait and see! For a while at least we've got you well and truly in the bag! Let's have a little look at what's going on down south. Yup, we're pretty confident that on this single-track train line it won't be so damn easy for you folks to escape! But in order to make absolutely sure that this goes according to plan, the old man orders us to attack a small bridge. Several attempts fail until finally we score and the railway bridge blows up.

We now set course northwards, heading toward Bryansk at a leisurely pace. We can't make out more than one train on this route, and this one has already been destroyed by a direct hit. They must have aced it. The engine, the middle of the train and the rear are all piled up into one huge metal wreckage. Rail traffic on this route will certainly come to a complete stop for several days.

We draw a respectful circle around Bryansk which will make it impossible for flak to open up on us. Truth be told, we have no appetite whatsoever to confront Russia's best fighter planes, the I-18 [he probably meant the MiG-3], stationed around here. The airbase is located north-west of the city. But the distance is too great and makes it impossible for us to determine any additional details.

We fly south over a fork in the path where it splits into two, and a bomb has been dropped smack in the middle of the fork. What a hit from our right wingman!

In front of us we spot our trains. Toni still tapping his keys incessantly. Diving down onto the last train, Richard gets him right in the middle – these were his last two bombs. Four wagons keel over, they've been hit at full speed and those behind crush into one huge ball of entwined steel. Meanwhile the left wingman targets the track right just in front of the engine, which puts this part of the route out of commission as well.

We've fulfilled our mission and we fly straight back home. Our results from the reconnaissance outing are truly stupendous, which means that the remainder of the available machines are set to go. When, after barely four hours, we touch down, the airbase has practically been cleared of all aircraft.

We make a brief oral report covering this operation to the service centre, gulp down some food and off we go, following the others.

Down below, the area has been completely razed by our raids. Hardly one train remains intact. At several points we see brisk troop movements going on. They're in such a hurry to escape down there, they don't seem to mind disruptions. The minute one train is full, it hurtles down the tracks at full speed – with us at their heels. A railway bridge in front of me attracts my attention. If we're able to destroy it we'll definitely be able to obstruct traffic on the rails and all train changes would be considerably delayed. In tight formation we circle the bridge. Unfortunately, we're facing a rising wind and not a single bomb hits its target. Richard is the only one who scores, with his bomb destroying the strategically important bridge. The right railway track has exploded into fragments at some 10–20 metres short of the bridge. What we need is a bunch of Stukas, or a team of our aircraft demolishing the crossover by plastering it with our bombs.

Flying home, we follow the road, where we note some insignificant traffic which doesn't cause us too much worry, but nonetheless we engage in some low-level strafing, with several vehicles set on fire and knocked out.

Day after day we carry out attacks with bombs and guns, pinpointing specific objectives for precise targeting. Unfortunately, we can't prevent the Soviets from repairing the tracks during the night, nor can we hinder them from scramming. In some places they dismantle a double track by lifting a single track measuring several kilometres, with which they fix the disrupted line. Yet, the overall result is that a large part of the 5th Army's rolling stock has been destroyed.

During our subsequent sorties and through sustained dive-bombing we attack all larger railway stations and junctions.

— • —

Flying our thirty-eighth combat mission, we take the Shukavka railway station. Leadership has been entrusted to the old man and myself.

Weather conditions over home territory couldn't be better. With some initial cloud patches we gradually head towards a thick layer of clouds and I give the signal for our tight formation to split up and for each aircraft to continue on its own course.

I break through the clouds and, as luck would have it, come upon the railway line threading its way through to Shukavka. We have come too far south, so I decide to execute a sharp turn to the left and follow the tracks. At all altitudes we pass through wisps of clouds, but cannot come down lower due to the risk of being hot by splinters from our own detonating bombs. Finally, at some 400 metres, the carpet of clouds affords me a degree of protection while still allowing some visibility of the ground. Bomb bays open, I climb down, coming in for approach. A thick mass of cloud obstructs visibility. I suspect that the railway station is straight underneath, make a mental note of the course, fly straight ahead for about one minute, turn round, and this time come in without any problems whatsoever. While before I was perpendicular to the railway station, I'm now flying at an acute angle. Some of the stationary wagons are under steam, some without engines on sidings – approximately twenty bombs are dropped onto the station – exploding in between or to the side of the trains. This is followed by massive shouts on the EiV [*Eigenverständigung*, the communications radio] until the chief screams for silence. But these eggs were beauties, it has to be said. Six trains have been hit and each one lost a long line of wagons which are now shattered to bits. Not granting ourselves a moment's rest, we move onto an engine hub, attack, it bursts into flames and then we drop our last eggs into some storage depots. Literally, a smash hit!

Above the station I nearly collide with another machine preparing to jettison his egg. This line also attacks at a shallow angle but from the opposite direction. Moments later the three aircraft drop their bombs, pelting them down vertically onto the tracks. Several trains are demolished in a series of blazing detonations. It's pretty much a certainty that no train will depart from here any time soon.

Following this mission the old man decides to carry out an armoured reconnaissance outing and before too long we're left to our own devices, as we've lost sight of each other, what with the deteriorating visibility due to the miserable weather conditions. Low flying towards the south, we follow the railway tracks. At times the countryside is too hilly, forcing me to climb higher to avoid contact with the ground, but then I worry about the risk of missing the turns – I always manage to get back on track.

I set my sights on a train rumbling across a bridge. Diving down towards the front, I open up with all the machine guns to hand. The attack leaves the engine sticking out like a hedgehog with steam puffing out from the punctured boiler. A future journey on this train is highly unlikely.

Conditions are improving and bode well for low-level flying. Clouds hang at an altitude of 50–100 metres. Once ground defence hammers away at us and it's becoming too uncomfortable, we simply disappear into the clouds. Let them chatter away as much as they like. A minute later I stick my nose out again and happily assure myself that I'm well away from the bedlam.

There's a train in front of us. We plaster the line, then make several low-level passes at the locomotive. Very soon jets of white steam spout from the holes and I'm fairly certain that the

A Polikarpov I-15 (Source: https://commons.wikimedia.org/wiki/
File:Polikarpov_I-15_(4321424501).jpg).

manufacturers hadn't inserted those … Ferocious machine-gun bursts are fired at us and a fierce exchange ensues, with us liberally spraying the enemy troop transports with a rain of fire.

Well, that about sums up our journey along the train line.

Suddenly, below us, an airbase appears with some fifteen stationary biplanes neatly placed side by side. These are tired old birds, these I-15s. Our tracers whizz down, but not a single of these beasts wants to burn down. Just behind the airfield lies a town with a large railway station full of personnel milling around. I change course towards home. Glancing at the fuel indicator, I feel this is a wise decision, though the old man himself insists on continuing his reconnoitring. I am confident that we'll reach our base with what we've got left in the tank.

I follow the needle of the compass, keeping to a set course towards the ground and soon the railway line is in my sights again. Low flying along the entire distance but I'm slightly more cautious this time round. In addition, they're on the alert down below. Each time I spot a train, I withdraw into the clouds, only to reappear shortly before my dive. This gives us the window to put the locomotive out of action and with steam already escaping from the perforated boiler: that way we add two more destroyed locomotives to the four already on our account.

Nothing much happening along the rest of the route.

Near a small railway station we spot a team of Russians digging trenches who immediately take cover in response to our firing. Doesn't look like any further excursions would be worth our while. At a distance, we see the Shukavka railway station. Quite a bit of lively firing happening down there. Some light flak welcomes us. They're pretty damn accurate with their well-aimed bursts of fire – and I decide to withdraw to the clouds again … I climb up and fly direction home.

En route we notice a V-formation of He 111s attacking a line of tanks that had previously been identified by us and duly reported. They're roaring back and forth, making it practically impossible for us to score a direct hit.

Our bombs, however, have managed to rip apart the tracks running both in front and at the back of these armoured beasts, which means that they've been practically wedged in from all sides for some time. Circling the area for a little while longer, we watch this cat-and-mouse game, not much amused, as their flak gunners are banging away at us four crates quite considerably and viciously.

Fuel is running low and it's not a minute too early to make a decision, which is to make our way straight home.

Towards 12 noon we touch down and the old man reports our successes. The two other crews had landed two hours earlier and doubts about our return had been growing.

— • —

With us leading and in tight formation, the following day we zoom down onto the two railway junctions of Barmatsik and Konotop and literally plaster them with our eggs. Little flak from either of the railway stations in response.

A chase is on just above Barmatsik with a I-15! But poor devil – he's so damn slow he's barely able to get close up. Seeing the airbase next to the railway station, which is still aglow, we recognise it as the area we attacked just a few days previously.

Some of those crippled biplanes are still standing around and our Staffel is certainly not holding back spraying them quite liberally with whatever we've got on board. Admittedly, our results aren't spectacular, seeing as we're shooting from an altitude of 1,500 metres, and not a single one of them has the courtesy to actually catch fire and burn down. Different story with the railway station, which is out of commission and will remain so for quite some time.

4.9.41

Yesterday we attacked a train line south of Bryansk and today the northern part is on our agenda. Importantly, we must ensure that no reinforcements come north via the city. Weather conditions are rather murky and the decision is to fly solo.[37]

After about half an hour we're above the target. Once again, I was the last machine to take off and I can only hope that the other teams haven't inadvertently alerted any fighter planes, as close to Bryansk there's an airbase with the most up-to-date fighters, the I-18 [MiG-3]. Our own weapons consist of one cannon and four MGs; we're heavily armoured. These boys are cut of fine cloth – no doubt about that, they seem full of high spirits … enviable. Many of our crewmembers have had experience with that lot.

Below us, we see the railway line. No defence. Richard drops a tiny little bomb just to test whether the values indicated on the instruments are correct. With a big whoosh the egg exits the shaft, twirls in the air and finally lands right in the middle of the lines. A direct hit. We had planned to drop our bombs today in strict adherence to our training manoeuvres and following a precise

Mikoyan-Gurevich MiG-3 (Source: https://aircraft.fandom.com/
wiki/Mikoyan-Gurevich_MiG-3).

course of action. There's to be no drop without thoroughly executed approach tactics preceding it.

We cross the train line. Below us a small railway station with a train about to leave northwards. A few bombs hit the tracks just before the locomotive – they were meant to target the train. Then, a bit further north, a train seeks to escape. Wait a second! We'll not let you get away. First attack fails because I hadn't made proper calculations. Renewed approach flight. One of our hefty eggs smashes into the tracks some 5 metres in front of the locomotive, lifting a good section of it into the air and onto the embankment, along with four wagons. The remainder crunches together. Three drops and three direct hits onto the line. We can be well pleased with our results.

Looks like it's heating up further south and we'd better check on that. A short train consisting of only some eight to ten wagons pelts towards us at great speed and Richard is hell-bent on eliminating that worm. Three approach flights fail miserably but with the fourth one we're in luck and two bombs strike right in the middle. That's the end of this train now as well.

I ask Richard whether he's still got some stock left.

'Yes, 2 x 250 kg.'

We're flying north again – a long freight train is making its way north and we wish to seal its demise with our fond regards. I calmly prepare to dive down when I hear Toni screaming: 'Fighter planes at rear above!'

At the same time shells burst and crackle around us. As Ivan usually shoots from a distance, I'm assuming he's still far away, and seeing that I've had experience with twenty-five fighters in my back, I feel pretty certain that the guys behind me won't pose any danger … well, so much for that thought!

Gosh – what's that? A thick whitish tracer chain flashes from behind and comes whizzing above our heads at only a hand's breadth distance. Karl's shouting can be heard.

'It's two I-18s.'

Oh, my God, let's just scram – and as fast as possible. Finally, our bombs drop but fail in their objective and it's my fault entirely as I had become too restless and didn't muster up the necessary concentration. The eggs smash into the ground some 30 metres short of their target. Richard closes the bomb aperture while I turn up the lubrication and try climbing at full throttle into the clouds. The two fighter planes attack like Blücher.[38]

Only once they're really close up do they shoot like hell, fiercely shelling my machine from all sides while I cling on for dear life, desperately seeking the protection of the bank of clouds. But while busy cranking up the various instruments above the destination I hadn't noticed that the clouds had all but disappeared. There's just the faintest layer of mist above me, not offering much in the way of cover. Nothing left for me to do but dive down steeply. Put my bird on its head and I zoom down. More cannon shells punch holes in the crate. Every salvo sounds like a sickening thud on a drum, while the chattering of the machine guns has more of a tinny rat-tat-tat-tat to it … How this will end is anybody's guess! I ask whether anybody has been severely hit – no answer. All pistons rattle away practically at the same time, everyone blasting away at the I-18. Richard looks back and reports that all men on board are behaving quite normally – so nobody seems to have been injured.

With roaring engines and at full throttle I plunge down in a steep dive. The quivering speed indicator needle rises: 530, 550, 580, 600, while a glance at the rev counter tells me to throttle back instantly as the revs have jumped to 3,000 – which is over the limit for engines seeing as they can only really take 2,500 rpm. I'm concerned and can only hope that they fly us home as soon and as safely as possible.

Once again, I hear the howling and shrieking of a shell punching a hole into the trunk while a tracer whizzes by, and damn close to us, to boot. Then, continuous hammer-blows to our wings and trunk, but finally, at long last, I see before me a dark shadow appear – a storm is about to break – hurrah! Full speed, I enter into the hub of the storm when I suddenly hear Toni's screams.

'He's on fire! He's on fire!'

I am near frozen with terror and actually only catch the last word, as Toni's screaming is too loud. I quickly look at both engines and there are no holes in the fuel tanks – so nothing untoward with our crate.

'He's crashing' – a gigantic tail of smoke streams out – well, thank God for that – we've got rid of one of their cripples, at least. We see him plummeting down like a blazing torch – then lose sight of him as I disappear into the storm clouds. Blinding rain squalls are actually in my favour but the other I-18 has become crazy, streaking after us in hot pursuit. Toni fires an explosive rocket at him, though I call out to him to put a stop to that as our tracer reveals our position. I change course again, rotating the aircraft direction home. No way Ivan can find us – we've thrown him off.

Richard cannot locate our position. Getting our bearings is no longer possible. The receiving set was shot to pieces, but if we stick flying west, we'll soon reach the Dnieper and from there it's no big deal to fly home.

Richard looks at the map again, compares it with the landscape. After a good deal of time has passed, he finally states that by his calculations we should be in German territory. Karl clambers to the front of the cockpit with a wide grin on his face.

Suddenly, flash bombs to my right, I instantly dive low to avoid being a direct target. We stay down, close above ground with Toni setting his sights on the identified target and opening up – the flak doesn't respond. But before too long life returns in the area below and we spot men milling around; Richard and Pitt let them have it, and good. We're down to our last ammunition. Some Russians have frozen in fear, others lift their arm, others still lie flat on the ground. Not a single one remembers to get up and fire. Meanwhile we literally blast them into the ground.

To our right: Yelnya, which tells us that we've just flown over a large pocket where several Russian divisions are locked in. A few moments later we identify some Landsers and hold fire. I climb up steeply to avoid being mistaken, as from the front the He 111 has strong resemblance to the Russian Martin bomber. Richard fires a white flare.

It's only now that I have an opportunity to congratulate Karl on his air-victory, with Toni already raising objections, claiming he too has had a part in this. With the I-18 Pitt too had registered a perfect bull's eye. From only some 30–50 metres away it can be assumed the guy got peppered with bullet holes. Pitt cannot respond because a wire connecting to the EiV has been cut. Everyone is black in the face and it is sheer good luck that none of them are injured, though several blazing fragments have torn their flying-suits to shreds.

The winding silver ribbon of the Dnieper glistens below us and soon we see the runway below us. Arms wave back at us – our technical crew is beyond happy. I dive low and wiggle the tips of our wings to signal our air-victories. Then I glide into our approach. Karl wants to release the undercarriage but it doesn't work – the transmission rope has been shattered – so ... nothing doing, I cannot seem to salvage it – feverishly we consider all kinds of options, but nothing is possible up in the air – so we're left with no choice and I prepare for belly-landing. We tighten our seatbelts, shoot red, make another approach.

Just short of the runway I switch off the ignition and the light and close the fire cocks. I pull the nose up hard; the tailwheel touches the ground, braking the speed. Just before I put the aircraft down in the belly-landing, I fling open the window in case we have to make an emergency dash for it. The good old 'I' finally smashes onto the field, through wooden posts, and chunks of earth hurtle through the air, with the crate skidding for a further 70 metres along the wet ground, I curve into a right half-turn and finally come to a stop. The thud has locked the window back into closed position but it opens easily and we drag ourselves out.

The fire engine is ready to receive us – those boys are obviously so tense that they've shown up immediately. A truck comes zooming across the airfield – that's our tech team all equipped with fire extinguishers. The old man rolls along as well and for good measure he's brought with him the doctor followed by the ambulance.

I light a cigarette, offer one to the others and we enjoy revisiting the events, telling the stories of those beautiful targets, the two I-18s, the bombings which invariably earned lots of applause and praise; we revisit the undercarriage disaster and our efforts to get down safely against all odds. As for the belly-landing – everyone had witnessed it. 'Farewell, beautiful good "I". You sure were the fastest bomber I've flown so far – but sadly, you didn't luck out when you came to us: three missions are far too few for someone like you.'

Richard and I drive to headquarters and report back. The commanding officer and his aide congratulate us on our success and the clean belly-landing. They want to know details: how many successful attacks had we made? Had there been weak spots in the defence? Heavy in other areas? How many bombs had been released? Did the I-18 catch on fire in the air and had we – this was the most important question – observed the crash? Sadly, we couldn't offer them insights nor did we know whether the pilot had bailed out – no, we hadn't spotted a parachute. There was probably no time for that as the other I-18 continued its waves of attacks, and with the sudden thunderstorm, visibility had been hampered – and we had escaped their view.

'Nice. I want each one of you to write up a final report including the number of planes brought down. Let's see whether the top guys will approve. *Heil!*'

We're dismissed. A truck takes us to the quarters which we moved to a few days ago after the concrete buildings had been de-loused. On our way we watch the wreck of our trusted old 'I' being carted away. A tractor pulls what's left over to the hangar where she will be scrapped, as here at the front there's a shortage of both equipment and time to restore the bird for her to fly again. Well, if nothing else, Ivan can count this as a victory.

— • —

The following day we launch a further attack. When we reach the target area, three fighters are already expecting us and they are so deft at their craft zooming around that it doesn't allow us to release the bombs properly – all going disastrously wrong. The enemy, however, didn't prove quite as adept as they had been the previous day and failed to get within 100 metres. They, too, miss the mark. Their only success is our failure.

— • —

The following operations see us at the battle of Kiev, where we do our bit by closing the cauldron from north to south while ground-strafing various pockets. This is a massive cauldron measuring some 100 km along the edge and with a huge number of troops crammed inside.[39]

We target trains and railway stations, motorised and marching columns, villages, towns teeming with troops and vehicles. We provide protection to our comrades on the ground by battering the trapped Soviets with a continuous barrage of attacks. Places like Konotop, Petrovka, Klmovka, Romny – were all areas of intense fighting. Beautiful targets, such as cannot readily be found on a typical day, were identified and promptly pelted. Columns of three to four vehicles in a line roll down the roads, and thundering back and forth we sweep them with bombs, dive down with our machine guns hammering blows onto flak guns which have opened up on us. In the end, the Russians no longer know which escape route to take in order to avoid encirclement. Our infantry, artillery and tanks, our bombs, but our iron-fist – Halt! – makes an escape impossible.

Looks like the Russians have completely lost their overview, as otherwise such headless and unprepared attempts to break out couldn't happen in the first place. There seems to be total confusion on the ground – everyone driving or marching in whichever direction he fancies, haphazard attempts here and there to force open the breach. They seem to be working under the belief that there's nothing to lose, and perhaps one of them would get lucky.

There are only six fighter planes which attempt to obstruct our many flights – but their impact is zero and they achieve nothing whatsoever. One young crew, when first attacked, unfortunately become intimidated and seem to lose their nerve, but then quickly come into their own. And on the next mission they are already seen flying with the same confidence and determination of the old crews. Eventually the enemy disappears, either escaping or downed. Places where the day before we'd still been met by heavy flak are now firmly in German hands. Gradually, the cauldron tightens and for a while we're having good fun. The enemy was shooting with everything they had while tension on our side mounted. We carry out a series of attacks wiping out concentrated flak positions, which gives us no end of satisfaction – but, truth be told, these Red sergeants made several of our missions hellishly difficult.

At long last the Russian lowers his defence. Our twenty-one attack flights, each one of them lasting over four hours, had supposedly contributed to putting an end to this battle – the upshot is that every member of my crew is decorated with the EKI (Iron Cross first class) and the Front Flying Clasp in silver.

— • —

One flight, heading for a different destination, deserves special mention. That's the attack on the artillery positions near Yelnya, some 80 km away from our airbase. Well camouflaged in the trees of a forest, these batteries make the lives of our Landser a misery. Our mission is to smoke them out.

Groups from our Staffel take off in quick succession, with my Staffel now bolstered by a further three machines. Above the target we're provided escort, one of the rare incidents where all goes to plan. We near the narrow patch of woodland while a different unit runs into heavy flak and disbands. Bombs detonate in a different forest still. We're flying at an altitude of 3,000 metres, then go lower to prepare for the approach flight and are the last ones in this operation to eject our bombs. They rip through the trees and shrubbery and parts of the wood are set on fire. Somewhere a fuel tank must have been hit – clouds of black smoke darken the horizon.

The following day we receive a long letter of recognition issued by the army. The chief of staff has been briefed and it was these last bombs, that is those released by the last Staffel, which are said to have destroyed eighteen battery positions. As a result, our infantry is briefly granted a period of rest while we can take pride in our achievements. Our success means that headquarters specifically requests our squadron to be spread and allocated to various dispersal points along the Eastern Front, even to as far as Leningrad. But that's definitely too far and the weather is too lousy – so we have to decline. The south also requires our support, and seeing as it's all supposed to kick off in October, we stay put in our Middle Section.

— • —

We've been assigned to a new combat zone – in the proximity of Moscow. It's only about half an hour's flight to get there, so it means remaining on special alert in case of enemy fighter planes which are obviously consolidated right in this area.

A further hard attack on the railway bridge near Balov leaves it totally destroyed. Three fighter aircraft. In addition, we employ our usual tactics targeting trains, and though fighters are continually roaming around in the air, we deftly make full use of the cloud banks in order to remain undetected and plaster their rolling stock without being spotted. We seem to have specialised in this, with Richard destroying wagons and several lengths of track every time he dives low to attack their rail traffic. My Staffel alone chalks up thirty-six trains – with long stretches of the lines disabled for long periods of time.

We record a mammoth attack on trains running west of Suchinitski – a miserable pocket of flak resistance. There's quite some commotion up in the air, but no Russian fighters. Too many of our own crates buzzing to and fro, simply hanging in there waiting for their colleagues on the other side to emerge.

We're on our flight route towards Suchinitski. A Staffel consisting of Ju 87s is ahead of us. Their target, a stationary train, stands in the middle of a forest in a narrow and awkward curve. Not for long, mind you, as our low-diving comrades quickly dispatch that worm into the air with very little left of him but smoke and flames billowing up from below. His cargo consisted of ammunition, which explains why the locomotive had already made its escape.

Further orders see us targeting a fuel depot. A gigantic column of black smoke streams high up to 3,000 metres, then, dispersed by a strong wind current, it spreads into a pine-tree-shaped form.

We, too, are forced to deal with several trains. While two are hit by our bombs, the third one gets away due to Richard's flop but our leader quickly makes up for it and smashes the guy to smithereens by jettisoning his last egg. Our men have ripped apart the tracks just in front of the train thus enabling Lieutenant Beckmann a neat approach flight. I admit to having attached myself to his tail as I can't help being curious as to how he'll finish off his victim. His egg, a lump of 250 kg, lands spot-on, precisely in the middle of the train, with the immediate and grandiose unfolding of a firework display. Looks like this one too had a full load of ammunition.

During our attack on the town of Suchinitski that same afternoon, we observe more train wagons detonating in quick succession, causing death and devastation in the area. This amounts to the track line measuring the entire length of the train now being reduced to scrap. And with the last wagon blasted into the air, we get to see a beautiful mushroom of black smoke and debris drawn up above in the sky.

Just over the town a timid little bird attempts to attack, but doesn't dare come sufficiently close. Too bad … he gets his wings scorched. Lots of heavy flak but bad aim – we're starting to get used to that. This now amounts to my seventy-second mission – slowly moving towards 100.

The battleground is being extended north. Somewhere in the middle of the route leading from Roslavl via Naro-Fominsk to Moscow, a small town is situated off a well-built road. Laid out in a square, the place stands out because of its wide avenues, all neatly arranged in a grid. The place is called Madyn.

This morning, we're informed that traffic along the route leading to this town is supposed to be shut down. The Staffel attacks and strafes the enemy. Convoys of heavy trucks are spotted on both the main and the back roads and are thrown into disarray on becoming aware of our bombs. We don't hold back and indiscriminately spray them with fire. Tracers dance amid the Russians, who hop between vehicles in total confusion. We're at some 1,000 metres altitude and ahead of us, below, a few vehicles. Seems a shame to waste an egg on them, so we just bash them with our machine guns and soon half of that lot lies on the ground. Madyn ahead of us. It's jam-packed with Russians seeking shelter in houses with columns of vehicles lined up against them, partially camouflaged. But it's too late for that bunch. Our bombs come hailing down onto the street, among the buildings, many of which burst into flames. We can pride ourselves on our impeccable aim. Each Staffel posts ten to fifteen destroyed trucks onto their tally sheet. Houses too were set alight.

We then continue on our way for a good long stretch beyond the city, passing over two field airbases, but other than a few bomb craters we can't identify much, certainly no aircraft that has stayed intact. Indeed, some of them seem destroyed beyond recognition.

In a wide sweeping curve we dive down once more. While we hadn't spotted flak during our first attack, it is quite different this time round, with a number of those tomatoes darting past us –close shaves the lot of them. These lads have pretty good aim. With our array of forward-firing board armament we hit hard and Richard releases his last bomb – it's getting wild. We manage to dodge their first blasts, but two of them come pretty damn close at our rear while blazing away unperturbed, even though our tracers come whistling past their heads. Gracious me – these guys are definitely persistent if nothing else. But they haven't succeeded in hitting anything.

In impeccable close formation we follow the street to head home. Along the way we continue spraying with our machine guns roads and ditches where Russians have dug themselves in.

Then, just below us, an aircraft approaches. What the hell is the silly Ju 52 roaming around for? Surely the old boy has got lost. But, hold on, this guy looks weird! That beast has four engines, so it must be a TB-3 or 'Maxim Gorki'. Let's let loose another drum and smash the guy!

All I can see is the tracers from three machines converging and penetrating his wing and fuselage and yet, hard to believe, that beast simply won't disappear. Stubbornly he flies on. In any future

A Tupolev TB-3 'Maxim Gorki' (Source: http://wio.ru/tacftr/spb.htm).

sortie we'd sure be able to overturn this apple cart with ease, but not now as the old man is headed towards home and we're obliged to follow him. Richard curses like a trooper and only later on does the old man succumb to showing his true feelings – total fury.

Ahead of us: our own advance platoon led by tanks and followed by trucks. Behind them, a bridge. Gleaming white flames come belching out from its various sections with columns of smoke rising from the explosions and spreading across the countryside. No wonder, the old man had done his job! Below us we see flak personnel scampering around trying to get to their gun positions. Let's just hope they don't get there in time to pull the trigger. Good thing we're pretty much hidden from their view, as in the bright sunlight we could easily be taken for Martin bombers. Streaking the sky with a few white tracers does it – the agreed signal for the day identifies our peaceful intentions. In response, white flares are fired and Landsers point to the smouldering firebombs. The bridge has stayed intact.

— • —

Below us the roads are thick with troop movements. We've never seen so many tanks massed in one spot, columns of trucks, infantry, artillery – tanks squeezed in between – streets teeming with army units and, where there's no space to push forward, groups spill over into the surrounding fields, advancing towards Moscow. It's a fabulous spectacle! If our Landsers can keep up we'll have reached Moscow within fourteen days. But that nut still needs to be cracked.

— • —

That afternoon we engage in another attack on Madyn, as units over there have annoyingly displayed determined resistance. Landsers stand poised; bombers attack!

We're going full guns, literally, with our bombs raining down in quick succession and plastering the entire city, already set alight by a previous unit. Black columns of smoke come billowing up from all corners of the northern section. Bit of a pity to waste more bombs on this place, so we swiftly turn our attention to the southern sections.

Shortly after our opening salvo, this part of the city also bursts into flames. Makeshift ditches have been dug all across the town, but are far from sufficient to offer the Russians any decent protection.

Just short of our approach flight we'd fended off an enemy double-decker. Would you believe it – this bird had attached itself to a V-formation of Ju 88s which had already set course back to base. But since the Jus are significantly faster than this guy, he suddenly pushes the throttle and, with engine blazing, comes racing towards us like a madman. We're happy to let him have some fun and move to attack, have him come quite close up and then smash him to bits. We can sure do without this loser. Ivan unfortunately views us as impolite folks with whom he wishes to have no dealings, so he puts his crate on its head, zooms low and escapes. At first we thought, gosh, perhaps we've caught him, but he then flares out and soon disappeared.

6.10.41[40]

It's my seventy-fourth mission today. For a change, I'm to attack a train line – the one from Kaluga to Vyazma is on the list. We're ordered to do our all and cause severe disruption, if possible blowing up some train wagons.

Due to the filthy weather conditions, the old man disbands the Staffel shortly before reaching the objective and it's now up to each individual team to pick the section they want. Us lot are keen to concentrate on a double-track line running through an open field and focus on just the point where it bends into a curve and into a forest. We know that this bit would be hard to repair as curves are a notoriously difficult affair, when it comes to attacking as well as to fixing them.

We soon pinpoint the spot, I haul back on the stick, prepare, and enter a steep dive, dropping two eggs that hit right between the tracks. I think I'm done.

Turning round, I whizz along while, in front of me, judging by the great clumps of dirt and mud being spattered into the air, a team is busying itself with the railroad embankment. Once I'm above a railway station where a freight train stand waiting, I'm forced to sweep into a wide turn because of considerable quantities of light flak from some ten gun positions. Soon we come across a particularly interesting bridge traversing a river. A freight train winds its way towards it. Tracers dazzle our eyes. Just you wait, you bastards! While we dive down, Richard discharges an egg which explodes in the middle of the train. Toni reports that two wagons have crashed and are blocking the line. Pity, the air pressure would have meant us being able to cause much more damage, but we're forced into delayed action bombing. Nonetheless, this way, the resulting crater is much deeper. Richard misses his target when it comes to a second train, but strategically drops an egg just in front of the locomotive. The train comes to a stop just short of the pit.

But now, nothing but off to the bridge. Our first shots are failures. Darn! Renewed approach from a different angle. This time our bombs are spot-on but, recoiling upon hitting the steel construction, they fly through the air in a great arc and splash into the water. For Christ's sake! Why doesn't this God-forsaken beast cross the darn bridge? All we've got left is two bombs which we'd kept for the train in the railway station, which is spewing fire. Just weighing up the feasibility of a second attempt to demolish the bridge, Toni sights a fighter plane. And before we can even blink, the guy wings over in a steep dive, apparently ignoring our fierce defence. A few hits rip into our wings – looks like the tank is also gashed.

No denying – that boy sure has a dashing style. At full pelt I pull up sharply towards the clouds for protection. The I-17 embarks on a further onslaught, attacking from the back. Karl slams his salvos of bullets smack into his fuselage and with a white banner of vapour trailing from his tail he changes course. Within seconds I've reached the clouds but can't resist peeking out to see what Ivan is up to; enveloped in a cloud of smoke some good distance away, he's flying on. Well, he might be showing us the way to his airbase, we reckon, and we follow him. Sooner or later he'll be on the receiving end of our two eggs. Sticking just below the cloud cover, I race after him, all the while maintaining a certain distance. However, due to the streaky cloud cover I soon lose sight of him, but I continue flying in that direction. If we're lucky we'll get to that airbase at some point.

As it turns out, we're indeed in luck. Richard spots the fellow below us, just on our right. With the cloud blanket now thick, I begin the chase. Can't see anything except for the double-decker at the far edge of the field and for good measure our last two bombs zap down. What with the air pressure caused by the two eggs, which miss their target by some 20 metres, his crate, hit by several fragments, teeters on its side but, though eventually riddled with bullets, that beast still won't catch fire. One last glance, but we can't see any more aircraft.

I withdraw into the cloud and set course for base. Before too long I poke my nose out of the mist and at a distance of some 50 kilometres north-east of Madyn we spot the head of the tank convoy. Gracious me – these comrades of ours have certainly made fantastic progress in the last twenty hours, close behind them our reinforcements are rolling up. A swarm of Me 109s blocks the flight path.

I wave and one of them, now joining my squad, flies level with me for a while. Wildly gesticulating, I'm trying to communicate to him that we have had some close shaves with the enemy further back in the rear areas, but he just shrugs his shoulder – seems he doesn't understand. Well, so be it! We cruise along above the road, which gives us a good idea of where we're at with our advance and what the supply and reinforcement requirements are. After a further half-hour the operation comes to a stop.

— • —

We push further towards the gates of Moscow and en route bring devastation and destruction to absolutely all of their supply routes. But this is precisely where the Russians, who're practical and totally on the ball, come into their own, ensuring that all repairs are swiftly carried out during the night, thus allowing for their supplies to get through the following day. Even when at one point we hit a train that was loaded with ammunition, which explodes as track sections are flung into the air, the trains just keep chugging along.[41]

— • —

Flying solo, we attack the double tracks of the Tula–Moscow train line on 8.10.41. At an altitude of some 1,000 metres, we have risen above the thick cloud bank and, coming out into a beautiful clear sky with the sun shining upon us, we're prepared for approach. At the indicated time, I spiral down, push through, and have near-perfect visibility of the ground below. The first snow glistens on the mountain peaks – heralding winter. A few moments later the railway tracks lie in front of us.

Direct hit on a train transporting ammunition
(Source: Atlantic Bilderdienst. PK Luftwaffe).

But just before, I very nearly collide with another machine, also flying very snug underneath the cloud bank. While I put my crate on its head, the other one vanishes altogether, swallowed up by the murky blanket.

Approach. We drop two test bombs in order to ascertain lateral deflection as, judging by how our aircraft is being buffeted from side to side, strong crosswinds are blowing. And with this, the eggs land 10 metres shy of the tracks, in an open field.

'Left-hand curve,' I hear Toni screaming all of a sudden. I immediately come sweeping round and straight ahead of me I see bombs tumbling down. Gracious me, luck was on my side once again! Could have been the end of us. The area is too well frequented for my liking, so I'm on the lookout for a different section.

Our own bombs are jettisoned some distance away. A bit further on we see a man equipped with a long hammer seeking shelter at a telegraph post while looking on as six out of ten bombs smash the tracks. He must be a linesman and scared out of his mind, as he zooms across the field as if crazed and vanishes into the woods nearby. We whoop with laughter, he looks ever so droll; I therefore decide to put the fear of God in him and steep dive. Poor devil, there he is … plonking himself lengthwise on the ground and burying his head in the mud. Spiralling into a curve, we wave to him as he escapes us evil Germanskis and flees to the forest.

I swerve down to the tracks just in time to observe an entire row of bombs explode in the air. This section sure seems to pull in the folks! Richard unleashes the last bombs, but it's not his day by any stretch of the imagination. They all plop into grassland. Nonetheless, we're quite satisfied with six hits and there's nothing left for me to do but take to the clouds and get rocking home.

PART II

With Kampfgeschwader 53 (continuation)

[11 October to 16 December 1941]

11.10.41

Today is my seventy-sixth air operation against the enemy. Six machines of my Staffel are to be deployed to the double-track Mozhaisk–Moscow train lines.

Take-off is at lunch time. Weather conditions on our side are perfect, but towards the front line some scattered clouds appear at various altitudes, gradually gathering strength with cumulus clouds closing in on us. We're flying the usual path, along the highway to Madyn, where a number of trucks are parked, then on to Naro-Fominsk, a small town situated on Moscow's outermost defence ring and embroiled in hot battle.

We make a few sharp turns and loops and wonder whether this peculiar dump is finally in German hands – but not yet, it looks like, as we run into heavy flak. The old man ahead of us makes a gentle turn to the left and a bit further on we circle past this hornets' nest. At the outskirts of the city violent street fights are ensuing, tanks thrusting forwards on both sides. Some enormous Russian monstrosities have turned into burning hulks. Bright flames raging, then black pillars of smoke. The city is aglow.

We note brisk traffic along the highway and the railway line. Just you wait, you won't be rolling along for much longer! It's about time we put a halt to your handiwork. We have another twenty minutes until we've reached our objective. Joining up close together, we push through cloud banks or plough through thick fog.

Then, in front of us, emerges the road, it's the highway to Moscow. If we had assumed that we'd be confronting heavy traffic, we were certainly wrong. All we observe are a few isolated vehicles with a fair bit of distance between them. A few bullets, and the Bolsheviks disappear into the roadside ditches like lightning.

The double-track railway line emerges some kilometres further along. Not much traffic here either. We prepare for our approach flight – bombs are dropping. They spin in the air and become tinier as they home in on their target. Perfect hit along both tracks. We register five bull's eyes. A long freight train is ahead of us. If we manage to hit it, the rail workers would certainly be kept busy for at least a little while fixing the damage – so freeing up the line will be delayed. Short of the train, cumulus clouds drift towards us and cause our crates to be violently tossed around; as a result, all our bombs miss their targets. We engage in a renewed approach when, all at once, my three guys start screaming: 'Six fighter planes from below!' Looks like this is going to be wild. The score right now is 1:1. Shell-bursts come whirling down on Ivan from all directions – but hey! What's that? One of our machines isn't opening fire. Might our brothers in there be asleep, or don't they realise the danger we're in? Toni grabs his flare gun, firing off a red signal, and seconds later it seems the guys have woken up, banging away at Ivan with considerable vigour. The Russians close up to within 200 metres but then sod off, which gives us only the tiniest window of a target, awfully difficult to hit.

By this time the captain is on his homeward course. Richard hasn't yet had a go and, much like all the other observers, he's now bent over the bombsight, releasing one egg after another, wherever he's identified a likely target down below. At three spots he disrupts the tracks and at one he also demolishes a truck, sending it toppling over and then smashing into a ditch. After that Richard gives all his attention to the fighter planes who're still pestering us, with one of them being pretty gutsy. Despite vicious defence fire, he comes as near within 50 metres of us, firing wildly from all sides. He proves so adept at his manoeuvring that the other Hes are prevented from firing back at him.

Toni lets out a slew of swear words as his loading mechanism is jammed. The I-17 comes nearer still and because Toni can't fix his problem, he decides to reload his flare gun, zaps Ivan with a red shot and flings down a handful of fliers. Ivan drops away in steep spirals, then keeps his distance, following us all the while. He seems to have a fair bit of respect for the He, because, who knows what this malicious Germanski has up his sleeve? Toni feverishly tries putting things right with his gun and finally declares her fit for action.

A thick wall of clouds looms ahead. Regardless – we push forwards. One He after another vanishes into this murky soup while I immediately yank my bird round to the left to avoid colliding with another machine. I steadily climb at 3 metres per second and then fly onwards in a straight line. My cockpit MG ices up, with ice also settling on my wings and windows. But who cares? As long as the crate remains in one piece, all is well.

But further icing makes it more dangerous than I had initially thought, with my crate now swaying from side to side like a drunk and my joystick no longer responding. Nothing I could do but to set my bird at nose-heavy and push the throttle to its utmost limit – I needed to get out of this inhospitable washhouse. At an altitude of 2,000 metres I see the ground below me. Dropping just a wee bit lower, we have a good look around. Ah yes, wouldn't you know it, but back there to the left of us two persistent Russians are circling the area, and the minute they catch sight of us they whoosh across. Shouting out to my crew that they should allow those lame ducks to approach, I prepare to pull the trigger, climb to hug close beneath the cloud bank – they are at 100 metres away from us.

'Fire!' and with that we keep up a continuous drum-fire. The comrades make a sharp turn and disappear. Cowards! We don't even get a chance to aim at them properly.

I stick around underneath the bank, but of the enemy there's no sign or sausage. Not far from us an He emerges from the clouds, then vanishes with some beautiful red tomatoes flung in his direction. My crate is having a grand old time being buffeted about, with the wings quivering under the strain, which forces me to break away, if for no other reason than to give those down below the pleasure of believing they had shot me down. I disappear at an altitude of about 1,000 metres into thick clouds and the Russians stop firing.

But no rest for the wicked … I swiftly emerge as here the danger of icing up is even worse than at 3,000 metres, leaving me with no other option than to return to base at some 750 altitude. We spot some trucks down below, fire at them, but the result is close to nil. After some ten minutes we sight flags with the swastika on them – our troops at long last. I return to base, flying at an altitude of 500 metres. This is turning out to be quite the operation. My crate is being buffeted by severe turbulence like a boat driven off the high seas. Can't say it's fun flying in such conditions. Struggling to find the optimal altitude, I then carry on to my destination – our airbase in Sohabalovska to which we had been moved several weeks ago. We pass close to the edge of the Vyazma cauldron.[1] Down below, all hell must have broken loose – everywhere one looks, great holes are being punched into the ground again and again. The artillery is busy ploughing through the entire landscape – reshaping geography. I'm certainly relieved to observe it all from up here.

Far to my right, a one-engine He 111 is headed towards home but some light flak is attacking her. Engulfed by a tight web of bullets, I fly headlong towards her to silence the flak with my guns. At this point I also recognise the other crate: it's the 'ET', which returns home today for the fourth time with just one engine. Together we were able to cut off the flak and we left the cauldron. I circle the 'E' but can't pinpoint a hit. Looks like they've been damn lucky, that lot! Flying at an altitude of 500 metres, using one engine and flying obstinately and slowly in a straight line, and then not suffering even a single hit – that flak can bury itself in shame!

I throttle back and fly level with the 'E' towards home. Soon after my own landing, the old duck also waddles onto the tarmac – Jonas puts her down at precisely the landing cross and keeps rolling towards the hangar. Looks like this was the only He who'd been attacked by the fighter plane. A gunshot had punched a hole into the right-hand engine, disabling it – but it's not so easy to take an He 111 down!

This He 111 deployed to KG53 was seriously damaged during the attack on Vyazma and had huge difficulties returning to its airbase, where it was engulfed by the muddy soil (Source: Werner Held, *Die deutschen Jagdgeschwader im Russlandfeldzug* (Friedberg, 1986)).

Another team had discovered the airbase from which the fighters had taken off. At the command post we identify the base with the help of maps and photographs as the Kubinka airfield. Would be a lovely target, that!

12.10.41

It's an early start the following day. In fact, it's still pitch black. Engines are rumbling and the tech team has been busy for some time getting the birds ready for take-off. At the command post we meet up with the two other Staffel. After wishing us a good morning, the commander briefs us on the objective for the day: target is the Kubinka airbase identified yesterday and our captain will lead.

Soviet airbase under attack, 1941.

We take off while it's still dark outside. The unit lifts off at precisely 0600 hours. The runway lights are turned on and we identify who's at the front and next to us, and after one wide curve, the lot of us are on course. Dawn gradually breaks in the east and seeing as we're headed east we're fast approaching the new day.

Bit by bit the entire Staffel comes into view and, quite frankly, we're still a considerable force to be reckoned with. What's ahead promises to be quite the shooting game and we're simply hoping for the best. May it prove to be a rude awakening for these comrades of ours. The plan is that with the first light sufficient for shooting we'll be all over them – well, actually only if the ground fog doesn't get in the way.

After exactly one hour's flight we've reached our destination. Ahead of us: the indicated airbase. The Staffel fans out and our eggs drop soon after. They drop one after the other in an orderly, unbroken sequence and with a distance of 20 metres between them.

Buildings are smashed, barracks collapse, machines explode and huge columns of black smoke rise. Our own rack of bombs smash straight across the Soviet quarters, with the last one detonating some 10 metres in front of a timberyard.

Manoeuvring us into the right position, Richard pulls on the lever to drop our 500-kg bomb strapped underneath the machine – but this heavy beast won't budge. The old man flies around the base in a complete circle and, with me at his back, this allows me a good view of the devastation down below. Everything seems to be on fire, a number of four-engine bombers or cargo planes are alight, fighter planes standing at the perimeter of the base crumple into a heap of molten metal – and others have been heavily damaged by bombs which have crashed into the ground just barely missing them. These are what's left after a hurricane of fires and explosions.

But, hey, what's that! A good number of them are still standing in a clearing, close to each other and in good nick. I assume it's a fuel station or a hangar and the ideal spot for our heavy load, I reckon. Cutting away from the unit, I prepare to dive down. Shit! And shit again – it's a damn complicated manoeuvre what with carrying such a massive monster and, once again, the beast doesn't oblige. The bomb technicians will get an earful from us, just you wait and see. Richard swears like a trooper and Karl is shooting incessantly at the parked machines. The others are already way ahead of us and I've got to get my wits about me, not a moment must be lost, to catch up with them. In front of us the double-track railway line which we'd blasted the day before. Richard, meanwhile, is still busy trying to rid himself of this tedious load we're heaving about – I'm damned if we don't manage it. And wouldn't you know it, this is precisely when and where that tart hits the ground, exploding just shy of the railway embankment. Inside the cockpit all hell has broken loose and we're fit to be tied with fury. We've just about had it with that bombing business and are far from pleased with how this whole operation has turned out. Had that egg dropped as calculated, we'd have wiped out eighteen machines in one fell swoop.

A stick of bombs punches craters through parked Soviet aircraft (Source: John Weal, *He 111 Kampfgeschwader on the Russian Front* (Hinckley, 2013), p. 8).

And then, suddenly, far behind us we identify smoke from anti-flak guns coiling up into the air. Apparently the Russians have recovered.

After landing, I call the bomb technician to inspect my crate. Some idiot, who doesn't have the faintest clue, dares tell me that it's our own fault. Well, Richard and I certainly let him have it, we didn't mince our words. Attracted by the commotion, the old man comes strutting along, chases the engineers back to work and us onto the trucks, and off we go to the command post. What's the result of this operation? Three main buildings, twelve airplanes, three-quarters of the sleeping quarters and the entire landing strip destroyed. The commandant seems fairly satisfied with the outcome.

At lunchtime the bomb technician shows up again, reports that the fault had been identified and is now resolved. He had not been able to diagnose the issue before – but subsequently, due to his alarming lack of any ability whatsoever, the guy was dismissed soon after.

14.10. 41
Seventy-Eighth Operation against the Enemy

Armoured reconnaissance in the Naro-Fominsk–Moscow area. That's the order we've been given. Take off individually, the captain allocates different sections to the teams and before long we're airborne. The unit flies in tight formation close to the front line, then we climb high solo due to miserable weather conditions. My bird performs splendidly and has me leaving the others far behind. I've even overtaken the old man, who until now has flown the fastest machine and I've got to admit, my 'FT' truly stands out, being a good 60 km faster than my lame duck, the 'D' which I've used for over thirty-five flights. 'D' was by far the oldest bird in the entire squadron, but definitely a sweetie and very reliable. The 'F' can well manage 335 to 340 km/hour – a fine achievement for a fully loaded He.

Low flight above, or rather in between, the buildings of Madyn. This continues for quite a while until, short of the front line, the clouds suddenly begin to stick together, lightly at first, but then gradually forming a thick wall. Right now I'm 1,000 metres above the front line and continue climbing until below the cloud cover. Toni briefs us as to the weather conditions in the target area. Below us, to our right, a hamlet, not much flak but it's aimed with precision. Richard jots down notes on this battery and circles the position on his map. At 3,000 metres we follow the path to Moscow. Lying ahead of us is a haul of twelve long cargo trains and Toni immediately radios this information through. The first one, by all accounts, is standing 20 kilometres in front of Naro-Fominsk – shouldn't be a problem. Three attempts and finally bull's eye close behind the locomotive, dragging not only the locomotive to the ground, but with it several carriages. Good, seems this bit of the line will be out of service for a while and the other trains will be sitting in the trap. Some 20 km ahead of Moscow Richard jettisons some more bombs onto the tracks – and lo and behold – another bull's eye. Looks like we'll be keeping the Russians busy fixing the damage for quite some time. I turn round as I've come as far as I can and it's not really advisable to continue flying solo to Moscow.

On course to base, I take the route following the road as some reconnoitring is also supposed to take place. I note some traffic. Let's go, then, and I eject a few bombs, hitting vehicles and Bolsheviks who're hopping around. Two hits on the road. Once in a while, very far down below, we observe thin banners of smoke rising and then bending the corner – seems like it is all coming from the woods to the left of the road. We criss-cross above it. Gosh, there's definitely lots of commotion down there, let's flick our last bombs into that pack and be done with it, Toni all the while tapping away at his reports.

I make a big circle around Naro-Fominsk but flak tries to pepper us with bullets nonetheless and wildly chases behind us ... it doesn't much bother us, seeing as we've now got close to home territory. One last weather report, I flip over, put the crate nose to the ground and zoom down. Traffic is heavy on our roads. Every 200 metres there's a security post as the threat by Partisans, who are in their element in this area particularly, aren't to be ignored.[2] The area hasn't been cleansed thoroughly, as our Landsers have literally gone crazy and are running like mad towards Moscow.

Just short of the base I come across the captain along with his wingman. I take my original position and soon we're home. If I may say so myself, I end this operation in the most expeditious manner. In an almost vertical nosedive, dropping my left wing, I swoop down to base, navigate at breakneck speed, low flying across the entire airfield, then yank up the crate at the boundary of the field, flip out the undercarriage in a steep curve and with that the 'F' wobbles across the airbase. Oh what fun such a great show is!

Thoroughly briefed thanks to our reports, the entire group takes off two hours later to attack the targets identified by us as rich pickings. However, two units have taken off a bit earlier and will surely cause ground troops positioned there to become apprehensive. It means that strong fighter planes are to be reckoned with, not only hefty flak defence.

Both weather and visibility have somewhat deteriorated in the target area. The old man signals for us to fan out and with that we're all on our own, distributed across the entire space, and we hunt and chase to our hearts' content.

Just below the cloud bank we liberally spray one objective after another, roads, paths, edges of forests and bunkers – make no mistake, we certainly give them a good pummelling. There's absolutely no flak; MG defences are few and far between and our approaches suitably calm. One of the villages, teeming with vehicles of all kinds and makes, has taken our special fancy. An entire bomb line comes smashing down, with some of the rundown shacks immediately going up in flames. Ten trucks are also ablaze. In a steep turn, I watch as a large number of the vehicles have escaped to the open field and are rumbling towards the edge of the wood. You'll get the what-for in just a moment! Some nasty hits from light flak, with smoke trails framing us, but we're stubborn and push on. Richard makes some slight adjustments to our course with the rest firing madly with all their guns. Bombs drop – it's the last one of our racks. Spiralling steeply upwards, I watch as the scene unfolds – smoke and flames billowing up from the wood and its edges. Numerous explosions and heavy columns of thick smoke rising. The forest is burning at several spots despite significant humidity. We can't see any flak defence. Seems that the impact of our bombing is such that the comrades are scared shitless. Richard notices that four bombs have not been released, but we're off whooshing criss-cross through the landscape. These four eggs, however, certainly need to find appropriate targets. Suddenly, nearly scraping our right-hand wing, an I-17 speeds past us as if it had dropped from the clouds. Man – is this guy out of his mind? Has he tried to ram into us? Or has a novice been let loose and escaped the mayhem? Karl, just to be sure, directed at him a dedicated drum magazine full of shells. I carry on just below the cloud cover. Ivan meanwhile climbs up behind us, attacking us from the rear down below. His engine smoke trails at about 20 metres away from our cockpit, I reduce gas as I'm certainly not going to do him the favour of flying into his shooting range. Instead, Karl slings Ivan half a drum, which the latter considers an act of impoliteness and prefers to call it quits.

Richard has discovered some elaborate bunkers down below. We're talking more of a hedgehog defence with a bunker in the middle from which radiate out defensive trenches with anchoring strongpoints dispersed along the lines. I continue flying straight ahead for a bit, then reverse to eject four eggs which swish down onto their dugouts. Pity, we haven't hit the bunker. We see some silhouettes, people leaping out and flinging themselves to the ground or looking to shelter somewhere else. I go full circle and return and my bullets have the last word.

It's not too long before Ivan reappears. This time he attacks from the front. Richard responds with a few shells but speeds are too high

An He 111 hit by a 'rat'.

and before we know it – it's all over. He's probably new at the job as so far we've never seen such silly behaviour in the air by a Russian.

Just short of the front line Karl shouts to us about a machine having made an emergency landing. I turn immediately and circle the emergency landing site several times. It's a two-engine machine, its descent marked by long smoke marks. At first we can't even quite tell whether it's one of ours or a Russian machine, but then we spot the red stars. A pack of Russians run to the accident site – good opportunity to let loose a few drums. Down below, they're withdrawing, albeit quite slowly. The area is rocked by an artillery explosion and large columns of mud fountains spew dirt and rubble into the air. I change course towards home and soon arrive at base. Tomorrow we may well go sightseeing and inspect the battle scene in Vyazma –if it's a solo flight, that is.

16.10.41

We're off to pastures new, to the northern front line. The entire squadron is deployed and the targets identified are the street and railway junction of Vizhnig-Volochek. We're even being supported by an entire group of fighter planes whom we have to pick up from their own airbase.

In rapid succession one line takes off after the next, eventually coming together in Staffeln and units, until after some ten minutes the entire squadron flies as one. We count a good sixty-five He 111 machines – an awesome force to be reckoned with. In V-formation, there are three columns of us, we're sent on course to the fighters' base. To the left of us the second group is taking off, in the middle we have the first, and we've positioned ourselves to their right. We're the perfect target for enemy flak. All they have to do is take aim – and they'll down a few of our lot for sure.

The fighters' airbase is mostly shrouded in a cloud bank but, managing to peek through a few gaps, we identify the approximate location. We fire the agreed signals and circle the airbase twice. A fighter Staffel climbs up and signals that the rest of them have already left for the combat zone to help their comrades escape the enemy planes. Fine by us, as it's quite unlikely that Ivan would dare approach us. Our colleagues, fast and efficient, strategically position themselves around the perimeter, securing it in all directions. As for us, we continue flying north. Below us a dense carpet of clouds. The only way we manage to orientate ourselves is by tracking the route through some cloud holes. We're not moving very fast, and the group has to adjust to the speed of the slowest machine! For quite a while we've been cruising above the cloud bank, at an altitude of 2,000 metres. Above us: clear blue sky with sun glaring down onto the white clouds. Flying in tight formation is not a simple matter, but far to the right and to the left, the cloud bank finally tears apart. In a wide sweeping curve we head towards the airbase, now gliding along below the cloud bank. We're at about 1,000 metres and continue at this altitude; it's certainly a bold undertaking and what we'd anticipated indeed occurs: we're being shelled from all directions, bullets tearing through the midst of the unit. Some machines cut away, not before releasing their bombs in desperation, and disappear, making their way home. One of them must have had its engine hit, as it is trailing a long plume of smoke behind it. Well, one can only hope that these lame birds reach the other side in one piece.

Our squad meanwhile flies in tight formation through the clouds, but once we emerge above the carpet, we realise that we're scattered all around. Slowly we gather once again and each unit receives radioed messages as to our intended and secondary targets. We disperse, with each captain going his own way and obediently followed by his own flock of sheep. We immediately take the lead. Soon the old man pushes through.

Windows are icing up, with the old man ordering us to return because of that, but I've just broken through the cover. A few machines zoom past, barely a hair's breadth from me; I want to keep on their tail but soon lose sight of them all due to this lousy weather. Flying low, I continue onwards, though haven't got a clue as to our bearings. At long last we spot a road winding its way through this stupid forest and marshland and we note some heavy traffic. Looks like lots going on in the villages as well. Not long afterwards we know exactly where we are – and we've arrived precisely above the alternative target. Sometimes one gets lucky! Nothing left for us to do but approach and get to work. One bomb after the other drops from the bay, swiftly hitting their target. Never mind if one fails. Cautiously, I approach a different target, allowing me to make a surprise attack and indeed, once I do, the defence is negligible.

The thought of being shot down 400 km behind the front line doesn't make me feel cheery. The scene is chilling: there are plenty of other machines around, judging by the masses of dirt fountains rising into the air and the clouds of smoke. A number of vehicles on fire testify to the excellence of our troops. Many hamlets are burning. The Russians seem to all be taken by surprise and don't even think of defence. My mission is to blast the villages as lots of vehicles are lined up there. Fabulous targets! Bombs are hailing down, those at the back shoot like crazy. Richard, too, does his bit, flinging down a drum of ammunition before ejecting a bomb, and then repeats the routine. He sure doesn't lose a moment. Like no one else I know, he works by rule of thumb. After every detonation the machine jolts upwards, that's how strong the air pressure is. Behind us, all drums have been emptied and Richard is also running out. I ensure that the last ones are kept in reserve for potential chases. Our operation has terminated and I withdraw into the clouds.

The MG of the cockpit ices up instantly. A coat of ice also settles onto the windows, even the warm engine cap isn't immune. The wings are dangerously exposed as the cover thickens by the minute. Despite me revving up the engine to the max, the crate climbs only sluggishly. Eventually I lose height, forcing me to embark on my descent. The weight of the ice, by far exceeding that of the bombs, becomes a real issue. My machine sways back and forth as if drunk. Pressure on the rudders yields zero and I'm forced to make a pause. After a quarter of an hour which feels like an age, the monotonous grey blanket thins out and it's gradually getting light, then all of a sudden gleaming sunlight bursts out. Looks like I'd hit the absolute densest spot.

I fly close to the cloud bank and scan the area. Aircraft are everywhere, in between some fighters, but they are ours. Gradually, as the sun beats down on us, the ice melts away from the wings and the cockpit, and the crate behaves normally. After what seems quite a while, we can see all the way to the ground and spot the source of the Volga surrounded by lakes and extensive woods. A block house is located just alongside the source and a few Landsers wave up at us. Two tanks in front of them. Looks like our troops have penetrated up to here and, given that the entire landscape seems very uninviting, it's fair to assume that pushing through this morass

The blockhouse located at the source of the Volga close to the village of Volgino-Verkhove. Picture taken in the 1930s (Source: https://www.faltboot.org/wiki/index.php?title=Datei:Wolga,_Behning,_1.jpg).

could not have been a great pleasure. I descend steadily, lower and lower, and observe everywhere small Russian units embedding themselves. Won't take long to put an end to that, seeing as we've already disrupted the connections between Moscow and Leningrad. Kalinin is in our hands as of yesterday.[3]

A Staffel is ahead of me. As it's getting darker, I'm reluctant to join them but instead fly on at greater speed, still only reaching the airbase once it's pitch black. It's advisable to be cautious. There are planes flitting back and forth – recognisable because of their navigation lights. Since I'm already on course to land, I lower the undercarriage and touch the tarmac before the others, who decide to circle the base just one more time. This sortie has lasted for over four and a half hours which brings me up to precisely sixty thousand [*sic*] hours flying against the enemy.

17.10.41

In order to support our troops on the ground we're ordered to fly once again into the zone of Naro-Fominsk. Lots of rivers, small and large, run through that area and are severely swollen due to the heavy rain. Flooding covers large parts of the battleground, which is now soggy and muddy, causing tanks to get stuck and make only slow progress. During the night the attack has come to a halt. The Russian once again is inside the town. Muck and sludge are in cahoots with the Bolsheviks and seriously impede our advance.[4]

Our mission is to break the enemy defence and to this end we're attacking troops and freight depots both at the front and behind it. The weather conditions are lousy. Snow and rain showers severely reduce visibility. As a result we keep to flying low, so that we can at least see to some extent what's happening below us. The Bolsheviks in this area have mobilised to defend their capital city.

Even civilians, women and children have been called up to join, as we see them digging the trenches. They barely look up, knowing full well that we're not waging war against them; they work sluggishly and seemingly against their will. Toiling away, within reach of our weapons and driven by commissars, can't be a great pleasure. A bunch of Bolsheviks gather round, so we swoop down and fire at them – not a single one escapes unscathed. Soldiers assembled behind their fortifications are our next target – a few shots, followed by two or three bombs dropped in their midst and our wild chase continues. I've come up too far north. Protected by some clouds, I climb up and at an altitude of some 800 metres I'm granted clear views. My position is 20–25 kilometres south-east of this beleaguered city. In the same village we attacked yesterday we come across more lorries, some parked, some wildly fleeing in all directions. We throw two long rows between them. With the smoke trails dissipating, we're able to get the full picture of the effect we've caused. Several trucks have toppled due to the air pressure, three are on fire. In addition, some houses are ablaze. I fly on. Increasingly the weather is clearing up but I decide to remain at this altitude as Richard feels comfortable with his continued attacks. He flings his last bombs onto marching or driving enemy columns. Emptying the remainder of what he has left in his magazines, we then note that our cannon is stuck and all that it can muster is a few shell-bursts – that's when we call it a day. There's no point in continuing and I therefore set course for home.

At 1500 hours the same afternoon we take off, again heading towards the same area, but this time our focus is the railway line to Moscow. Just short of our destination we spread out and continue flying solo. We're met by serious flak defence. Avoid some damn close shots by vanishing into the clouds.

After a mile [sic] I poke my nose out of the muck and can identify the railway line below. First attack fails, the bombs fall short, some distance away from the target. My performance the second time round is better, but still the last one drops over 5 m shy of the tracks. I prepare for the third offensive – I'm determined to ace it with this one. Four bombs wobble out of the bay, falling in a steep curve towards their target. Finally, two hits and the line is interrupted. I continue flying and enter the combat zone.

We've still got ten bombs on board and we're positioned 50 km before Moscow. I make a sharp turn and head towards base, not before taking on the railway one more time. Suddenly I recognise three fighter planes flying in impeccable formation just below us. Friend or foe? Richard is busy ejecting three bombs and before you know it the Russians are at our wings – as that's who they turn out to be.

An I-17 is in the lead, two Ratas follow as wingmen. The leading machine wobbles, with the rest of them diving down to the right, attacking from behind and down below. Richard ejects a bomb, causing a rat to swerve – that was certainly a near-miss.

At full speed I make for clouds – I try to adjust pitch control and Richard swiftly cranks shut the bomb bays to switch over to his MG. Karl is busy firing, while tracer ammunition whizzes close above our left wing. A grazing shot leaves a 20-cm trail. Pitt makes a note of the last bombs which Richard had ejected, and it looks like there are two hits to the railway line, a hit to the left-hand track and the other one some 50 metres further along on the right-hand track. And again tracer bullets pass close below our cabin. I pull up and the next minute sees me well protected by the clouds. I immediately change course and have a near-collision with a rat which zooms past me like a rocket. Richard pulls out all the stops, firing madly. I keep changing course and only poke out my nose after some time has passed. But then I'm immediately chased by six fighter planes – so it's off to the clouds again. However, this time I'm not going to allow you guys near me! I turn east, direction enemy territory. After some time has passed, I peek out. The air is clear and we've got rid of Ivan.

Beneath us we recognise long columns marching direction east; whipping round and banking steeply, I continue shooting while Richard drops his last bombs. Didn't even know he still had any. A few of them land very close to the road, two are direct hits – wiping out the middle of this black worm. The last two also explode next to the road, eliminating a crowd of Bolsheviks seeking cover. A sensational success. Fragments and bullets do their bit. They'll have plenty to remember us by for a while to come. Breaking away in a steep dive, I disappear into the clouds, as the shooting down below has become quite ferocious. I climb above the dust and the filth and fly home.

The old man seems to be equally satisfied with the success. Having disrupted this important railway line in four different areas, practically paralysed a fighter plane and decimated the column of marching soldiers – well, can one hope for more?

But before we're through I make a short detour to the Vyazma battlefield. Goodness, what a scene! Deep craters caused by shell hits have literally turned the landscape into a ploughed field. Scattered around are dead corpses of humans and animals, wrecked vehicles, burned-out tanks and armaments, all bored deep into the marshy ground. I then climb up just above the Vyazma train station which we attacked not too long ago. No train on earth could travel along those tracks. Scorched sheds everywhere, and all that's left of a large supply depot complex are some half-destroyed brick walls. One bomb crater after another. The city itself doesn't show any serious damage except for its train station, thus seems not to have suffered terribly from the recent fighting. I then criss-cross above the sites of devastation and take in paths and fields littered with destroyed and charred vehicles. The Russians have already erected some repair depots where they store piles and piles of armaments and stacks and stacks of rifles and grenades. Covered lorries, trucks and tractors transport the stuff to Vyazma. The booty is absolutely huge, but the amount of material that was destroyed is a hundred times larger. Entire forests have literally been turned into firewood. It's obvious that our artillery has not been fooling around. Some lost Bolsheviks scamper around, raising their arms when they see us approaching. Others look for cover. A number of our own machines circle the doomed area and we are left concluding that what has happened here below must have been hellish. Soon, we've had our fill and we return to base.

— • —

Due to heavy fog and miserable weather conditions we're unable to fly for the next few days but make good use of this pause for rest and refit – our machines desperately need to be thoroughly cleaned and overhauled.

22.10.41

Today's agenda includes attacks on assembly points and troops en route to the front line, all in the proximity of Moscow. Squads take off from our good old runway. Direction front line. Weather conditions aren't at all favourable. Wisps of cloud at different altitudes obscure my view to the ground. Naro-Fominsk finally in German hands; I can make out some flags with swastikas fastened to vehicles driving through the town. The Russian attempts to clear out – trying to escape some 5 kilometres away towards the north. We can only hope that he doesn't then pose a threat to our flank, as our troops have penetrated all along this strip up to about Moscow – they're only about 40 kilometres away. The old man is filing a report on the direction the Russians are marching in, while our squad radios the ground troops.

After some minutes we've reached the combat zone. For a moment there the old man disappears from sight. Toni informs me that the old man has ordered us to disperse. That's fine by me, as in this foul weather this is a much better strategy. A long distance away, I spot some aircraft. To my left, I see reinforcement contingents from our own side coming up – it looks like our advance is making good progress. The first Russians appear ahead of us.

Congested traffic at a big road crossing. Rather convenient timing as it gives us an opportunity to drop a few of our babies. Six of them smack in the middle of the bunch, cause massive confusion. Steep diving turn to prepare for the next onslaught. A further six bombs whistle down – this time not aimed with perfect precision. They all end up exploding right next to the road, causing a few fires, with Russians leaping up and making a desperate leap for cover – but that's it. Just you wait, we'll flatten the lot of you! Another outing. Four bombs tear the road apart, causing isolated fires, among them a fuel truck has been hit. Two tanks thread their way through the countryside, digging broad grooves into the marshy soil.

I turn my head to scan the sky for unwanted guests, as at some distance away is situated a large airbase with three wide tarmacs and a considerable assembly ring. Suddenly, an I-17 zooms down from the sky, whizzing straight past my crate at just 10 metres to the right of me. Damn! That guy wants to hit us. I pull round sharply, virtually standing on my left wing – neither of us has a chance to pull the trigger. The Russian has discarded the roof of his cockpit and I can distinctly make out his eerily enlarged eyes through the goggles. Then the phantom has vanished. I've no desire to meet up again with this lad, who seems prepared to go to the end, while I'm sat in this clumsy machine of mine.

Put my hand on the stick, a hard jolt forwards and I'm gone. Just before disappearing into the clouds, I observe several more fighter planes dotted around the area and I decide that I should get the hell out of here.

I change course towards home. We're still nursing six bombs but we'd dearly like to jettison these as well. So I push my nose out of the bank and lying before me is a small town. Seems to consist largely of impressive industrial plants with sizeable storage sheds. Flak is attacking us – violently banging away, causing our machine to shudder and sway dangerously. I have to admit, the heavy batteries have perfect aim. With stubborn doggedness I prepare for approach. Richard advises some changes to our course. Behind me there's a wild exchange of fire. Again, fighters at my tail: smoke and tracers streak past my window – most of their shit targets my left engine. The propellers are punched several times. I clearly see bullets ricocheting in a wide curve. At long last we empty our bay and let the bombs rain down. Despite heavy flak and the fighters, I remain below the clouds simply to observe their impact at closer range. There! They're detonating, with fountains of debris and dirt spurting into the air, bomb after bomb exploding, each 100 metres apart. A silo is aflame, a hall reduced to rubble. The fires spread rapidly. I've seen enough and climb back into the clouds, changing direction several times. Bullets whirling around my wings, some slamming into my crate. At one point I hear a tinny sound and a flak splinter flashes through the cabin. At long last I escape this hailstorm and fly home, quite relieved. It's taking a long time to reach the other side of the front because it takes a considerable amount of manoeuvring the machine, which is being buffeted by strong winds. I keep above the roads, to get my bearings. Just above our reinforcement troops, our own fighter planes block off the airspace. Two of them want to take us on but we immediately fire off recognition flare signals, which leaves them to waddle past. Why don't these boys take themselves over the front line and do some cleaning up *there*?

Shortly after I touch down, the captain also comes flying low, approaches the airbase, speeds down the runway and wobbles the wings. Aha, he's scored an air-victory. His radioman is the lucky protector who has shot down a Russian, smack above his own airfield, with the aircraft going down in flames. The pilot was able to bail out.

23.10.41

The operation ahead of us is a difficult one. A strong assembly point of tanks north of Mzensk, a place located some 40 km north-east of Orel, is due to be attacked and razed to the ground. Rumour has it that the village harbouring the tanks is protected to the hilt by light flak. Supposedly the army is paving the way for our troops to advance towards Moscow. They plan to push forward from the south, east of Tula, get that large industrial area surrounding the city into our hands, then continue north-east and join up with the other German units just behind Moscow. Our Landsers, meanwhile, are now close to Moscow, some 30 km away from the city. One can only hope that the advance from down south will work, despite the sodden ground, mud and slush caused by several days of rain. Roads are damaged, ripped apart and crumbling, and vehicles and tanks can barely inch forwards.

Our squad has already been there once before, early morning. Other units also circle above the target. Weather miserable. Clouds at all altitudes, from the ground right up to 15,000 metres. Just here and there a gap. Four machines haven't returned from the first operation. Weather conditions are said to have improved, but there's the saying: 'Trau, schau, wem' ['Take care in whom you trust'].

In order to avoid a collision – earlier this morning two Hes slammed into each other and went down like flaming torches until they crashed into the ground – we now take off solo, one by one, ten minutes apart. The flight path is mapped out with precision and

German infantry storming a village close to Mzensk
(Source: Werner Haupt, *Sturm auf Moskau: Der Angriff,
Die Schlacht, Der Rückschlag, 1941* (Friedberg, 1986), p. 206).

at the command post we're handed detailed maps on which each path is clearly marked. The commander adds that no one should fly too low, to avoid being exposed to dangerous bomb fragments from other combat units.

At 1210 I give full throttle, on course to Bryansk. It's unbearably sticky out there. Shreds of clouds everywhere. Above the Bryansk airfield I nearly collide with another He, who's just about to touch down on the runway. Tightly gripping the stick, I push it hard into my belly, hopping over the badly bruised He, nearly scraping it. The radio operator shakes his fists menacingly at me – it's a crate belonging to our 8th Staffel.

Not long after this adventure, we're flying above Orel, a place that's barely been touched by the battles, known for its comfortable quarters during winter. Even a tramline is still in operation. All that's left of some of the buildings are a blazing heap of ruins. But what's that in comparison with a whole city? The fact that the city was hardly damaged is due to it having been conquered by surprise. On we fly along the train line towards Mzensk. Weather conditions have improved somewhat and I'm able to cruise at about 1,000 metres. Some cloud banks cross the flight path and hang low towards the ground.

Mzensk is in German hands. A few white flares are fired into the air at the north-east edge of the city. Russian artillery emplacements in and around the city. Great dirt fountains gush up everywhere. Our own artillery bangs away. Tanks engage in the battle and a dense web of tracers envelops the enemy. He, as well, responds by firing tracers.

There are exactly 18 km separating us from this damned village. A reconnaissance plane suddenly appears, coming straight at us. For a split second we think it's a fighter attacking. He comes close up and for a while flies level with us – both sides waving at each other. In a steep downturn, the Henschel [126] dives and I too have to go down lower as a cloud bank below me obscures my view of the ground. Takes no time to pull through this bank but already the next one looms ahead. Can drive you crazy. I bet that above the target it's all sealed up again.

I now follow a road, and where it veers into a country path I make a right-hand turn. I'm fast approaching the target. Clouds. I fly as low as 300 metres. There – the country path comes into sight and I make a sharp turn. Bomb bays are open – the babies are ready to be dropped. Again clouds – I dive closer to the ground. There, a small tear in the clouds allows me to catch a glimpse of the village down below. Flak banging away like crazy. Everywhere red- and white-coloured chains, like pearl necklaces, come up. Must admit – never before have I seen such a great quantity of light flak amassed in one bunch. There must be at least twenty to thirty guns welcoming us. Feels like target shooting. No point trying to avoid them. It's actually too late to empty the bay. A moment later I get myself back into the muck. Now the machine is caught in the slipstream, tossed about and lurching side to side like a drunkard. There's no way of getting a reading from the compass, its needle spinning around like crazy on its own axis. Even the most exquisite blind turn counts for nothing. But we're determined to jettison our bombs onto the village. No view of the ground, though we're at an altitude of 50–100 metres. Filthy conditions. Below me a series of detonations and a fantastic scene of bright explosions illuminating the landscape.

So as not to be caught by fragments flying about, I immediately pull up the nose and climb higher before diving down again. Propeller slipstream flinging me about again, terrific detonations. Quite a few machines must be zooming around in this mess. Gusts of wind, this time particularly strong. Toni sees a shadow flit by the window. The aircraft comes quite close. I make a turn and flatten out to get on course and follow the road in order to find the village – by hook or by crook, even if I've got to come down to 10 metres. Whatever it takes, I must get rid of these bombs. I make yet another turn. The village must be situated ahead of us. Suddenly the bank of clouds tears apart and sees me floating along in splendid sunshine – and I find myself flying along as an ideal target for the

Russians. There's an annoying click in the crate. Now, a blanket of monotonous grey is covering the ground. Again, we're bothered by slipstreams, this time much heavier than before. I can only hope we don't collide with anybody. Barely have I finished this thought than we feel an impact and my machine begins to shake. We're all convinced: it's finally happened. A large dark shadow flits past, the left engine starts stuttering and the shaking has become violent, tossing us about. Cautiously, I pull up, pressing down on the rudder pedals. Yes, they're still working. Can't be that bad then …

But hey, what's that? I see blood and flesh sticking to the engine block. The windscreens too are flecked with bloodstains. Did somebody get caught in my propellers when forced to parachute down? What the hell flew into my engine? I can't make out much, what with us being cloaked in a veil of grey. At long last it's becoming lighter outside and the cloud bank rips apart – the next one looming at a distance away. Once again we're totally exposed to the Russians. Trails of smoke and tracers streak by us. But I'm relieved, as looking at my propellers I realise that blood and feathers come with a bird leg sticking out of the cargo bay. Little wonder that the engine was moaning, seeing as the bay must have crumpled to bits. Looks like the propeller has also been damaged, as I definitely note its sluggish rotation. MP [manifold pressure] fluctuates like crazy. Not great fun flying low with an engine that's failing. No other option than to set course for home. I fly direction the village where we had been badly bruised – Russians everywhere. Richard empties his bay with the entire load of bombs thudding to the ground. I loop into a steep dive to watch the impact on that dump. A barrage from an MG tears open my left wing. Those in the back spew out one drum after the next. Looks like most of the bombs sit nice and tidily in the village. Deafening blasts all around. Russians racing around like crazy instead of seeking cover. Fools, the lot of them … but what do we care – bullets thudding to the ground finish some of them off. Also a large number of vehicles, all parked close to the houses, explode into the air. That brings about masses of Russians spilling out of

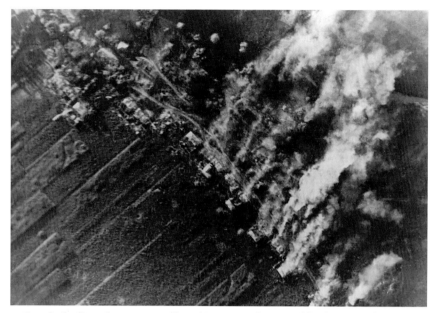

Bombs hailing down on a village (Source: Atlantic Bilderdienst, PK Horn).

these homes, dashing towards other sites that are still burning. The last of the bombs ploughs into the ground some 5 metres shy of a dislodged gun emplacement. Much as I would have liked to, it's totally impossible to carry on with such excursions, what with this spluttering engine of mine. On our descent the crew in the back shoot like madmen and scream with delight.

I crawl home. Before too long I've crossed the front line. In no man's land a machine belonging to our Staffel is on fire. Grinding through mud and filth, two of our tanks rumble in that very direction when I see five crewmembers, skipping between bursts of flak shell, running towards them. They're even carrying their parachutes with them. They arrive safely – the tanks withdraw.

We inspect the machine. Both wings totally perforated. Tail is also damaged. Flying home, I keep to the roads. Should the engine die and if the He can't be controlled in this sticky weather, I can always take a vehicle and return to the Staffel. But I'm in luck, the engine doesn't fail me – good German craftsmanship. The engine chug-chugs away, as if it knows what's at stake. At times there's a worrying pause, but then the reassuring droning comes back.

At long last Roslavl appears before us. It's only a few minutes' flight away from where we are and soon we see the airbase. The space is busy, with loads of machines hanging around, but I squeeze myself into a gap and go for a smooth landing. Close by, a machine from the 8th Staffel passes me at breakneck speed and touches down – with only one engine. Gracious me – will this end well? Far ahead of me the undercarriage of the He collapses, and the He slips along the wet, mushy runway for several hundred metres and only comes to a stop a few minutes later, short of a stacked pile of bombs at the edge of the base. That's what one calls being lucky, comrade! The ambulance and fire engine return, implying that none of the crewmembers have come to harm. I roll on towards the bay.

The chief maintenance manager and the first mechanic inspect the points of impact and the engine. Theo, the mechanic, climbs into the crate, turns on the left engine, but there's nothing – it's dead. He then lifts the hood and looks around. The supercharger was torn, parts inside the engine casing were damaged. New engine. We've been let off lightly, as the engine could easily have failed during the operation. A truck tows my machine to the hangar and the repair unit immediately sets to work.

The adjutant at the command post is worried about machines still missing. I report back and also report Lieutenant Beckmann's emergency landing. But the adju needs no briefing as the radio operator had been messaging him up to the last minute. Of all the machines who've returned so far, only two are unscathed. The rest are damaged due to having been hit. Two are missing altogether. Our group has lost seven machines in total, all because of that damn dump; the other group is also missing a few.

A few days later the group commander reads out a message written by the tank unit deployed near Mzensk.[5] He has particularly complimentary words for our squad. Thanks to the devastating impact of our bombs and attacks by aircraft armaments, the Bolsheviks have suffered huge losses and their defence is severely dented. This allowed our ground troops, so it says, to obtain considerable stretches of enemy land and bring them into German hands.

For us lot, it was a cursed day, recording the highest number of losses in the entire eastern campaign.[6] The crew of Lieutenant Beckmann as well as some members belonging to other crews return after a few days.

27.10.41

Rain, snow flurries and fog have prevented us flying for four days. The airbase is flooded. But today, the Staffel is finally able to take off again. My good old 'F' has been given a new engine. Holes in the wings and the fuselages caused by the heavy shelling have been repaired, the petrol tank, slashed through and through, has been replaced with a new one. Nothing stopping us from starting afresh.

We return to our combat zone in front of Moscow. Our advance is progressing only slowly, indeed is threatening to get stuck in the marshy soil.

Naro-Fominsk is once more in Russian hands. We're ordered to attack troops of all branches located to the east of the city. Group II has already arrived before us. We enter the combat zone, strictly one Staffel after the next. We must expect defence from fighter planes.

Weather nothing to write home about. Clouds hang down low, obstructing our view of the ground. We remain at a high altitude and fly in tight formation as a unit. Criss-crossing fields, forests, villages, there's nothing noteworthy to see down below. Russians have become cunning during the past intrusions into their territory and are well camouflaged. No sign of any marching columns, nor of vehicles on the road. But some can be seen standing hidden under trees. Here and there some bombs are being dropped, detonating on a stray vehicle, with flames spurting out from all sides split seconds later. Seeing as there's nothing to be gained from us focusing on the forests and there are no vehicles to speak of, we save our ammunition for the villages. There, close to the houses, trucks line the streets, and where there are vehicles, troops are never far away. So, off we go with our bombs stashed away in their bays. Many a village has thus been set alight; with our guns we go on pursuing the Bolsheviks who're trying to escape through the fields.

Then we chance upon an extensive network of freshly dug trenches with vicious defence fire erupting all at once. Attack! Let's dump those bombs! Three of our babies have pretty much covered the trenches but these guys keep on firing. Renewed attack and we let loose more bombs. The lads are stubborn! Their light flak simply cannot be silenced. Just you wait – you'll soon grow tired. I pull away in a wide sweep, the red tomatoes in hot pursuit, and go on another approach.

We're just about to dive down when three I-17s suddenly appear on the horizon and engage in immediate attack. They're not to be deterred and come quite close. They put up some light flak, effectively setting up a barrier between us and the fighter planes. This brings a bit of relief and I can't help but feel joyful. Banking into some crazy curves, the fighter planes turn and offer themselves up as a good target. The Staffel fly in tight formation and, beset by a sort of frenzy, empty their tubes on the three Red guys. Light flak realises their mistake and resumes firing at our group. From the hull, with their MGs, the aerial gunners try to control the flak, who're shooting right into our midst, assisted by the observers in the cockpit. Then all six Hes eject the last of their bombs at nearly the same time. They settle perfectly, exploding right inside the positions. Flak was also affected. That sure was a made-to-measure operation by the observers!

Three fighters are attacking. We twirl our MGs around, spitting bullets down on what are rather hardy boys. They come up close. One of them seems to have taken a fancy to me. His four Russian tracers flash across my wings and I'm forced to cut away, then

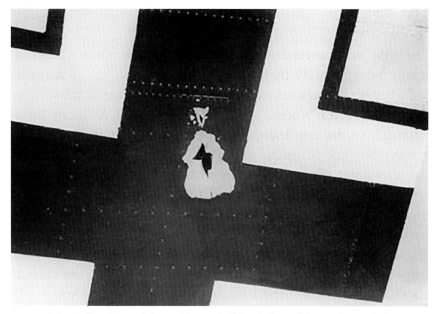

The Balkenkreuz [the emblem of all branches of the Wehrmacht]
shot through the middle.

I zoom across and press the button of my MGs, never letting the enemy out of my sight. We've already been hit several times, but there, suddenly, a few bursts and the Russian is trailing flames. Swinging down, he takes his leave and glides away direction home. The other two keep him company – they've probably had enough.

It's hard to pinpoint who the skilful gunner was on our side, as it was all of us who were letting the bullets rain down like mad. Of course everyone claimed success for himself. Downing the plane was therefore chalked up for the Staffel and not the crew.

Flying in formation, we approach the airbase, with our photographer imprinting our impeccable arrival onto his plate. A brief tour of our crates reveals that we alone have suffered six hits fired by the fighters and they sit dead centre in our Balkenkreuz. Light flak missed us altogether. What an achievement by the Russians, I say!

28.10.41

Today we have a special target: Moscow.[7] It's meant to be a nuisance attack, nothing more than a sort of bluff. The weather conditions are a dense blanket of clouds hanging low, reaching to about 3,000 metres. We're to proceed towards radio beacon X. From there, approach to the line leading to the Red metropolis. From radio beacon Y check proper bearing and eject bombs onto a precisely calculated line. Take off at fifteen-minute intervals. No chance of any fighter planes appearing, as they're unable to penetrate the cloud bank. The likelihood of heavy flak defence is a fair assumption. Not a single approach or attack below 4,000 metres.

I'm in receipt of one of the most recent aerial photographs of Moscow, with all flak batteries circled. Crikey, the Soviets have certainly done their homework. I try counting how many emplacements in total, but soon give up. In the top left corner it says: 197 flak batteries. Well, that sounds ominous. That flak defence has called in the big guns. Looks like around 700 gun positions – there'll certainly be some killings to be made.

Richard and I set to work and do some proper flight planning. Finally, we seem to agree on all points. The old man checks over the maps and the measurements we've come up with after carefully calculating them and with that checks out his Staffel. The other Staffel are supposed to take off after us, which will have Moscow on the alert throughout the day.

I'm meant to take off at 1035. I've got loads of time; Richard and I go over the entire flight path and each and every phase of the attack. It absolutely must go smoothly. Nothing should nor may go wrong. I check the aerial photograph once again. I note that they have plastered the left part of the city with flak as a priority. I discover two barriers. One situated some 5 km in front of the city, the second one at its edge. On top of that, battery positions inside the city.

One might hope that we'll escape what promises to be hell more or less in one piece. Seeing as the Russians have no visibility, we'll

Aerial photograph of Moscow, October 1941 (Source: Werner Haupt,
Sturm auf Moskau: Der Angriff, Die Schlacht, Der Rückschlag, 1941
(Friedberg, 1986), p. 78).

make sure they fall by the sound detector. But … what can us folks do against such a mighty power …

1030: We climb into our machine, accompanied by the good wishes of our mechanics. I switch on the ignition, warm up the engines and roll down the tarmac for take-off. Pushing the throttle right on time, I make a steep turn, direction north-east. After a few minutes I've disappeared in the clouds. The bank reaches up to 1,500 but keeps increasing in altitude towards the front line. After a while we get a proper bearing indicating we're close to the beacon. Then, a further bearing and we're on course to Moscow.

The right engine is giving up. The supercharger doesn't want to budge. This means our heavily loaded machine is barely able to get above 3,500 metres, and that's the altitude I continue to maintain. If we're hit, then frankly, it won't much matter from which height we go down, from 4,000 to 5,000 metres or 3,500.

We've set course, and several checks to establish our bearings confirm that we're headed in the right direction. According to the chronometer we should have reached the front by now. Visibility is appalling – we can't see the ground. Sun gleaming onto the white, dense cloud blanket. It's comfortably warm in our cockpit although the thermometer measures an outside temperature of -17 degrees. The combi-heater works beautifully. All seems fine at the back.

Below us some small rips in the cloud bank. A quick glance at the map. Yes, there are about 80 km to destination, not quite twenty minutes' flight. Constantly measuring and reading the values with our instruments to get our bearings – we're only about 10 km away from Moscow.

Before me an He. She's a good 1,000 metres higher. She's now flown across the destination. Suddenly we see ahead of us countless black dots appear in the clear sky. That's the first barrier. I detect a few gaps and commit those to memory. After five minutes I've reached the first flak belt encircling the city. Russian barrage of fire – nothing more. Changing course continuously, I target a gap in the second barrier. Our machine is surrounded by the crackling of hundreds of flak shells. Once in a while a light tracer from the middle flak streaks through the sky – they don't quite reach us. Roaring flak increases after we penetrate the second barrier and fly across the city. Richard has cranked open the bomb flaps, eagerly keeping a watch on all the instruments at all times. With the machine shuddering, I know he has jettisoned the bombs. They'll be detonating down below, 100 metres apart. Soon, the entire cargo has disappeared into the clouds. The bays close shut, a steep right-hand turn and we head back the way we came. Those gaps in the barriers were just too good to be true – indeed they were perfect for us to do the job and get away unhurt. It was pitch dark around us. From the hurricane of fire bursts, clouds still hung in the air. The Russians must have tossed some 1,000 shells at us. The other machine has long since returned home; meanwhile bright flashes of lightning, seeming to pierce the darkness all at once, envelop the city. Our bombs must have exploded, as beyond the city, in a line reaching from its centre to its surroundings, the flak unleashes an inferno of smoke and flames which I'd never want to witness from within, it has to be said. Had I continued flying straight ahead after dropping the bombs, who knows … I might well have been caught out.

I hadn't considered adjusting the propellers – but suddenly I find myself in the middle of a bank of hundreds of smoke clouds. Goodness me – these dogs shoot sharp. I quickly reduce the speed of my left engine, bank into a steep left-hand turn and – would you believe it – we just missed being hit by a hair's breadth. That very nearly went wrong. Gradually I manoeuvre myself out of this mess, put my crate upside down and at terrifying speed I streak through the last barrier. We breathe a sigh of relief. Let them all go to hell …!

We're homeward bound. Music to our ears. Right ahead of me: my frontman. Suddenly, a small dot above me approaches. Fighter planes. I radio this through at once and coordinate defence. My frontman spirals off, disappearing through the clouds. The comrade pursues him, but soon emerges and circles the area from which the He has escaped. The guy must be fuming.

I approach him while remaining close above the cloud bank. He recognises me, comes straight at me. Richard opens fire. This fighter plane of ours then pulls his plane up into a steep climb, has us fly beneath him and then zooms into our back from up above. But Toni and Pitt slam a salvo into his crate and for a brief moment I disappear into the clouds. No visibility to speak of. Lowering altitude by a few hundred metres and I emerge, with Ivan pushing through the carpet at about the same moment. He hasn't yet set eyes on me. A few rounds of fire and off I go once again. Eventually, I poke my nose out, hoping this might be the end of it. But Ivan seems the stubborn type. He doesn't let go so I have to empty a magazine and again retreat to the clouds. We seem to have fun playing cat and mouse, making me peek out more and more often. At the front or the back, wherever Ivan is hovering around, we fire at him. He himself barely has the opportunity to respond in kind. Every time he's in a fairly convenient position, I've cleared out. After a while – some ten minutes have passed again – I see another cloud bank below me. Off with me to my next hiding space. He must be fit to be tied as he never really gets an opportunity to fire.

The area now under our control isn't far away. This time round I pull up and cruise at 1,000 metres altitude above the clouds. My wait for Ivan is long and drawn out. Finally, he appears and opens fire from quite a distance. What an idiot – you're not going to score a hit this way, comrade – and with that I dive into the clouds. Below me, another carpet; I nosedive and the whole thing starts all over again instantly. I poke out of the clouds, Ivan swoops into the cloud bank, sees us at the last minute and spews out his ammunition. Toni and Pitt respond and I leave them to it. According to my calculations we must by now be flying above our own territory. The few holes in the cloud blanket allow us a quick peek. Indeed, I'm right. We've long passed the front line. A collection of 109s are zooming around. We weave in and around them while firing shots into the clouds, with our fighter planes immediately catching on. Two of them plunge through the bad weather while the rest of them wait down below. Let's hope they've stopped this Bolshevik busybody in his tracks.

We certainly had fun playing this game. Richard turns on the music again. Karl joins us in the front with a bright grin lighting up his face. I zap him, a fist-fight ensues, while the good old He cruises along without much interference.

The engine has returned to normal and at this altitude is once again running smoothly. Flying low, we follow the roads, passing over the heads of Landsers and farmers. The former wave at us, the latter hurl themselves into the mud. Pitt, shrieking with joy, has completed his sixtieth enemy operation and mayhem erupts in our crate. Not surprising really. To surface from this inferno intact, not having suffered a hit, and then be in the doldrums wouldn't be appropriate.

The airbase appears in front of us. Approach … flying low – technical ground staff run for cover. My traditional steep dive follows and a moment later my 'F' hurtles along the muddy runway towards its bay.

A huge welcome awaits us, followed by raucous laughter when we tell them the hullaballoo with the hide-and-seek game that has gone on. We congratulate Pitt on his sixtieth enemy mission and drive to the command post. The old man and the commander listen to our report with a smile, upon which we move to the mess and voraciously devour our lunch, while also emptying a bottle of cognac.

29.10.41

A quick glance through the window has us shudder. Brrr. Clouds are hanging low. Filthy weather conditions and it is freezing cold in this pad. Let's just snuggle a bit longer in our sleeping bags – it's quite bearable inside them.

Gradually, we feel hunger pangs, but 'Where's breakfast?' is responded to by peals of laughter. Alerted by the commotion,

Schmeling joins us from the next room, smirking. A moment later he reappears and, plop, I am drenched in ice-cold water. Just you wait, you rascal! I leap out of bed and, lunging at him, I scream: 'Let's get a hold of him!' A chorus of those lying in the other beds chimes in 'Let's beat him black and blue! We want to see blood!' And with that Schmeling receives his comeuppance, getting a bucketful of water hurled at his neck, with the rest of the cabin then clambering out of their bunks.

A warm fire burns in the kitchen. We heat up some water, glance at some broken mirror and realise we've grown beards. Off with that facial hair, otherwise Papa Stalin won't pick me for his entourage.

I'm done and hand the wash bowl to Karl as if it's the holy grail – we actually stole it in Radzyn. Karl, however, has put himself to bed again. But not for long. One not very gentle pull at his arm and he tumbles out of bed. Growling, he shuffles into the kitchen. Soon, we're all gathered there, have breakfast and curse the weather.

We'd barely finished when the sergeant enters and hands out the orders. There's no arguing; we pull on our uniforms, grab our parachutes and report on the double at the command post. We're informed of the destination. It's a railway line south-east of Tula. We're to interrupt the route or disable the trains. Take off solo, at five-minute intervals.

The weather has really become crazy. Because of the low temperatures and the rain, the machines are caked in ice. Lieutenant Ramminger takes off for weather reconnaissance to see what impact this might have – as for us, we feel there's absolutely no point embarking on anything.

The old man's radio operator messages that Bubi is returning because of a serious risk of icing. We hear the rumbling of his engine, but suddenly the airbase is completely shrouded in fog and snow flurries. Only half of the water tower situated at some distance away peeks out. Signalmen shoot white and green light tracers into the air. Bubi is familiar with blind-flying and there he is, emerging onto the base, he throttles back, executes a blind turn, closes in, the wheels

He 111s flying in formation over Russia
(Source: Bundesarchiv_Bild_1011-641-4548-24, Russland, _He_111).

touch down, he puts on the brakes and comes to a standstill, albeit a bit off from the landing cross, but the runway is empty anyway. After he has turned off the engines he informs the old man that any operation is bound to fail as within fifteen minutes of flying, a thick 2-cm layer of ice had coated his crate. Nothing doing. Let's get onto the trucks and go home. Shortly thereafter driving snow is sweeping the landscape. Bubi was lucky to come down before that.

Towards lunchtime the cloud cover lifts, with a blue sky looking down on us. Ten minutes later we arrive at the command post together with the 2nd Squadron. Crews of the other two Staffel have already gathered there. It's the same target we were told about this morning. Tight formation and we're off. Apparently we should be getting fighter plane protection above the target. We're slightly sceptical – Russians might appear. Our captain is in the lead.

Incredible how weather conditions can change within three hours. Totally clear blue sky, not a cloud in sight. Gradually we climb to 3,000 metres. Watching the instruments, Richard takes measurements to assess his strategy.

Before too long the front line is below us, the large industrial zone will be ahead of us shortly. We're quite sure that we'll be met by heavy defence. Tula is situated far to our left, veiled by ground mist. Industrial plants and small towns dotted around all over.

The old man swings into a wide right-hand curve, indicating that the squad is to attack the target coming out of the glaring sunshine. A few fighter planes appear – at long last we're given protection. Here we are, we're all ready for you, you Russian folks. We're flying straight above the industrial zone and the railway line is below us. The old man loops into a sharp turn, cranks open the bomb flaps, and Richard follows suit.

'The old man is jettisoning the stuff!'

Richard waits a moment, aims with precision and ejects the bombs. Ammunition is spilling out of all machines … the old man has discarded his entire load all at once, Richard still harbours six of his eggs.

'Oh, just be done with it and fling that last bit on any old industrial plant we pass by,' I say to him, and he nods in agreement.

Flak salvo bursts flash up at several spots, fifteen hits straight onto the train line and the battle is in full swing. There are many misses. The route has been destroyed along a length of 200 metres. With the bombs having barely left their bays, concentrated flak opens up. Those shells really are a smash hit – if I may say so myself. A perfect formation drop and with that the unit fans out – that's why the old man had been in a hurry to get rid of his bombs all at once.

The fighter planes who'd escorted us now clear out and have us battle through the leaden sky all on our own. Richard is hunched over his instruments while informing us of changes in the route. I veer slightly off course to approach a blast furnace installation. It presents itself so beautifully, just straight ahead, and all I need to do is keep my crate steady to eject my last bombs. Two detonate just short of their target, the others are bull's eye, with two barracks exploding and fountains of debris hailing through the air. My last one slams into an empty building still standing and sets it alight. Well done. The old man lets his machine wobble its wings to show his appreciation. I join the others and after five minutes we've escaped the heavy flak. We're all together, no one's missing.

Our descent is leisurely with our airbase in front of us before we even know it. Close up to one another, we circle the field. I can bet you there's no other unit who can be prouder of their flying in formation than us! We disperse without any issues. All runs smoothly.

Looks like some crates have been hit, especially those from the 7th Staffel. Well, as the saying goes: the devil takes the hindmost. Explains why the rear positions are not first choice, really. My good old 'F' is due for a check-up. She's clocked up her hours and deserves some proper looking after in a repair shop back in the Reich. Kuddel Jonas, who's been by far the unluckiest among us and has earned himself some rest and relaxation – was ordered to fly her back to Germany. I'm given another order: to fly a Ju to Warsaw in order to pick up an He for our lot. That's it for me, then, adieu to the front line! A brief interval can't hurt after eighty-eight enemy operations.

— • —

My stay in Warsaw lasted for over one week. We had a jolly good time there.

9.11.41

My Staffel has put quite a number of operations behind them – as for myself, I'm still in the lead with respect to my number. My new machine is the 'E'. The technician is a pro and knows his craft. While the 'F' was only able to carry smaller bombs mounted to the exterior, this one is fitted with a larger bay that can manage heavier bombs. A comforting fact.

It's noontime when we get our orders. At the command post we're informed that our next mission is to intrude on the Tula–

Venev area – which apparently has already been heavily damaged over the preceding days. According to the reports delivered by other crews, a huge amount of heavy flak has been massed, especially in Tula proper. It smells of disaster.

A good hour later sees us flying at 3,000 metres from east to west, approaching from the enemy hinterland along the roads. I decide to stay well clear of the villages where an inferno of flak bursts is creating mighty havoc. Heavy traffic below. Have the boys even spotted us? In a larger town a collection of vehicles are lined up on a square and that's precisely where the old man is headed towards. The bomb bays were opened a while ago – they rain down at the very next moment. Our heavy blob zooms down, becomes smaller, disappears and we hope for a whammy. It was. Further five dropped onto the square of this dump, six crossways and only one misses. Not a single one of the parked vehicles will ever drive again. The place turned into a blazing heap of wrecked metal. Long trails of black smoke rising into the air from all corners. Flak blasting away.

The old man veers off, flying along the road towards Venev. Busy around here as well. Here and there bombs rain down, dropped by individual bombers, and they block off the road. Crates punched – one after the other, and we swoop over vehicles turned into flaming wreckages. Nothing to be seen from up above. We take care of the trucks in Tula and then return. Several plants dotted around the area are set on fire, probably hit by artillery shells. A few kilometres short of Tula several concentrations of vehicles are reported. One last attack gets rid of the rest of the bombs. Heavy flak is the response and what the Russians are mobilising is awesome. Down below our eggs pack a lethal punch in the village – but not quite as effective as the first time round. Nonetheless, pillars of flame all around.

Crossing over Tula, we fly home. The major part of flak defence is aimed from too high up above or from too far on the right. Unchallenged, we pass this important armament centre and none of these plants is actually a priority as sooner or later they'll fall into German hands in any event.

10.11.41

We're deployed to the Nakafü [Nahkampfführer, close combat leader], which means that to support our troops we're flying towards destinations situated close to the front line. Apparently, we're told, the crossing over the Oka, north of Tula, should be properly prepared for. At that point the embankment is rather steep, the river itself some 100 metres wide. Won't be an easy nut to crack.

The main defence, as per reports, is amassed east of Alexsin. That's where we're headed. Weather is gorgeous, not a cloud in the sky. We take off one squad after the other. Attacks in waves in order to tire out the defence. At 3,200 metres we decide to zoom. Before us, neatly arranged in rows, lies Alexsin with its broad streets and American high-rises. I'm a bit surprised at not encountering any resistance. Straight behind, two villages emerge. The first one is ablaze, looks like the 8th Staffel had good aim.

Bomb bays ajar with a drawn-out and precise approach flight. We've fanned out slightly with a view to carpeting the entire village. Every machine targets through a gap in the thin veil of clouds now drawing across the area. The distance between each of our lines measures about 100 metres. The guys ahead of me eject their stuff, while I remain at the back and have a good overview. After a slight adjustment to our course, we let our bombs drop as well. Basically nothing misses the village. It's all been well peppered, in my opinion. Fires erupt, fragments of burned wreckage are hurled into the air. The strong winds will do the rest. Making a wide left turn, we sweep past over Alexsin, the front line and then back home.

Our bomber-squadron is rolling. There're continuous comings and goings in the air. Barely have we touched down, and already the two other Staffel take off. An hour later it's our turn once again.

— • —

My engines are cold. The battery's on low and the ignition won't switch on. We need the heating truck and a burst of hot air injected into the cylinders. The Staffel has long ago disappeared into the air. At long last the engines start by spluttering, roaring and then settling to a monotonous drone while I gently increase the revs until the required temperature is reached. My left engine is still ticking and must have sooted up the spark plugs. But these can be changed after the flight. Release brakes, push throttle forward and we're airborne. Gusts of snow whirling high up behind me.

At full speed I race after the group. Impossible to catch up. I only climb to 1,200 metres. That should be plenty. I just hope I can eject the bombs in time; our infantry wants to kick off the attack. Just above the Oka I meet my Staffel who are already on their return flight. I've another five minutes until I reach that dump. In six minutes, the attack is supposed to get underway. I give full throttle, the distance decreases and soon I prepare for approach to rid myself of those eggs. The dump is burning at all corners. Steep dive, Karl is taking pictures. There's not much to see for all the smoke. Our line is diagonal to the rows of houses along the road. To go easy on the engines, I gently throttle back. Flying low, we cross over Alexsin. Nothing noteworthy to be seen. No defence, suggesting that the Russian is still lurking.

Just short of the airbase I finally join up with my unit, the last one to touch down. We discard the old spark plugs and replace them with new ones. But the engine keeps faltering and choking. After two days they're running smoothly and everyone's content.

11.11.41

Weather conditions have changed violently. Low-hanging clouds, poor visibility – all in contrast to yesterday's brilliant sunshine. Heavy ground mist.

We're informed at the command post that we're supposed to engage in a free for all, which means that we're at liberty to do as we please within the zone allocated to us. No other option really, what with this weather. I receive a crate which belonged to the 7th Staffel and off I go.

Filthy weather conditions. No visibility beyond 500 metres. Ghastly. Let's just be thankful if we get clearance of up to of 5 metres. Inside the cloud bank we're experiencing serious icing.

After about half an hour I cross over the front line, encountering light flak. Ramming back into the clouds, I change course. A bit later, I poke out my nose. Zero visibility. Only once I lower my bird by some 50 metres do I gain ground visibility. Though the terrain around here lies lower, it's rugged and treacherous. Often it's too late to pull up and it's only if I yank and tug at the wings that I just about scrape through. A road is ahead of us – it appears as dark and blurry in the filthy grey mess which the icy landscape has turned into. No traffic. MGs fire at some individual Bolsheviks and when there are several of them, a bomb comes zooming down.

At long last Richard is in full control of the instruments. I can't pay any attention to these, seeing as I'm awfully busy with the machine. A turning point: we've reached the dump but it's too late to drop any bombs. The minute we become aware of it – it's already behind us. No option but to perform our finest blind-flying manoeuvres. Richard now notes some troop movement. A bunch of Bolsheviks escape into buildings – we've got to fumigate this junk pile.

I dive down to attack anew. Richard follows my orders and keeps the bomb bays shut, which allows me to have better control over the crate – the weather is making things increasingly difficult. The eggs will find their way down in any event. There! Let's get this over with. A slight pressure on the release and the first stick of bombs crashes into the dump with a monstrous explosion. Satisfied, we watch several huts going up in flames.

Racing on, we recognise down below a camp consisting of several barracks. Looks to us like there is heavy traffic within and we decide to jettison our heavy charge. I loop, return and attack. But I'm too far to the left to target the area effectively. Renewed approach and attack. I fail again. A barrage of MG fire from the barracks. Finally, we score a clean hit with the third attack. The massive lump smashes into the road at the edge of the camp, slides a short distance towards a barracks, whooshes through it, slides further and crosses the entire camp to finally detonate some 100 metres behind it. The detonation causes my crate to be thrown from left to right and, flying low-level, I can barely hold her steady.

But we're still nursing a few bombs on board which must be dropped on the barracks. Yet for the life of me, I can't find those blasted wooden huts. After fifteen minutes I decide to give up. Weather conditions are simply too awful and I have no reference points available. We're furious that the lump now lies somewhere in a field.

At long last we make out a well-paved road which can guide us. We fly low and three trucks go up in flames while two stick to the trees. Well aimed. The chase isn't over, and we fly north. The road leads towards Tula. We need to be cautious, as our own troops are embedded just 20 km south from there. Apparently, they've advanced a good distance along that road.

It's time for our drop. Four trucks, one behind the other, and they must have heard us, as the vehicles come to a halt and the passengers jump out and fling themselves into the road ditch. Three bombs smash down. One lands smack in the middle of the fleeing Russians, one crashes into the road, alongside the vehicles, the other one ploughs into the mud. Pitt reports that two trucks blown by the air pressure had landed in the ditch. For good measure Karl rattles off a few bullets.

A moment later we recognise at some distance away a few German tanks and fire off the recognition signals. They respond from down below. The lead tank shoots yellow smoke tracers in the direction of the heaviest defence. Ah! Gun emplacement. Bombs come hailing down. But before Richard ejects them, he first lets off a barrage of gunfire and Pitt presses the button of his cannon, but only manages to fire a few shots, as during our take-off it had been splattered with slush and mud. Bombs have hit their target – precisely in between emplacements. Well, hardly surprising what with us flying low. We turn round and blaze away with our machine guns until their barrels are hot. Thankfully they work beautifully, with bullet after bullet finding their mark in quick succession. Breaking away, I'm very aware of the impact of this attack of ours. One field cannon has been overturned, the other one must have been seriously damaged by fragments, as a bomb had landed only 10 metres away from it. Two eggs smashed into the camps and they seem to have disappeared under the debris and rubble. I return to dive into the muck again, targeting the gun emplacements in the trenches. Three of our own tanks thrust forward, rumbling through slush and mud while our weapons get to have their say yet again. They strafe the trenches and we follow up by firing our tracers. We make a swift escape only to return instantly and this time there's no defence. Tanks are close up, with tracers from all sides converging on a specific target. We dive down and I hear Toni screaming that a bunker has exploded – a direct hit – spraying great masses of dirt fountains into the air. A number of Bolsheviks climb out of the trenches, raising their arms above their heads. Slowly they stump towards the tanks, which roll back with them on board. Another circle above the column and then it's homeward bound for us lot.

13.11.41

Weather conditions have improved somewhat. Cloud base at about 300–400 metres off the ground and visibility at 2–3 kilometres. Perfect, considering the current circumstances.

We report at 0900 to the commandant and are ordered to go into action. Once again we're to attack assembly points located south-east of Alexsin. We take off solo and are dispatched at customary intervals of ten minutes. We were instructed to follow a precise route: attack a bend in the river, dead south of Alexsin, swing right towards a village surrounded by armed positions. I am to take off last. Not exactly ideal to have to face an anthill, veritably crawling with fighters, which has received prior warning thanks to our previous attacks and will thus be ready to defend itself. There's to be only the one attack, followed by a steep right-hand climbing turn. With everyone gone, my team boards the plane and we roll to the take-off runway. I give full throttle at the indicated time. My machine belongs to the 7th Staffel and only sluggishly gathers speed but eventually I have lift-off. As we're roaring across close to the roofline and despite take-off being rather a mundane occurrence, many faces are turned upwards. Only slowly gaining a bit of height, what with the engines not responding properly, I'm not progressing. These mates of mine certainly haven't blessed me with the best crate. I bank cautiously and continue flying below the cloud bank. Almost horizontal, the plane now catches up and proves me wrong. She's not at all that slow in the end. At a speed of about 300, I thunder towards my destination. I've adjusted my course and Richard fusses

Army quarters of an airbase located in Ukraine
(Source: Atlantic Bilderdienst. PK Baast).

around the radio. Some great jazz music plays loudly through the earphones. In our seats, we all sway to the rhythm, which makes the crate start rocking as well. Toni objects, moaning that he can't adjust the communication unit properly, but we're in high spirits. Karl, as usual occupying the emergency seat in the cockpit, grins and slides around on his narrow stool. This is how we listen to one record after another. Once in a while Richard turns down the volume and regulates the sound … before we know it, we've arrived just short of Oka. Karl moves to the back of the plane, the music is turned off and we're prepared for battle.

Alexsin lies to our left. And we also recognise the bend we were informed about. We veer off to the right, open the bomb bays. From behind us our guys are discharging barrages of concentrated gunfire, targeting the trench positions built on the high embankment of the Oka. Targets are also being fired at from down below and no less viciously. Every now and then we hear a crack. A hit. Causing quite some damage. A stray bullet whizzes through the bomb bay but fortunately ricochets off the chunky fragmentation bombs.

The village now lies in front of us. It's surrounded by quite a number of bomb craters. A few houses are on fire and we note some light flak fire. Little red mice streak by – quite close. It's not exactly comforting to see those devils dart past you. I try pulling out my machine from the thick of the heavy defence, but Richard vents his anger. I should keep the machine steady, for heaven's sake. All right, so be it; if we're hit, that's it then. Karl bangs away into the flak positions, but to no avail as the brothers down below are thick-skinned and don't give up. I'm actually surprised that so far we haven't been hit. Surely it can't be that difficult to shoot down a machine from 300 metres away? I too dig my heels in and aim for the gun emplacements. The village is right behind them and heavy MG fire keeps attacks at bay.

But the time has come. In quick succession bombs go hailing down.

I briefly withdraw into the clouds, climb into a steep right-hand turn but then immediately come out to observe the impact. Down below, the last bombs erupt. Bravo! One has crashed right next to the flak positions. Weapons remain silent – looks like they've been hit. The other clump has landed in and between the positions and the village. Salvos burst out and with that I escape into the clouds. Mission accomplished. After a few minutes I emerge. The Oka lies behind us, at a distance of some 300 metres. The sky above and far away is streaked with vapour trails. Let them keep shooting away – they'll not hit anything as it is.

Karl reappears at the front. Richard brings along some music and our return flight turns out to be as jolly as the beginning of our operation. We relax and are in a good mood.

14.11.41

Today we're expecting a special operational assignment. The advance infantry units have run out of ammunition and supplies have been delayed or can only be delivered with great difficulty due to miserable weather conditions. Every vehicle gets stuck on roads and paths that have turned into gooey mud, sludge clinging to the wheels and slowing them down to a snail's pace. It's therefore down to us to look after reinforcements and make sure they get through.

That's the reason for our flight via Borisov, the nearby airbase.[8] We're en route to Smolensk in order to fill up the machines. Every available machine has been deployed. Today, I'm back again in my good old 'E' as at long last the engine has been repaired.

Once we've arrived in Borisov, it turns out there are no hoists to be had and seeing as I'm the last one to arrive, I'm immediately dispatched to procure some. I radio through the order and request they be ready for me to pick up on arrival. It all goes to plan. They're all lined up and loaded onto my plane, full throttle and I'm up in the air – no time is wasted.

Upon landing in Borisov, we unload and special units take over our machines. As for us, we're picked up and taken for lunch.

Outstanding. Back here, they sure know how to live. Our inspector, what with his boring *Eintopf* [stew], can take a leaf out of their cookbook, so to speak. We then return to our machines and some of them have already left. My 'E' hasn't yet been given the all-clear. A group of prisoners unload the provision containers, and the packers then don't lose a second in doing their bit. We all help. It's already late and towards 1600 hours it's getting dark.

Just before taking off, I receive the exact coordinates for the drop. With darkness falling rapidly, I spot flashes of light dotted around the sky. Artillery fire opening on both sides. Richard fires a recognition flare. Where the hell is the drop point? Ah, over there, they shoot white tracers up several times in quick succession. Gosh, that must be another one of those ramshackle villages. The drop point is supposed to be marked at the western exit. Spiralling down, I can't see a thing other than a collection of vehicles standing alongside the road with many Landsers gathered around them. An empty field not far away. So, that's where we'll throw our bombs. A few curves, then approach. Bays are open and with barely an interval between them the containers descend. Two parachutes unfortunately don't open and the mines detonate while spraying ammunition all around the area, much to the annoyance of our Landsers, who'll have to scurry around in pitch darkness to collect all the stuff.

From an angle I can see them running to and fro trying to salvage bits of armament. But then I scram.

My crate glides along peacefully as darkness continues to fall. My feet barely have to touch the rudder pedals. Richard lies stretched out in the cockpit and tries giving me directions. The dark lines of roads still stand out sharply against the snow, the forests appear as gloomy patches of black rags. Kaluga is to our right and from this spot I plot my exact course towards the airbase. I note the time.

Toni fiddles on his wireless, trying to set up a connection to the base. But it's all in vain. By the light of his torch he disassembles it and realises that the transformer had blown. He then adjusts the radio compass and Richard tries his luck. It seems as if it's all jinxed – we can barely make out anything for all the disturbances. Ah, finally, a reading – but then it's gone. All the turning, twisting, adjustments – nothing works, no way to get any reading whatsoever. Finished. It's closing time. If we don't catch a road soon, we might just as well bail out.

There's still a tiny bit of clear sky in the west, but below us it's pitch black. If it's not raining, it's pouring. The gyro horizon also fails. The only instrument available to me is the turn-and-slip indicator and stubbornly I keep to the set course. Richard lies stretched out, desperately trying to recognise something – anything. Not a landmark in sight. Fortunately, we've noted down the time at Kaluga. At one point we simply must reach the road leading from Roslavl to Smolensk and with any luck there'll be some traffic. The light of the circulating vehicles will then guide us.

The time has passed and we must have flown far beyond the road. I'm giving it another few minutes and then keeping north to approach the runway Minsk–Smolensk. We're relying on some traffic lights perhaps, and with any luck, headlights as well. Indeed, from afar we can make out some lights and they become more frequent, with a town eventually appearing below us. From that point, one road leads north and another one east. That'll be Roslavl. Very convenient that the town is not completely sunk in darkness, and we breathe a sigh of relief as we'd become quite nervous. Toni keeps hammering on his keyboard and finally is connected with headquarters. We're only getting very imprecise directions but enough to have confirmation that Roslavl is the town situated below us.

Quite heavy traffic going in the direction of Smolensk, which allows us to follow the road as the trucks haven't dimmed their headlights. I remain at a certain altitude to get a good overview of the situation. After twenty minutes the road makes a sharp left turn, which tells me that the airbase can't be too far away. Brightly coloured lights on the horizon. I bear down and before too long the airbase stretches out in front of me. Richard fires off some recognition signals and I prepare for landing. The beacons are barely visible, they're so faint. Well, here's hoping it'll work! The gyro horizon still isn't working, but I swing round towards the barely lit flare path. A white and green flare shoots up, the airfield is empty. My wheels are out and gradually ground is coming closer. I switch on the landing lights, while Richard gives me directions as my attention is fully focused on the fast-approaching ground. The crate hovers in the air for a short moment before touching down with a few harsh bumps, to then briefly bounce up and down and finally roll down the runway towards my bay. I flash my lights and ground crew respond by swinging their torch lamps, which lead me to my allocated bay. Finally my crate is at home where she belongs and we disembark. Everything is prepared. The fuel truck has arrived, my oil is being refilled, and the mechanic notes down my list of complaints. By early morning tomorrow, the plane should have had a thorough check-up. We're still in a queue, waiting for the tech team to finish up the paperwork, and then we drive to the command post to report. After that, at long last, we're off to our barracks, where we're received with a warm welcome.

An amazing operation is behind us and I'm well and truly knackered, ready for bed.

15.11.41

Destroyers ordered to safeguard the outer flanks of troops located to the east of Tula and pushing towards north. Due to bad weather, we fly solo. With the customary take-off interval, we make a start. Clouds are hanging low, visibility is so-so. Once in a while we pass through a rain shower with visibility deteriorating to only a few hundred metres. I fly as low as possible so as not to lose sight of the ground. After about one hour we're close to the front line. We all strain our eyes to recognise our own lines. While we're still a good distance away from the front line, Swastika flags are fastened to our trucks, but our mates of course remove them shortly before the front so as not to be shot at by the Russians. For us up here it's a difficult task to tell friend and foe apart, especially given the current filthy weather conditions.

There, just below us, some Landsers wave their hands up at us. We're still above our own territory, it seems. For a few minutes we see absolutely nothing. Once we regain a bit of visibility we notice individual units moving in fits and starts across the fields, immediately throwing themselves flat on the ground when they become aware of us above them. We're gone the next minute, only to become the target of Russians shelling us without mercy. The ugly enemy is rearing his head. Looks like our own units have pushed ahead much further than we'd been informed back at the command post. It must be awfully difficult for those poor devils to drag themselves through marshland and mud.

The battle can begin.

Weather conditions steadily deteriorate the further east we fly. We're at an altitude of barely 50 metres and can only see about 200–300 metres ahead of us. Shreds of cloud hang in between – it's filthy outside. Often, when taking sharper than usual turns in order to observe targets which suddenly appear, I slip and bank, and more often than not it's too late to drop any bombs as, given the high speeds, we've long missed the target. In fact, we only just manage to fire off some shots. This kind of business goes on for quite a while, sometimes we're close to the ground, sometimes close below the cloud bank. Little visibility. At times the machine starts wobbling, spitting and doing all sorts of tricks, I then straighten her out again, but the bomb flaps are open and because I keep my eyes trained on the ground rather than on the blind-flying instruments, any forms of manoeuvring are considerably reduced. But I'm still able to pull her out just in time before it's too late.

At long last we come upon a bit of a larger hovel. A few vehicles are parked there and it seems worthwhile to drop some of our eggs.

After two failed attacks we finally succeed, but as for the surprise element – well, that certainly didn't materialise. We get rid of a row of bombs, among them one big hunk. That cheeky thing jumps up from the ground, rolls around but finally settles in the dump. Diving down, we can clearly hear the detonations, a few seconds later a huge bang. The big fat egg has exploded. We've never gone down that low to eject. The time fuse works perfectly.

The bright light of the shelling makes it easy to find the village. Our eggs have been well placed. Goodness, looks like an anthill down there. Full of civilians, but in there with them loads of Bolsheviks, and one drum after another blasts down among them. Sometimes MGs respond but eventually that dies down as well. The wild chase continues. I can hardly make out anything – so I must be closer to the front line. I set course north, flying on. But guess who can't be spotted anywhere? The Bolsheviks. Damn, where are those guys? No matter how hard we look, we can't detect anybody worth a bomb or even a bullet. After some time we return to our own line, where our Landsers have gathered in larger and smaller groups, warming themselves at the fires from some shacks they've just burned down. Some wave at us – others barely look up. For a while I fly along the front towards the east, but nothing noteworthy to be seen. I turn round, back home.

One thing remains certain: the planned flank protection has not happened; nothing could be further from the Bolsheviks' mind than attacking us from the south.

On my return flight, short of Sukhinichi, I chance upon an He 111 which has made an emergency landing. No sign of the crew. There are some twenty Russians surrounding the crate and, calm as a cucumber, they disassemble her. One has ripped apart a parachute, trying to stuff the silk into a bag, others break the glass window panes. Just you wait, we'll wipe the smirk off your faces.

I put my machine in a steep dive. Some Russians duck while tossing something upwards. We can't make out any markings on the He as she had been blackened for night flights. Those idiots hurl stones at us but we're having none of that. We turn round yet again and this time we let our onboard ammunition do the talking. Diving low, the chase is on. The bunch of them split apart but don't let go of their haul. Some beat it, others fling themselves to the ground, a few of them shake their fists. But a bullet swiftly takes care of that and has them tumble into the snow. We swoop down low and Toni fires into the heap. Another turn, another attack. Goodness me, what is it that I behold? Here in occupied territory? Some human rag is waving around with his gun. Without hesitating, I aim directly at him, one shot and he crumples to the ground, his wrecked body engulfed in smoke. Everyone still alive after this episode bounds down an embankment towards a nearby hamlet while firmly gripping their loot, but looking for cover when our bullets come spraying down, turning the white carpet of snow into a sieve. My next target is the hamlet itself and the house where the looters have taken refuge. With fire spouting from the building perforated by our guns, my only feeling is that of satisfaction. 'You won't be looting a German machine forced into an emergency landing any time soon, you buggers.' Richard is so furious that he's determined to throw his last bombs at that dump, but I forbid him to go ahead as these bastards don't deserve our precious ammunition. They've been punished plenty. I report the event at the command post after we've landed and am informed that the machine belonged to our 2nd Group, forced to make an emergency landing the night before.[9]

— • —

Over the following days we fly several operations tasked to protect our flanks while also ordered to set all villages we come across on fire, thus depriving the Russians of finding any accommodation.

We're still leading and pushing forward. The ground is blanketed in ice. We're to circle the Oka emplacement in order to avoid unnecessary losses and are to roll up from behind while also forming a new cauldron. Bases located in the south are Tula, in the north Serpukhov, in the east Kashira on the Oka, which winds its way from Serpukhov towards the east.

Kaluga is situated on important railway lines and a road leading to Moscow. We're always flying solo, as weather conditions don't permit an operation in close formation.

24.11.41

On 24.11.41 we attack troop emplacements and heavy field fortifications north-east of Venyov, situated on a road towards Kaluga. At the command position we weren't able to get the exact position of our tank groups, so it's now down to us – to fly along the road and bomb the lot of it, anything which turns out to be enemy troops or fortifications.

Our flight path has us flying above roads and rail-tracks, left wheel aligned with right-hand track. Follow each bend if possible. The return flight is to follow the same path. The aim is to ensure that, should we be forced into an emergency landing, we'd always be close to home troops. Lengthy, time-consuming searches could thus be avoided. We're fine with that, but the constant banking turns are annoying. My own strategy is to skip those, in order to reach the destination faster.

At points the railway line consists of only one track, with no trains visible; it has many twists and turns and is barely visible, what with this filthy weather and a landscape covered in snow. At times we lose sight of this narrow band and suddenly it has completely gone. I stay on course in order to make it easier for Richard to give directions. We spend a long while fighting frequent snow flurries and once they're behind us, a town appears straight below us. This must be Tula and, just as soon as we've confirmed this, we're engulfed by a hail of fire. We run into heavy flak, with the enemy proving to have perfect and precise aim. And that's with us flying low level all the way.

My 'E' banks and I too move into low-level flying, seeing me skimming low over the house roofs, then going deep into the wide streets, flak chasing me all the way. Clouds of black smoke from the explosions below engulf us. Finally I've reached the edge of the town. Streets are teeming with civilians and soldiers who flee into the houses. Richard and the three guys sit in the back, guns ready, trying to make out the exact flak positions in order to shell them. Richard is just about to shoot into a horde of Bolsheviks who've gone wild and disperse. Many fall over and forget to get up again.

Crossing the edge of the city, I go as low as possible, just a few metres above the ground. My eyes are peeled for obstacles in the shape of pipes and chimneys, but in one short leap I zoom over them to go low again immediately. Land to our right rises steeply, with a few houses planted on top. It's the valley path for me, but suddenly, wafting by my windscreen is a smoke trail. Behind me, a clicking noise from the tank. I've flown straight through a burst of fire. Toni and Pitt have immediately noticed the four-barrelled MG and deliver a concentrated attack on the beast, eventually silencing it for good.

Firing off a further bunch of shells onto the Bolsheviks, who look up in shock, we continue our barrage, but subsequently see nothing that would unsettle us. At long last a few Landsers appear, which has me break away instantly, and Richard shoots his recognitions signals.

Actually, that could easily have gone wrong. We're quite relieved it didn't, and I draw a wide circle around this inhospitable dump to then fly above the territory occupied by our troops and along the roads leading west. Toni confirms that we've been hit a good number of times in the ventral gondola, but this is of little consequence. The machine remains fully operational and just as strong as before.

Venyov is now in our hands. We spot the first white flares rise into the air just before the north-east exit, and recognising their signs of identification, we respond in kind. Moments later we recognise the leading group of our tank brigade.

Flying just below the cloud bank at barely 100 metres high, I follow the road which we'll be shelling the moment we sight the enemy. For a while, we can't see anything, but then gradually we notice trenches appearing to the right and left of the road, which turn out to be deep crater pits. Looks like those who preceded us have done good work.

Ahead of us: a village. Flak is at work, as well as MGs. That means we'll drop our eggs with the first line smashing down in a rapid cadence straight across the village. Flak continues blazing away with their guns. Seems like folks down there haven't yet had their fill – well, just you wait and see!

I swerve away, cut into the clouds, fly straight ahead, then swing off to the left to attack the village from the opposite direction for a second time. Perfect approach. Richard has sufficient time to rid himself of his bomb cargo – as I am zooming straight towards the entry to the village. Richard manages to keep defence at bay and then lets his bombs clean up. The first one lands just short of the target, the second one crashed into the middle of the village, right into the street, next to houses which disintegrate into flaming ruins. We keep at it. Russian defence is most certainly broken in this part of the country, and we're well satisfied with our success.

Close below the clouds I'm ready for my return and follow the same flight path that got me here. Blasting away at everything that comes in our sight, we grimly look on as very few get back on their feet. Catching up with the lead tank, we fire off the white flares and come down lower. Further back, Landsers seek cover behind buildings and a large barn. Wobbling my wings, Richard again fires white and, recognising us as one of their own, they wave their hands. In a wide sweep round Tula, I then set course home.

Upon landing and inspecting our machine, we tally up quite a number of MG hits. Several bullet holes in the undercarriage – off with the crate – into the hangar – she should be fit and ready soon. The repair detail is working day and night trying hard to fix the damage on my He – and the others also require extensive repair. Their main aim is to return the machines to the Staffel as quickly as possible – we've got superb ground crews. They are good and tough, our 'men in black'!

— • —

Our next operation takes us south of Kashira, targeting motorised columns and villages brimming with soldiers. Our own emplacements are located some 20 kilometres south from there. Our runs back and forth go ahead at full pace, we pick up speed, flatten out, inflicting as much death and devastation as possible. Hardly a single bomb, dropped from some 100–200 metres, misses its target. On our return, still firing away, we're pleased to notice that our tanks have advanced a fair bit, and our hunch is that Kashira will fall within the day – which means that a central position is in the bag.

26.11.41

Today's operation is to attack the Kashira–Moscow railway line. This being an important area, one must understand that the enemy will quite probably bolster their defence considerably by dispatching reinforcements coming from the north, thus placing further obstacles to our advance, already much hampered by the winter fast approaching.

After a short briefing we once again take off individually. This time round I speed straight up at full throttle and break through the cloud bank, minded to dive down some five minutes prior to the assault and, based on weather conditions, either attack flying low or from high altitude. Richard pores over the map, trying to figure out the perfect position from which we can drop our bombs while remaining undetected and not confronting strong ground defence.

After some time he points to a spot on the map – where the railway track makes a sharp bend and runs through the forest, consequently hidden from view. If we're able to blast the line right there, we're in for a colourful spectacle with an accordion effect unleashed at the point where the train rolls past.

I'm in agreement with Richard and set course towards that position. The sunshine up here creates a good mood and it is

Attack on a factory for military production and on railway hubs in
Krasnopresnensky, south-west of Moscow (Source: Werner Haupt,
Sturm auf Moskau: Der Angriff, Die Schlacht, Der Rückschlag, 1941
(Friedberg, 1986), p. 231).

pleasantly warm in the cockpit. The heating also does its bit. We're due to reach the line and an unbroken blanket of cloud extends below us. No ground visible, not even other machines in the sky. They're probably below the cloud bank.

According to our watches, we should have crossed the front line and there are another 100 kilometres to reach our destination. Our eyes darting around, we still can't identify any emplacement that would suggest enemy defences. After a while we see some holes in the cloud bank, but not large enough to help us orient ourselves.

We're reduced to navigating by dead reckoning alone and decide to dive down. The greyness of the sky gradually lifts and we can see the ground. Clouds still hanging low and somewhat limiting our view, but not seriously and after about three minutes we see a dark line running along ahead of us. That must be our railway. Circling around a village, we're met by heavy flak. The place is riddled with troops. We quickly annotate the map and follow the train line. We've drifted a bit too far south. Not wanting to drop our bombs too close to our own lines, we swerve to the left, catch up with the railway tracks and once below the cloud bank we plunge down to the target. We recognise the train station with some trains lined up, no locomotive. A bit further on, white steam puffs in the air – aha! Must be a train rolling south. Well, you won't be getting anywhere far in a hurry … We fly to within a few metres and let the heavy egg thud to the ground – straight in front of the locomotive. But hey! What's that? The beast refuses to explode. Puzzled, we work over the area – but conclude it was a precision attack – so the fault must lie with a faulty fuse. What a shame – could have been a direct hit right in between the tracks. The train meanwhile happily chug-chugs along. To think we missed a storm of metal being hurled through the air … but let's not give up hope or let him get away. We make another run, and this time we hit the tracks 10 metres in front of him. That'll do – he won't chug-chug any longer.

We're minded to disrupt the train line at many more spots so don't waste any more time with the train. The Russians will already be kept busy trying to repair the line to make it operational.

Ahead of us is the indicated sharp curve. We rapidly bear towards it, holding the machine as steady as possible. No need for any course adjustment – the He lies in the air like a plank of wood.

'Bombs released! We've got another four!'

Richard bends over and watches his eggs disappearing until they're just small dots. After a few seconds we hear, albeit weakly, four detonations. Behind us terrific excitement and joy erupts! Two direct hits on two tracks! Let someone else do any better! I switch off the navigator, break into a steep dive so as to get the full picture of the scene and verify that the hits were carried out with absolute precision. From what I can see at 800 metres altitude, two tracks have been ripped apart and the other two bombs were placed 10 and 20 metres in front of them.

I continue on my route in order to discharge the last few of my babies. Forced to circle a seemingly empty train station, due to light and heavy flak, I briefly spiral off into the clouds and immediately change course. No point wasting my precious load on this station. Four eggs don't achieve much and track disruptions can be fixed in no time, as surely they've got the necessary stock. More worthwhile dropping them on the open line. More time-consuming to report disruptions, it'll take some time to find the more remote areas and even further delays in repairing them.

After a while we come across a small bridge. I decide to attack, dive in, but sadly miss. One bomb crashes right in front of the bridge, the other just behind it. Same result with my second run. Well, let's leave it, then.

Richard winds shut the bay flaps and we climb above the clouds, emerging into the bright sunshine direction home. We're satisfied with the results of our drops.

27.11.41

Our troops have nearly reached Kashira. The tank unit turns west and pushes towards the Oka river from the east. Their advance moves along a broad road. We're ordered to secure the flanks and fly reconnaissance.

The battlefield is situated south-east of Serpukhov, right in between that road and the Oka, where the river makes a bend to the east. So basically, we're talking about covering a large triangle. One line after the other takes off. Should weather conditions deteriorate, we're to thin out and it's every man for himself. That suits us down to the ground – who wouldn't enjoy flying all over the sky at a whim, albeit with the disadvantage of being very much exposed to fighter planes hunting us down?

Weather conditions aren't splendid, as it happens. Cloud patches all over the place and the old man is buffeted by winds while a good distance away from the front. We disperse and I immediately take to the clouds where, just occasionally, the sun manages to burst through a few holes. Perhaps we'll come across some gaps in the cloud cover, offering us an opportunity to drop some stuff.

Flak busily shelling away above the front line. But seeing it is located too far left, we're not bothered in the least. The clouds break up more and eventually they fade into a faint curtain of haze spreading out beneath us, allowing us a perfect view to the ground. First, I fly along the road leading to Kashira. Not much traffic around here. Villages are pretty much empty. We glide along for a while until we recognise our lead tank steadily advancing towards the Oka in order to tighten the cordon. We turn back and run back and forth in between the road and the river. There's damn little to behold; the Russians must be well camouflaged. No wonder, actually, what with masses of fighters and machines roving above the combat zone. A collection of tiny black dots twisting and turning all over the sky, different aircraft and our own fighters. There definitely aren't any Russian machines in the air, as they're quite petrified at the sight of our Me 109.

We're headed towards a town which I first circle to determine whether there's something worthwhile. Suddenly Richard spots quite a number of vehicles, all well camouflaged, grouped together close to the houses. They're barely visible due to being painted white. Not a soul or sausage around. I swing my aircraft round. Let's just see whether we can kick up some dust by dropping a few eggs. After a brief interval, I make for the town and within seconds four bombs come crashing down, separated by only very short intervals. The moment they've detonated, the place is swarming like an anthill. Not done yet, you guys! There's plenty more where that came from! In a steep diving curve I attack again. Ah! Some trucks attempt to escape. Well, we'll be taking care of that, and a full drum load comes hailing down across the town. Flames are coming out of the houses, licking at the stationary trucks. Eventually there's resistance. Bursts of machine-gun fire lashes out at us – quite inhospitable really, but seeing we're politeness personified, we respond in kind. Additionally, air-dropped leaflets whirl towards the ground. Renewed approach and the last bombs are whistling down.

The village is engulfed in flames. Looks like our aim was good. Burning vehicles wherever you look, trucks and lorries are overturned by the blast or lie smouldering by the roadside with columns of thick black smoke rising from the streets. Smoke and flames erupt from several more vehicles set alight, not many seek to escape beforehand. Guns blazing, we keep firing brief bursts of fire before sweeping into a tight curve to give Toni, who until then was sitting in the radio operator seat, a chance to make his own mark in this onslaught of ours.

I make a climbing turn and then fly several zigzag runs across the area. Eventually the weather closes in and I cut through the cloud bank. Barely through, we face heavy flak. Serpukhov below us. Let's get out of this mess. I push the throttle fully home, pull hard on the stick and dive into the clouds for cover. Tracers come whizzing by close to our machine, bursts of bullets punch holes. The Russians are shooting like crazy. A fragment hitting our fuselage with a dull thud has the machine shudder and vibrate; unable to stand it any longer, I make for the clouds. Black trails of smoke darken the sky. I must get away, there's nothing left for us to do around here. After a few steep climbing turns and twists, the unfriendly dump is behind us. Soon the cloud bank lightens. We hardly notice troop movements. But let's dip below the clouds and make sure we haven't missed anything. Richard marks all our observations on the map. Some villages are heavily occupied.

The fuel indicator warns me and I must turn back. In any event, our mission has been fulfilled long ago and we set course for home.

Once we've crossed over the front line Richard extends his congratulations to me. I look at him in surprise when it dawns on me that I've just completed my hundredth enemy operation.

The other three members of the crew join them. To celebrate the day, we take a bearing on the Smolenks soldier radio station and fly home to dance music. As usual, I sign off with a steep turn, which is a little steeper than usual today, and then switch to low-level flight. I push down steeply and race close to the ground towards our parking place, where the entire technical crew of the squadron is already standing and waving all sorts of things. Then I pull up steeply, extend the landing gear and land in a hairpin bend. I roll slowly to the parking lot. A large crowd has gathered there. We climb out of the plane, and I am immediately surrounded by our mechanics, lifted onto their shoulders and carried around as if in a triumphal march. Laughing, I grab them by the ears until they finally give in and let me down. A large fir-wreath is placed over my shoulders. I can barely see my head out. I have to squeeze countless hands as everyone wants to congratulate me.

A photojournalist from the PK [*Propagandakompanie*] takes a few pictures, then I have to say a few words. God knows what kind of rubbish I have talked. Then the old man lands and the theatre starts all over again. He congratulates me and hands me a bottle of cognac. Pictures are taken again. This time with my crew in front of our "E". Then we get into the lorry and drive to the command post. Here the commander shakes my hand, congratulates me on my 100th and wishes me good luck for my next hundred missions.

Afterwards, we report our successes and drive towards our quarters, where we empty a bottle in the company of our squad and the technical team, as well as smoking tons of cigarettes while chatting, enjoying some biscuits and chocolate.

28.11.41

Once again we're deployed to the same combat zone. This time we're to fly in close formations.

When we're just about to leave the command post, Pitt gets a telegram pressed into his hands: 'Hans-Peterle has arrived!' There's a big hullaballoo as Pitt has become a daddy and everyone congratulates him. He's over the moon and keeps re-reading the joyous message. I commemorate this moment with the aid of my camera, just when he glances at the telegram yet again in front of our machine. Then it's time and the squad takes off. Soaring high, we're headed east.

It's a bit hazy, the cloud line is at 1,800 metres. Before too long we've crossed the front. Three dots are approaching us head-on but we soon recognise them to be our own fighter planes. We've got to be extremely cautious as, based on our experience to date, the Russians will soon appear with their fighter planes. In tight formation we continue east, then change course and head west, open our flaps and attack one village after another. Seems like they're all huddled up inside, as no Russian would be camping outside, what with the freezing cold.

In one of the villages, we spot trucks that have not yet been camouflaged so I break out of the formation to spray the village from one end to the other. All three of our machines drop their ammunition with clouds of smoke rising above the individual fires. Some of our bombs drop too far to the side, but those which crash cause devastation, with dust, debris and splintering planks flung into the air. Several houses burn down altogether.

Ahead of us a second village with houses neatly built on either side of a long road. Seeing as we're now straight above, I pick off a few vehicles and Richard drops his eggs in quick succession. This goes extremely smoothly – the bombs hit their target perfectly, smashing into roads and houses, just shy of a row of vehicles at the edge, with only two of them catching fire. Excellent results overall.

The two other machines fly level with me but far on my right. I close the bays, throttle back and am minded to join them.

Suddenly a large collection of aircraft appear from down below on the right. 'Achtung! Fighters in front!' I scream. They've whizzed past and Richard doesn't get to shoot. I actually can't figure out how many of them there are – it lasted just a split second.

A whole bunch of them have come up behind us in a steep climb and go on the attack; I make out Ratas, I-17s and an entirely new model which I've never seen before. Looks like a Rata, but its build is much slimmer and more elongated. It might well be a I-180, a prototype, or an American model, who knows?

Tracers streak across the sky, in between long smoke trails rising from the ammunition.

Toni has taken over the firing, as from where he sits he benefits from the best vision. I've joined the squad and we fly in tight formation. We fire off one round after the next. 'Goodness, there must be ten of those Ivans!' shouts Toni and lets out swear words while adjusting the jammed release mechanism. Our squad commander, Lt. Bumann, is still keeping his flaps open, not considering shutting them even for a moment. He approaches a village. Aha, so that's where he wants to place his eggs. I get my bearings, dive down, see a number of vehicles lined up, but he isn't attacking. Has this guy gone mad? Isn't he aware of the superiority – so why fly in such a crazy manner?

All of a sudden the wingman swings wildly from side to side. He's been hit. Swerves from right to left then plunges vertically into the clouds. I hope Mohrhardt and his crew get home in one piece.

175

Bumann continues his flight path. I glance at the instruments and I realise that the coolant temperature in my right engine is rising at an alarming rate. Checking my back, I see a banner of white smoke trailing behind us. Toni wires it through. Damn! Another 100 km and our engine is dead. And ten fighters in my backside to add to my woes and to liquidate us!

No, gentlemen, this is not for me. I'm out of here. At full speed I climb up as fast as I can. The protective clouds still seem far away. Bumann continues gliding along, calm and collected. Something is not quite right.

My right engine is conking out. Meanwhile, performance of the left one drags so massively that I trim the machine. Behind me an inferno of shelling. Richard joins the shooting, several times emptying his drum magazine in one fell swoop onto the Russians. Smoke coming out of my right engine, spluttering and choking like nobody's business. Smoke is turning blueish-white then gradually getting darker. Time for me to turn off the engine altogether as, if it starts burning – we're finished. We might as well bail out immediately. Our options can be counted on one hand. Not really a reassuring thought.

Clenching my teeth, I climb ever higher. Behind us, it looks like they're selling our souls for the highest price. Three fighter planes turned back, slipping away in a steep dive. The other six subject the group leader flying below us to concentrated fire. Nobody's attacking me, which surprises us all. It wouldn't take much for Ivan to down me, as my capacity has been considerably reduced and I could be plucked out of the sky like a ripe plum dangling from a tree.

At long last I've reached the clouds.

I'm mightily relieved and switch off the stuttering engine. It's getting dark around me, with ice coating most of my machine, I feel rather content as up here no Russian will catch me. I bet the engine will pull through, seeing as it'll only be another thirty minutes until I reach our own lines. I climb steeper and gradually my poor old 'E' gains some height. My speed isn't picking up much but, everything considered, the old crate is holding up nicely.

It's gradually getting lighter. I'm above the cloud and continue homeward course. Should fighter planes appear, it will take me no time to dip into the grey mass. But no sign or sausage of anybody.

A machine comes streaking from the clouds. He levels, then circles me, and the propeller slipstream of his engine catches my aircraft, making me stall. Flattening out after some 100 metres, I climb up again above the clouds. Bumann is still circling. This guy is pretty much ramming me. Again caught in a slipstream with the crate being tossed around wildly, but this time I'm more in control and keep steady. Bumann approaches again, and I am so mad at him and menace him with my fist. Richard is bending over his MG and would love to slam him with a short burst and get rid of him.

Nothing doing, Bumann flies parallel to my machine, albeit keeping his distance as he finally seems to understand that I'm signalling him to get away from me.

He keeps me company up to the front line, approaches me again, but then swerves away to disappear into the clouds. Once more I'm buffeted by slipstream and I'm furious. Just you wait, old mate, I'll give you what for, you watchmaker!

Slowly I limp home. My journey must have lasted for another half-hour, what with the left engine spluttering away and me moving at a snail's pace. Though severely strained, we pull through in the end. Gradually I drop in altitude and Richard is taking pictures of the immobilised engine. The airbase lies in front of us, I come in over the field with Richard firing off emergency signals. Swinging off to the left in a wide arc, I float in.

On my orders Richard and Karl lower the undercarriage, seeing as the hydraulic is connected to the perforated engine. Lowering the wheels is a different matter. Using their body weight, they brace themselves against the lever and the crate plunges. I give her full throttle and we approach. At long last the undercarriage is lowered; Karl tries to operate the wing flaps, but they won't function. Never mind, this has to work without them. I put down the machine at great speed, some 200, with one side sagging to the right. Gently I ease my foot off the gas pedal and straighten her out. I land precisely at the white-cross line, briefly hop up and down, then touch down and, turning slightly left, I speed off towards the hangar still a small distance away. I want to clear the field as quickly as possible for other machines – there're already two of them in the queue for take-off, only waiting for me to roll away.

Suddenly my machine wants to break out to the right. The right undercarriage slumps, which means my tyre must be flat. I press down on the left brakes to avoid the undercarriage slipping away. Nonetheless I can't avoid a cartwheel. I fear my wheels are falling away – but nothing happens. The machine finally comes to a full stop. I attempt to roll the few kilometres to the hangar with the one engine, but it's impossible what with the flat.

I switch off the engine and we disembark. A truck has already been dispatched and the senior foreman and part of the ground crew, which includes the team from the control room dealing with the 'E', come running to inspect the damage. I'm congratulated for the one-engine landing. Then we look more closely at the machine and find four hits in the radiator. The hole is about as large as a fist, with the rest of the coolant dripping out. The wheel has been strafed twice and burst on touching down. We mount the trucks and drive to the command post, while the 'E' is towed to the hangar.

30.11.41

Attack on Moscow.[10] Individual take-offs at fifteen-minute intervals.[11] A dense cloud bank above the target. Approach according to communicated navigation, and jettison of bombs based on calculated position. One can hardly miss the target because of the wild shelling by Russians piercing the cloud cover and them thereby giving away their exact location. No complaints from my side.

I'm allocated some crate belonging to the 7th Staffel as mine isn't yet ready. My intention is to climb to an altitude of 4,500 and begin throwing my bombs at the very first attack.

Airborne, I take to the sky, then climb further and set course for the beacons, where we arrive at the appointed hour. From there we follow a direct line of route to Moscow, and making precise calculations we figure out the exact position. After some fifty minutes we cross over the front. Another twenty-five minutes' flight. Gradually I climb to 4,000 metres. The right engine drags a bit, but then runs smoothly. It's uncomfortably cold up here. The heating scarcely works. I read a temperature of -38 degrees. Ground temperature was -15 degrees.

Ahead of me a machine cruises at some 5,000 metres and I too go higher until I've reached 4,500, which in my mind has to suffice. Richard continually reports our bearings and we near our target. Suddenly the He in front of us finds itself in the thick of heavy flak. The sky is blanketed by a hurricane of bursts with barely a hole visible through which to escape. The Russians must have fortified their flak positions, as we didn't witness such a barrage of fire the first time round.

I turn towards one such hole in the clouds and have the engines run irregularly in order to confuse the Russians listening to their sound detectors to pinpoint our location. I manage to get through the barrier but in front of me towers a wall of fire and lead. Shells slam through the air like hailstones. There's no let-up and no escape. But we have to get through somehow.

Orienting myself by the thick smoke rising from the explosions below, we must be on the line towards the Kremlin. Clench your teeth, full throttle, both engines at full speed and into hell's cauldron. Richard opens the flaps and at intervals of 100 metres flings down the entire stock in one go. Adjusting the propeller blades, I'm flying and don't encounter any problems. The moment we've jettisoned our bombs I tear into a fabulous steep dive and escape to the south. Below us, through a tiny hole in the bank, Richard and I see the Kremlin and a bit further large industrial plants lying in the outskirts north of this Bolshevik stronghold. One might hope that this foxhole won't be spared.

Zigzagging my way through the air, I try and escape the flak, which is growing to horrific proportions. I make use of any gap I come across. Suddenly I find myself engulfed in a mass of some 150–200 shell clouds. The acrid stench of gunpowder and burned rubber filters through to the cockpit and my machine is engulfed in a barrage of fire rattling something awful.

At full speed, I push the nose well down, dive vertically like an arrow and get out of here. What an unfriendly corner it has turned out to be.

At long last the fireworks are behind me. We breathe a sigh of relief before inspecting the machine for holes. Wings and fuselage are perforated. We've been damn lucky and it could all have turned out quite differently.

Throttling back, I turn back, homeward bound. Just before the front line, I push through and immediately recognise our own troops. Keeping down low over the road, then cutting across the field towards the base. Brisk drop, then touch-down followed by a report at the command post. Turns out the aircraft in front of me had also sighted the Kremlin through the gap and shelled it.

2.12.41

Once more we return to the old combat zone, Naro-Fominsk–Moscow. The weather is miserable and doesn't let up, clouds hanging low. Suddenly they tear apart and the most brilliant sunshine welcomes us. Slowly we climb to above 3,000 metres and sooner or later are above the front line. Again, it's Lt. Bumann in the lead and I'm curious what'll happen today, as there's always something afoot with that poor sod in charge.

For a long time we fly along the road towards Moscow. It's mightily busy down below. I've eventually had it up to here and I make for the road. Richard drops four bombs, but they miss their target. Ahead of us, quite far away, is a small town. We note some lively traffic. So, that's where we're headed. Before that, Richard still jettisons two eggs, this time there's one hit onto the highway, just short of a column of trucks rolling direction front line. The real mushrooms drop onto the town. Boy, oh boy – the impact is terrific! As a result, an oil refinery plant explodes, the right wingman flings his rock onto an ammunition warehouse which is demolished in a series of tremendous detonations and a dense rain of sparks swirling around. The same guy also hits the main road, stuffed with trucks and lorries. It's been a worthwhile attack.

Lt. Bumann still has his flaps wide open. Stubbornly he pursues the road leading to Moscow which appears clearly on the horizon. Visibility perfect – a rare occurrence. Scanning the area, we recognise factories and railway stations with their black and white smoke rising up. Part of the city is alight. Artillery shelling in the north-western district. Our Landsers are only some 15 km away.

Suddenly a white dot appears and approaches at alarming speed.

'Achtung! A fighter from the front on the right!'

It's an I-17. Behind us Ivan pulls up and attacks us from behind and above. We draw closer together in order to optimise our fire power. Toni and Karl have lined up their sights and empty a drum magazine of ammunition. I descend a bit lower so that all three machines can crush that guy in one swoop. Just behind the squad, he wings down in a steep dive, but, pursued by the gunners in their canopies, he seems unharmed. Sweeping up and to the right, he's met by my own well-targeted defence fire. Bumann, his flaps still open, doesn't consider even for a second setting course for home. Instead of flying above the road, he hovers along the side, then skims the forest where there's no sign of the enemy. He's either pretending to be a real fool, or indeed is one.

The I-17 reappears on our flank and comes up dangerously close. I can clearly see the four points flash at his wings, yet his barrages miss their target.

Richard once again lies stretched out in the cockpit, his camera propped up while taking a few photographs of this high-spirited Russian zooming past us. In a tight left-hand turn the Russian yanks up his machine, to then come immediately zooming down from left up above. This time he's caught out by six barrages forcing him, mid-approach, to spiral away, showing us his brightly coloured underside. He turns back, but Toni and Pitt still manage to hurl a magazine full of ammo at him with Toni suddenly exclaiming: 'He's on fire!'

Trailing a long white smoke banner behind him, which then turns black, he plummets down vertically. We pursue him for quite a while but then lose sight of him, due to his white paint camouflaging him so well – until swathes of smoke and fire reveal the site of his crash.

Suddenly we found ourselves in the thick of a barrage of shooting, grenade shelling and firing. Damn – we're in the middle of the flak belt surrounding Moscow. Bumann, whose left engine was hit by a fighter aircraft back when he first flew his attack, now trails behind him a long white vapour stream, flings down his last bomb on flak batteries and then sets course for base. I see him flying across the road, hotly pursued by medium and heavy flak. We wingmen zoom in and out, making it difficult for the Russians to attack their targets. Bumann suffers a direct hit to his left wing with a dense rain of sparks swirling around. He nosedives, then straightens out and, throttling back, he flies home.

We peel off to fly alongside him and in a steep descent we finally reach our airbase, not before our machine gets buffeted by squally gusts. Bumann is mighty busy with his damaged machine. But that can't hurt him – let him sweat it out for a while. Why he can't keep to his orders is anyone's guess, and what on earth made him cruise into Moscow in fine weather carrying four bombs?

After landing I climb onto his roof, Lt. Ramminger the right wingman joins me, and Bumann certainly gets a piece of our mind. Let him choose different wingmen – I'm out of the game when this guy is leading. Red in the face, this goner clears out and additionally gets a severe telling-off from the captain and the commander. Then, to top it off, he claims to have downed the fighter plane. But we can give proof that instead it was our crew alone who had fired the hit. The right wingman confirms this and so this point was awarded to us.

4.12.41

On 4.12.41 we fly into the northern sector of Moscow. Tight formation. We're given our destination, a bridge close to the Volga reservoir, and then we're to hunt down anything in sight. Villages should also be razed to the ground with the purpose of depriving the Russians of any possibility of finding quarters for the night. Civilian population must not be spared, as they're joining the fight against our troops. At an altitude of some 2,500 metres we're approaching our target. Clear blue sky. No need to target the bridge as it already lies demolished.

We attack all villages along the Dimitrov–Moscow road. Several villages go up in flames. A large number of vehicles lie burning by the roadside. The road is teeming with our own troops, who are ready to assault following our attack. No sign of any defence, not in Dimitrov nor on the road. This area consists largely of marsh and woodland. Several rivers thread through the landscape. Due to heavy frost, however, fields are covered by a thick sheet of ice yet pose no obstacles to our forces.

It's hellishly cold up here. I'm frozen to the bone. Richard does some stretches to warm himself up. Shortly after the attack the group flies into warmer regions and before too long we've touched down again.

— • —

That afternoon there's a further attack. Villages and concentrations of enemy troops are the target. Once again we climb to 2,000 metres and fly in formation, targeting all the villages we can make out. A whole group of them have already been turned into blazing heaps of ruins. Reddish lights flickering on the dusking horizon. Our squad sets two villages alight. As our advance has been halted due to the severe Russian winter having suddenly broken out, all we can really do is snatch away winter quarters from under the Russians' noses. The front line is being aligned at various spots. Vanguards of troops which had advanced far ahead are now withdrawn in order to facilitate reinforcement efforts.

We disperse after the attack and everyone heads to their base as fast as they can. At full throttle we race home.

Night has fallen. Vyazma is the last place we can still see in the fading daylight, and after that we have to rely on radio navigation.

Toni receives a message directing us to a different airbase due to bad weather conditions around our own one. But I ignore that as at our base we've got a quiet radio beacon which we can rely on when approaching the alternative airport.

It'll take us another fifteen minutes to get there, but more frequent snow flurries make flying difficult. With the snow becoming denser around us, we can only see some red and green light flashes reflected in the white. From time to time I catch a brief glimpse of the stars but mostly snow clouds scudding across the sky obscure the view. Nonetheless I put my nose through the thick blanket and approach the airbase at about 300 metres. Finally, red lights flashing ahead of us plus a beacon signalling the alternative airbase. We can now recognise the ground lights on either side of the runway. As visibility is fine at the moment and the cloud bank relatively high, I prepare for landing. A bit bumpy, of course, but we've made it and not a moment too soon. With heavy snow now coming down, visibility is poor. Once again, we've been lucky.

Back at the command post the old man hands me a cigar to recognise the achievement of landing in such foul weather conditions. I go on to explain to him how it all came about and immediately sense him becoming quite tense, which I understand completely. Crews still up in the air haven't been trained, or not sufficiently, in night-flying. But they all return in one piece, landing at the alternative airbase either that same night or the following morning.

5.12.41

Attack on a railway station north-west of Moscow. Apparently the station is showing heavy artillery emplacements threatening our units, who're as close as 5 kilometres and anticipate bitter defence. That's why we bombers are to come in and fumigate the nest.

Weather conditions are beyond disgusting. We can barely make out the edge of the base. Clouds are hanging low, heavy snow still coming down and reducing visibility to a few hundred metres. This should be fun. Rumour has it that it's not getting any better, not on the route nor at the destination point. Sheets of ice cover the ground. As is customary with weather like this, we take off solo. The first squad departs. As I am the left wingman it's my turn next. The minute I've lifted off and retracted the undercarriage, I'm engulfed in muck. Carefully I lean into a curve and then follow the route indicated, switch on the pilot and zoom straight towards the destination, mostly flying low. Richard lies in the cockpit and navigates. Sometimes I've got to pull up, barely hurtling over treetops, wooden towers or ridges.

Gradually the cloud bank lifts and visibility marginally improves, but not much beyond 100 metres. Thick lumps of ice form around the wings, coating the MG and the windscreen, with my crate becoming sluggish under the weight. It's cold. Heating is not working.

Slowly we come closer to the front. We keep our eyes peeled in order not to miss the one-track railway line along which we're meant to fly and which would take us to the railway station. We've reached the tracks. Visibility near nil and the next minute the tracks disappear altogether out of sight. We bank right and I go very low down. Behind us snow whirls up high due to the slipstream. There, the tracks appear again, we follow them for a few kilometres and then lose them again. I keep flying close to the ground; maybe we can still find the railway station, though I think it is hopeless. But it's all in vain, as the visibility is too poor, and we can't find the railway track, which is completely covered in snow.

Hence, I decide to go over to free hunting and bomb villages and troop concentrations, and continue flying until we arrive at a canal. Surely no German troops have assembled around here. Instead, we discover large camps with barracks lined up ... our gunners get busy – no resistance. Looks unoccupied. Hardly anything to be seen. We fly over the canal one more time, there are no traces visible in the fresh snow blanket. Onwards. In order not to come too close to Moscow, what with its awesome flak, I turn north. Below us lie vast forests and snow-covered clearings. Glancing at the map, we can't see markers for any villages. I put the machine in a left-hand turn, course west. Must be mindful not to inadvertently hit our own troops. There! Russians below us! With their white camouflage, they barely stand out against the dirty grey landscape. Man, they're waving to us! Could these be our troops? The others have seen this too. Nobody is shooting. Nose down, I dive into a wide curve and target. All dodge for cover, tells me that they must be Russians. We get a response to our light signal. I pull up in an almost vertical climb and continue flying. Maybe these are our own units and none of us are inclined to shoot at unidentified targets. Before too long we recognise our Landsers in their *Feldgrau* [field-grey] uniforms.

I bank into a right turn and see MGs shooting. Ahem, Russians! Our infantry responds with light tracers. It's our cue and we zoom down. Four bombs jettisoned. They explode directly below our machine. A number of bullets into that cluster and the hunt continues.

A larger village appears ahead of us. Keeping straight ahead, we drop a row of bombs, then pull up to avoid being hit by splinters. Barely having reached 150 m, I watch a series of detonations down below through gaps in the clouds. Terrific banging going on. Almost all hits lie in or between the straw huts, which instantly go up in flames. Well, there'll be somewhat fewer of these lice-infested cabins and fewer winter quarters for those Russians now.

I press on. Light flak guns appear and I give them my attention to then vanish into the clouds. Red radishes come flitting by us very close. Toni and Pitt rattle away at their guns but then I become invisible to the Bolsheviks.

After a while I put my nose down again. Smack below me lies a village where troops are assembling. Too late for a drop, but I memorise the coordinates, continue on my path for a few minutes to then turn round with the dump now straight in front of us. Small adjustment in the course and a drop of several bombs should do their bit. We can see the Reds squirting in all directions, desperately trying to escape hell, seeking cover in between and inside the houses. Terrific explosions causing much damage and fires spreading. Seeing as all bombs have been jettisoned, Richard closes the flaps and turns to the guns. We spray the hell out of the dump. The hunt is soon over as our own troops appear. They mistake us for the enemy and target us. We fire the recognition signal, they recognise their error down below, hold fire and wave towards us. Not really surprising, what with this terrible weather, nobody can tell friend and foe apart.

I climb up again to move through the clouds. Gradually we gain in altitude. Further icing on the wings. We're stuck for quite a while in this gloom until the greyness lifts. After a few minutes the sun comes out and we're homeward bound.

Richard wants to get our bearings but the instruments have failed. Toni reports that his radio has also crashed, right after take-off, and I reproach him for not having informed me sooner, but he just grumbles something and fiddles with it until his receiver is clear.

After half an hour I push through the cloud bank. Brief orientation. Another five minutes to the airbase. We know the area like the inside of our pockets, but landing is tricky in these weather conditions. Half flying on sight above the clouds and half following QGH procedure,[12] I move into my approach and lower the undercarriage. I've lost sight of the ground. I lower the wings as I'm sure I'm close to the base. There, on my left I see a machine out of the corner of my eye, but before I know it she sweeps past me. In front of me a demolished aircraft. I gently ease throttle and float in.

There's the landing cross and soon enough the crate wobbles down the frozen runway.

Once we've touched down, ground personnel come rushing up enquiring whether we've bombed the indicated target, to which I respond with a 'no'. They then inform me that these areas have actually been occupied by our own troops some time ago.

The old man who was standing in for the commander kicked up a fuss, we're told, as we hadn't been contactable by radio. No wonder, as of course our radio was down.

Once we report to the command post the old man enquires what targets we had bombed in the end. I inform him that due to bad weather we had not found the indicated targets, had continued flying east and conducted an air battle. He says that it had been exasperating that we couldn't be contacted. He immediately orders our instruments to be checked.

6.12.41

Weather conditions have improved somewhat. Orders received require us to attack a railway line leading from Moscow to Roslavl. The goal is to prevent reinforcement troops from Moscow rolling south. We depart in close formation, the old man in the lead.

At first the clouds are hanging low, but they lift as we approach the front line. Crossing above Tula, situated to our far left, we've already climbed to 2,000 metres. Far ahead we can see the cloud bank completely thinned out, with a blue sky appearing. Our vapour trails behind us are certain giveaways for flak to pinpoint our whereabouts.

Approach flight to the railway line runs along roads which are under our control. Heavy traffic. Excellent visibility which lets us see that here too our troops, who have pushed so far ahead, are now being ordered to turn back in order to shorten and align the front line. Pity that a fierce winter has set in, putting an abrupt end to the manoeuvre warfare. Also, the encirclement around Tula, practically sealed, is also to be abandoned.

At several points our rearguard are engaged in heavy fighting with the Russians, who relish the opportunity. Our withdrawal must be arduous just where our motorised columns previously advanced far into enemy territory and with the right- and left-hand sides of the road still in Russian hands. But nothing that our leaders and our Landsers won't be able to weather.

Far ahead a dark line with columns of smoke rising into the air. That must be the train line – our target.

Bomb bays open, the division disperses, observers prepare for the drop.

Ahead of us we locate a small train station. We fly above it in echelon formation with the bombs tumbling down almost vertically. One lot misses the target, the other two sit perfectly. Once the whirled-up mud and smoke have disappeared, we confirm the results. The bombs have demolished the train station, fires are erupting, several lengths of the train line have been ripped apart, and there's not a chance in hell that a train will roll along these any time soon. Not bad.

Sweeping into a wide left curve, we withdraw and bear down on a moving goods train. We're keen to make good use of the heavy piece of rock we're still lugging around – but the beast won't budge. Richard presses the release button several times and eventually the egg dislodges and zooms down. But it won't be a hit. Down below I see three wagons topple over, shot by the right wingman. Then I see an explosion in front of the train – Hurrah! Looks like our heavy blob has indeed smashed the target, and good – having punched a great big crater into the ground, it is now sitting pretty, right beside it. What luck! We move to attacking a third area, but this time round we're not successful. Not a single rocket lands where it should, either too short, or to the side.

We close the flaps and follow the old man, who bears down on a big train station. He drops the bombs he's got left over and they leave a gaping hole right in the middle of the tracks. Unfortunately, his big one fails as well, and just causes a bit of damage on the ground. At long last our ferreous messages have woken up flak from its slumber. With our mission completed and all drops captured on camera, we don't want to hang around. I turn and are homeward bound. Slowly we drop in height and the weather has turned ugly again. For a while we fly above the clouds, but then the old man disbands the division and pushes through. I circle a bit, then carefully feel my way down. 300 metres, then 200, 100 – still no visibility of the ground. Finally, at an altitude of just 30 metres I can actually see the ground. It's miserable weather. One snow shower chases the next.

Richard locates the beacon near the edge of the base and I approach. The ground seems to have disappeared from the face of the earth; what with the snow falling heavily, I have no visibility at all. But I won't let that bother me any more – we've got used to it by now.

After about fifteen minutes I see the signals flashing, I throttle back gently, lean into a sharp left turn within the boundary of the field, and touch down.

8.12.41

Yesterday the fog was such that flying would have been tantamount to suicide. Today, things seem somewhat improved. Forecasts predict better conditions along the front line. Believe it when you see it.

We're ordered to take off individually and once again our destination is the train line of the day before.

Due to the cold weather the control room only clears four machines, and once we've been allocated our targets, we're also provided with more detailed instructions. This time we're ordered to strafe train stations. My destination is Koloma, a notorious flak concentration which Richard knows only too well from his own experience when during one of the nights he had to stand in for an observer. And to make matters worse, we're to attack from an altitude of 600 metres as that is precisely the cloud ceiling we've been given. Should be fun!

I'm last to take off and, easing the stick forward on the dot, that's me up and away! Today, Pitt flies his hundredth enemy operation – he's the last one in our team to reach that number.

I fly below the cloud ceiling until I reach the front and only then do I climb up so as not to expose myself unnecessarily to the enemy over a stretch of 200 kilometres. But despite climbing steadily and steeply, the clouds remain distant. Fine by me; I can only hope they remain at this height at the point of destination.

At 2,500 metres I reach the lowest cloud shreds and remain at that altitude. I can take cover at any moment, should the need arise. The ground below us disappears from view. Richard measures the ground speed and reports 400 km/h, which means that we have the advantage of an impressive tail wind of 80 km/h.

Within a short time we've reached the train line. Banking left, course north, I focus on the railway and down we go towards the target. It's become terribly windy, making it hard to hold the crate steady.

Question is, whether our eggs will hit their target what with being tossed about by the gusts. But I've full confidence in Richard, who will surely wait for the right moment to push the release button. I want to come in properly to attack the target, which finally appears before us. We're facing immediate problems – those thugs know what they're doing. But we've got to push through this block. No success. Richard makes continuous adjustments, altering angles of approach as a strong cross-wind is blowing. But I won't give up and decide on a *Hundekurve*.[13] Richard then dumps the entire load successfully, I loop into a steep turn, put my crate on its nose and with full throttle escape the flak. Zigzagging to escape the fireworks, I get away without a single splinter. The ground is covered in a haze and not much is visible. But judging by the flashes of the explosions, the bombs have been precise and smashed right across into the train station. Sadly, we

191

can't remain to inspect the result. I climb up and fly home, keeping straight below the cloud cover. While our approach only lasted twenty minutes,[14] the front line doesn't seem to be any closer due to the headwind cutting down our speed. Meanwhile we strain our eyes to identify enemy fighters, but none in sight.

Below me a rather dense cloud bank. Diving down steeply, I keep up the speed – winds down below surely can't be so powerful. Close to the clouds, we streak through the sky, recognising through some gaps Russians down below. We hammer away at them, with the Bolsheviks enveloped in a dense web of tracers. Desperately they seek cover, throw themselves to the ground, but we chase them relentlessly down the road. We empty our magazines on the long truck columns, set vehicles on fire and cause mayhem.

Soon we've reached the front. In an area cleansed by our own troops, all villages are reduced to burning ruins. The Russians should not have any quarters for the winter. And on top of that our Landsers take anything important with them. Good on them! Why should Russians stuff their own bellies? – After quite some time has passed, the airbase finally appears below us. After reporting at the command post, where all other crews are already assembled, we drive to our lodgings.

11.12.41

Heavy snowfalls have brought worse conditions, including all roads cut off and preventing supply convoys getting through. We receive the order to supply our troops from the air with anything necessary.

Machines cleared for take-off have bays loaded with parachute mines, fuel and ammunition. We're to drop our cargo onto a village south of Orel.

Weather conditions miserable with a blustering wind. We're instructed to follow a flight path which goes along roads and railway lines, the only really useful orientation points. With the machines loaded up, we zoom off, climbing to 200 metres.

After one and a half hours Orel appears before us. The village earmarked for the drop can't be far away. Other machines are returning, must have already emptied their bays. And there's the village, just ahead of us on the left. Green lights come up flashing. We've reached the right destination. A great number of tanks and vehicles are expecting to receive their fuel, and our containers plop down to the ground near where our folks are located. Landsers come rushing up and quickly retrieve the goods. I circle the area a few more times, then go down a bit and skim low over the heads of the waving Landsers before changing course to return home. Here too, some troops who had penetrated further into enemy territory have now been called back and find themselves in Orel. In the wider surroundings all villages scorched. Russians are hot on our heels. It is time that our Landsers be supplied with fuel, ammunition and food and be housed in proper quarters.

14.12.41

To protect both the flanks and the back of our units who're returning to the winter lodgings, we fly back into the zone south-east of Orel. Everything should be bombed – anything we come across along the way or in the villages.

Before too long we're hovering above the combat area. We're roaming around for quite a while but can't make out anything noteworthy. Eventually we come across a road which is significantly darker than the others. Some movement must therefore be going on there. In a village, we spot a number of vehicles parked – we drop our 500-kg egg, which bores deep into the ground, and shatters several houses. The crater blocks the entire road and vehicles are overturned due to the enormous blast pressure.

We continue, firing at vehicles until we arrive at a bridge. It must be exploded at all costs. Our attacks fail, then a few bombs smash the planking and detonate on the ice. I must approach it differently.

Renewed attack, the last bombs drop and the wooden bridge collapses. That done, we return home content.

16.12.41

Our orders are to deliver supplies for the infantry. They're positioned in Klin, south of Kalinin. Weather is awful. We cruise around for a long time until we find the spot. Then, Russian tracers converge on us from all directions; we bear down on them, firing from all guns and don't let them get away with anything.

Our Landsers are busy setting fire to Klin, but in the meantime we find the pad where we're to drop the stuff. A bunch of trucks and tanks are heaped up, some are already ablaze – we destroy the lot, so they don't fall into the hands of the enemy. Fuel is desperately short, as we know. We hurl our supplies down. They then fill up their tanks, each one towing away three to four trucks and then they clear out, direction winter quarters. Landsers wave up at us with gratitude, we wobble our wings and sweep across the Russians a second time, spraying them with drum loads of ammunition. Then we too clear out.

— • —

This is my last flight this year. I receive orders to fly the machine to Germany before going on leave. When I return, my unit moves towards the Reich. On my return, the whole unit is being moved to the Reich. First, we stop off in Kovno, following which we're stationed in Ansbach[15] for three months. In the meantime [probably around April to May 1942] we have a brief layover in Anklam[16] which includes a training course in throwing bombs,[17] and are then moved to KG55 [on 4 June 1942].[18] We travel by train for three days across Russia before arriving at the location of our new squad.

[It seems, however, that Döring along with his crewmembers did in fact spend time at the front in February 1942, as can be verified

194

based on a handwritten note on the back of a photograph, showing him surrounded by some of his pilot comrades in front of the Hotel Miramare in Bordighera. This is not mentioned in his diary. It seems that Döring's crew had received permission for a four-week recreational leave in Italy after having been shot down on 21 February 1942 at the Mius river in southern Russia and reaching their own lines only three days later.]

The text on this picture, handwritten by Döring, says: 'Crew Arnold Döring at the transfer of 4.(KG53 to KG55) on 4.6.1942 Ansbach airbase'.
From left to right: Friedrich Brösing, Karl Krupitza, Anton Grimmer and Richard Wawerek standing in front of their He 111 H-3. In the background a new He 111 H-6 is visible. Döring had just been informed that he had been awarded the honorary cup (the award was confirmed on 25 February)[1]
(Source: Döring).

Another photo of Döring in Ansbach, spring 1942. From left to right: Anton 'Toni' Grimmer, Arnold Döring, Richard Waware[c]k (Source: Döring).

Just before the allocation of rooms at the Hotel 'Miramare' in Bordighera, near San Remo, early March 1942 (Source: Döring).

PART III

With Kampfgeschwader 55 [Legion Condor]

[22 May to 5 August 1942]

[Dnipropetrovsk] Airbase

The comradeship that exists within the 8th Staffel makes it a lot easier for us to get used to the new circumstances. In fact, after just a few days we're feeling quite at home. In the first days of 'sizing each other up' they want to push our lot against the wall and are keen to show off their superiority. Primarily it's the old guard lashing out at us, those who'd flown operations to France and England – but soon all calms down and what with all the missions we've got under our belt, we're counted as one of the old fighters.

Our quarters are some 18–20 kilometres away from the base. The road is paved, albeit in Russian style. Badly tossed about, one arrives there only after about half an hour. Curses all round, but we soon relax and don't let it bother us.

Quite often we're ordered to report, but don't get deployed. But, having just about had it, we kick up a fuss and finally get deployed.

The Griffin – the insignia of Kampfgeschwader 55 (Source: https://de.wikipedia. org/wiki/Datei:Geschwaderwappen_des_Kampfgeschwaders_55.jpg).

[22.5.42]

We're off to a place in the vicinity of Kupyansk, a flak concentration point despised by all and not held in high esteem at all. I'm curious whether this is actually true, seeing as I'm accustomed to rather strong stuff – much like I've experienced in the central sector. Towards midday we take off. I'm posted to the last group as a left wingman. The commander [First Lieutenant von dem Bongart][1] flies ahead. After an enormous sweep, we're on course. Rapidly we climb to 2,000, 3,000 metres. Why are we approaching from such an altitude onto some lousy dump? We cross over the front line. Kupyansk, the junction, lies ahead to our right. Much to my surprise, the commander steers towards it. Doesn't our target, I think to myself, lie to the left of it? Just short of the town we cut away, course north-east. The last groups run into murderous fire, deafening explosions framing our aircraft. Those crews back home certainly didn't exaggerate, I conclude. I'm kept pretty busy holding my crate under control but escape unscathed. A bunch of shells explode underneath my belly, flinging my aircraft into the air and sending splinters flying through the cockpit. But a brief glance at my wings, my engines and the instruments reassure me: all is fine.

At long last I've left this unfriendly dump behind. A few more minutes and the target should be ahead of us. Richard releases the bombs and leans far forward to observe the impact on the ground. They land perfectly, right between the houses and on the road. Two fires erupt. I then cut away to join my leader and the unit returns to base. After landing, we take a close look at our crate. Some flak fragments have scored major hits. Both water coolers are punctured, and the coolant is leaking out in streams. The engines wouldn't have lasted much longer like that. But once again it turned out well!

[13.6.42]

On 13 June it's my first actual night flight. At the command post I receive the order to attack Voronezh. Approach and attack to be kept separate and from maximum height, that's the order. The distance between the front line and the town is 220 km. No report on the weather conditions. I'm to go first, to reconnoitre the weather. Every twenty minutes there's to be a weather report. It's still light when I give gas and zoom into the air. I'm not keen on the weather. Large towers of cumulus clouds which are quite black. My only hope is that a storm doesn't break. My poor bird climbs ever higher. Right now we're flying between two cloud banks. Toni taps out a weather report to base. Soon I disappear into the clouds. Richard navigates to a beacon ahead. The moment has come to put on the oxygen masks, it's awfully cold up here. One twist of the lever and hot air blows through the cockpit.

Ice is settling onto the engine cowling and the front MGs. We're still climbing through thick layers of greyness. Further icing all the way to 5,500 metres when the clouds thin and then completely vanish. For a brief moment we get to see the sun setting, but soon clouds envelop us once again. The ice is melting away. A look at the thermometer indicates 3 degrees above zero. A bit later we've completely left the miserable weather behind us and soon have ground view. We're able to get our exact bearings, which are radioed through to the control room along with a weather forecast. But it'll take a bit of time until I reach the front. It's still daylight up here, but down below, heavy shadows lie over the ground.

We've crossed over the front line. I calculate the time it'll take us to get to destination. If we keep up the current speed, it's very likely that Ivan will have every opportunity to fire at us. For this reason I curve for a while along and above the front line at an altitude above 6,000 metres and only then set course to Voronezh.

Flak opening up just below us. But falls short by a few metres. I decide to have a bit of fun and perform a few turns – before climbing back to my preferred altitude to fool them. This should make the fellows below believe that they have adjusted for the right altitude. And they actually fall for it, not a single shell reaches higher – every shot misses. Below us a carpet of cottonwool clouds. Lucky we're not in it. That certainly would be quite a different experience. Turning north, I break away and quickly vanish direction south. I continue on to Voronezh and its factories and the large cargo railway station we're supposed to attack.

Below us, night is falling, covering everything. Navigating the bird becomes really challenging, with Richard weirdly enjoying this all the more. I keep my eye on the air space, but no fighter planes are around. Some areas on the ground are ablaze and we're nearly at our destination. What's on Ivan's mind? In front of us: a light-coloured line, it's the Don river. After a while we see its various bends and have pinpointed the one which is our target. Well, let's head towards it! Everyone tenses up. Below us lies a large airbase with two runways crossing each other. I scan the sky to spot potential danger. Richard is bent over the instrument panel and issues adjustments for the approach. Oh! What's that? Ah … searchlights. But they flit about haphazardly and can't catch us as it's still too light up here. The first shells come shooting up. They sit too far to our left, but are on our level. Damn, that one was close to the cockpit! I adjust the engine revs and pitch of propeller and that helps a great deal. The searchlights go crazy, zooming across the landscape, sometimes the sheaf of beams hovering fleetingly above us. The next flak waves also fall short.

Finally we let the bombs come raining down and in a steep left-hand curve I immediately cut away. Christ Almighty, they're shooting like mad. Lights flashing at a good one hundred locations. Continuously. Shells detonating in close proximity momentarily light up the cockpit and you can hear the explosions despite the engines running full throttle.

Suddenly Toni, the idiot, starts blasting away with his gun. I scream for him to stop, for goodness' sakes, but it's too late, our location has been revealed. The searchlights sweep across several

Targeted by bombs and ammunition (Source: Atlantic Bilderdienst. PK Janz).

times, then trap us and all the others lock on. In total we've got eighteen strong thugs who don't let go of me despite me looping and spiralling around. We run into heavy flak. Finally the bombs below us detonate. They take a whole minute to hit the ground. The whole lot of them land in the train station, causing three fires to erupt. We can't actually make out too much of what's what down below, as it's too dark and the searchlights dazzle us.

Suddenly the flak has gone silent. That means we've got to be aware of night-fighters. Our eyes try to pierce the darkness. There! Two, no three shadows suddenly appearing ahead and then diving down on us. Immediately, tracers come whistling close by our machines. These guys come up terribly close. Contrasting against the light sky in the west, we identify them as I-17s. Several thumps of fire and we manage to keep that scum away. Then I put a stop to the shelling, and dive down at full speed, nearly turning the machine on its nose. There you go – now try and find us! We certainly won't stand out against the dark ground. The mob is drawing circles above our heads, it shoots in the dark, and always misses. My bet is that the comrades are simply trying their luck, as where the tracers whoosh past, the likes of us are nowhere to be seen. At long last the guys give up the hunt and clear out.

I'm hugely relieved. It's not pleasant to be pursued by searchlights 250 kilometres behind the front, chased by flak and then, to top it off, by three fighters, without being able to do much more than fight for your life and for that of your crew.

We gradually drop in altitude and my lumbering crate catches up at greater speed. My aim is to get above our own territory as fast as possible. Way ahead, on the horizon, we discern flickering lightning. That's all we need. First an enemy attack, a mother of all battles, and now a storm brewing. I'm desperately trying to find a large enough gap within the tangle of threads of lightning but it's one huge firework lighting up the horizon. Wherever you look, from north to south, bolts of lightning crackle through the sky. As far as we're concerned, fair weather is still holding up in our corner as we're still some distance from both the front and the storm.

We continue flying at an altitude of 2,000 metres and I keep to that altitude until the front line. Shortly before that we're hit by extremely well-aimed light flak. No option but to give full gas. Soon the racket is over.

But this is where the merry dance begins: fighting the forces of nature. The wings rattle and make the entire crate shake from side to side. Clamping down on the rudder pedals, I'm trying to keep the machine flat. My hands ache. I switch on the lights in order to be able to see something despite the blinding lightning. We've put on our seatbelts. There! A gust of wind, the machine is barely under my control.

As I climb low, it all calms down at about 500 metres. Nonetheless, we sway up and down, like on a rocking horse, sometimes we bank to the left, sometimes to the right. Minutes drag on, each one seems to last an eternity but at long last we can make out some stars. Gracious me, looks like we've made it. But it is only the first storm front behind us, the next one already looms ahead.

I set course for south. Richard is trying to get bearings, but all he catches through the earphones are awful crackling noises. No other signs whatsoever, here and there some light whirring and whistling sounds, but there's no way to get radio bearings or positional reports.

In a foul mood, he turns it off. Over time one can literally go crazy listening to all that crashing and banging through the earphones.

Our aircraft is once again buffeted by heavy winds and we bob up and down like on a merry-go-round. Bracing my legs with full force against the rudder bar, I do my best to keep the machine on the straight and narrow – it works. The winds subside and we smoothly cruise along, with only the occasional lightning as a reminder of danger still lurking. With only slight pressure on the rudders, I carry on. Far ahead of us, where the airbase must be located, another storm rages. Who the hell knows how this will end? My hope is that the airfield is clear for a brief window as, if the storm is right above it, we'll surely crash upon landing.

Toni sits at the radio trying to connect to base, but his receiver remains silent. Richard churns the navigation instrument and finally we get some identification signs from the beacon. We note our bearings and swiftly change course. Checking again, we get confirmation that we're homeward bound. After the briefest feeling of relief, we're rudely awakened: the banging around us is infernal, but at least we're on the right course.

No sign coming from the ground for ages. Rain clouds hanging low hamper visibility. At long last it's clearing up. Far ahead of us, on our left, lightning illuminates the landscape. Well, was it lightning or signals from the airbase? Once again we're knocked around by a ferocious storm and there's no visibility. We follow a path, we're surrounded by hail and rain, but keep to the route. After a long time the weather quietens down.

Now [the signals] are clearly defined: red-white. Pause. Red-white. Hurrah! We're approaching the airfield. Toni gets his radio connection back, we get our directions and are informed that landing is within the next fifteen minutes. Looks like the storm has moved away from the airbase, I increase my speed and we approach the field.

We can now clearly make out the flashing red obstacle-warning lights appearing from the dark, and the base is before us. Flying control indicates the angle of landing, undercarriage lowered, a slight curve and down we go. Blast – the lightning blinds us and for some seconds I can't see a thing. A white flare is shot into the air and not a moment too soon, as I nearly drag a parked He [111] along with me. I yank the stick back, give full throttle, pull the bird up, then immediately down and then hit the ground, bouncing up and down a few times. I slam on the brakes, as the base is small and is standing practically underwater, but looks like the brakes have had it, the machine skids down the soft ground and at long last comes to a standstill. I roll her to the bay.

Holy smoke! This could easily have gone wrong. We've well-earned the cigarette. Toni, our mechanic, reports that the *Kuhsturm* [strong wind/gale] had wreaked havoc as recently as fifteen minutes prior to our landing. Strong gales had lashed the area, recalling the biblical flood. Arriving at our quarters, we realise that our tent has made off. We look at each other in silence, help the crew cover the machine and then stomp through deep puddles and the even deeper bog of this blasted Russian airbase to the tent area where the old man and the entire groundcrew are just about to tighten the last ropes and ram the stakes further into the marshy ground. I report the landing of our crew, get a handshake from the old man and a hearty gulp of rum. This noble liquid and a few cigarettes calm the nerves and while away the anxious wait for comrades still up in the air to land.

After some delay, we finally hear the noise of engines. [Lieutenant Heinz] Moldenauer arrives; initially he's floating somewhat too high, but at long last rolls his crate in to a stop. She'll be on her way tomorrow again, no doubt. After a while, Moldenauer comes marching along and submits his report; he receives what is left over from the bottle and hoofs it all the way back to the command post. The Moldenauer crew, too, had observed the three fires and had done its share of bombing. Barely uttering another word and totally exhausted, we stumble to our quarters.

[25.6.42]

We continue to push forward towards the east. Kupyansk, the train hub, lies not far behind us. Despite disrupted railway lines and our bombing, which was spot-on, the Russians manage to receive reinforcements coming from the east and south. And this is the hub where it all takes place. That's why we're ordered to cripple the Soviet railway system and do a job which will ensure that there are no supplies coming through for some time to come, and if possible to interrupt the rail traffic forever. In our belly rack we've stowed away massive eggs spelling doom and disaster; the bays are full of heavy bombs.

We're to take off very early in the morning. At first light, before the sun rises, we're meant to jettison our bombs. Shortly before midnight we mount our trucks and hurtle to the airfield. If we could just have avoided suffering from the heavy shaking on the trucks. It's still pitch dark when the captain, by the light of his torch, goes over with us the exact route that has duly been marked on the maps by each observer. Then it's time for us to locate our machines. We still have a bit of time, a last puff on the cigarette, and after a brief meeting we board 'Anton', who's in impeccable condition and specially brought in … and is known to be the best bird in the Staffel.

In the meantime the old man warms up the engines. We're ready. Several 1,000 PS [*Pferdestärke*, equivalent to 0.986 HP] roar up and run smoothly at low revs. A huge number of lights flash up in front of me. The 9th Staffel is taking the lead today, with its first squad lined up for take-off. Engines howling, and the birds streak along the flarepath into the night – a rising band of dark shadows. The second squad follows at a one-minute interval, as does the third. It's our turn now. Full throttle, increased speed, and my bird jolts along the flarepath. Fixing my eyes on the navigation lights of the old man and the flarepath, the group now speeds across the dewy runway and is airborne, disappearing into the night. It's no small feat to take off at night as a formation, given a small airfield and a heavy load in our bays. But it saves more time, which would otherwise be lost in assembling the whle group in the air.

In close formation we put our machines into a turn, set course and then gradually climb up. The stars fade away in the east, a pale pink sky appears on the horizon. But below us it's still dark. Via intercom the captain calls on his squad leaders, who in turn call on their wingmen. This communication works perfectly. Gradually, at very high altitude we approach the front line. We encounter some cloud banks, which, however, have plenty of holes. Day is breaking. First gradually, then more quickly, we recognise the outlines of the geography clearly taking shape against the sky. Down below it's probably still hazy, what with the soggy ground and marshy meadows, where only recently the bitter spring offensive around Kharkov raged. The landscape is dotted with craters, some larger than others, all testifying to huge explosions. Entire villages have

The railway hub at Kupyansk under attack.

been flattened – where once houses – miserable clay huts – stood, and what is left are dark, sooty flecks dotting the area.

Down below, at the corner of a forest, we can see the hits of our artillery, all belonging to us. The front line is ahead of us. We can't make out a lot, as low-lying mist and fog are now building up and obstructing our view. And amid all that, artillery is opening up. One can clearly spot that on the Russian side their Ari [Artillerie] is being thrashed by ours.

That's done. It's finished. We've actually crossed rather swiftly over the narrow section which calls itself the front. We'll have reached our destination in some ten minutes. The unit swerves south, in order not to be blinded by the sun later on when we're attacking. Far ahead of us to the left lies our target, still a dark spot contrasting with the landscape. We carry on a good bit further along in a straight line, then we swing left and dive down on the Russians with fury.

No flak response yet. Fighters can't be seen either. Probably it's still too early in the day for these comrades of ours. The first group is above the target and unleashes its bombs. Then everything happens all at once. One group after another drops its massive load and as the bombs hit the ground, flak shells are plastering the area. Gracious me, the group in front of us is getting smashed. But our approach flight is calm; we've thinned out a bit in order to press down along the entire length of the train station.

The dive-bombing onto the target is coordinated, and, as if on command, the first shells explode close by. Beware, you fancy gentlemen down below! You're using a rather foolish tactic. Instead of shooting ahead of time, you might be better served by bashing each individual machine only once we approach and so be able to escape the bomb aimed at you. Why don't you aim with precision, for God's sake? Oh, I see, you want to shoot us down, do you? Well, so be it, then! Go right ahead, keep trying, but here's a warning – I'll definitely not sit back and watch, 'comrades'! And I don't. I put the crate upside down, dive and bank to the right, spiral up, then continue a bit straight ahead, steep left-hand turn followed by an even steeper right-hand turn and at full throttle vertically down. Oh, shame … comrades, looks like you can't keep up … you seem to have forgotten all the little navigating skills you ever had. Gosh! I've been struck by a splinter … but just carry on, you lot, I'll catch up with you, don't give this a further thought.

I put them through their paces: in quick succession, a right-hand turn, followed by levelling off, straight ahead, then immediately banking left, pressing down, sweeping into a steep climbing curve to the right – the madness slows down only gradually and I clear the area – it's for the other groups to take the brunt. A bit below me I spot my captain – he's escaped unscathed – much like us. My right wingman now approaches from the right and we return as a close formation, setting course to base by following our commander. When we report back, it looks like every single crew has recorded a hit, wherever it be: among the tracks and the stationary trains, the station buildings and the storage depots. One of the crews attached to the 9th Staffel has chalked up the demolition of an important road bridge. Columns of vehicles are now piled up and can't get to the front. The following day we get to see aerial photographs and only then can we really take in the extent of the destruction and devastation we visited upon the flak concentration with the help of our huge eggs.

— • —

The Russian who've been pulled back from Kharkov to the east attempt to obstruct our tank divisions. These have arrived at a bridge crossing over a river which isn't as wide as it is deep. At the other end the first emplacements have already been dug in. Ivan is putting his efforts into a fresh defence. It is ourselves, the aircraft bombers, who now stand in for what is the extension of the Heer's heavy armament,[2] which is why we're ordered to annihilate troop concentrations in and around Senkovo.

Away you go! 8th Staffel! As always, when there's a hard nut to crack, it's us who go first. The briefing is short, everyone knows this section of the front, even in this particular war of movement. We're

A camouflaged He 111 enlisted with KG55 above Russia
(Source: https://www.google.com/search?q=kampfgeschwader+
55+-+980&rlz=1C1CHBF_enGB884GB884&sxsrf=APq-).

not able to fly high, as clouds hang at 900–1,000 metres. Doesn't matter, as it lets us tell friend and foe apart during this wild chase. And besides, the target is close to the front line.

Full throttle, and we're off! Flying low, we zoom over roads, watching as reinforcement transports roll along. Landsers, equipped with bits of fabric of all kinds, wave up at us; civilians stare and seek shelter. Below us the traces of war flit by. Discarded by the roadside lie destroyed tanks, charred remains of trucks and debris from vehicles and bombed buildings. Villages are half razed to the ground, half collapsed into heaps of rubble. But nonetheless, signs of life and busy traffic in between uninhabitable ruins and rubble and wood draw a picture of hardy folk.

Gradually we climb up in order to gain a better overview of what has been achieved. And while just recently we watched dust clouds whipped into the air, there's nothing of the sort right now. It means we need to pay attention as the front line will come up any moment.

And I'm proved right. Here and there we see blankets spread out, we fire off recognition signals, we're reaching our own lines and cross them a second later.

Some long-range artillery fire leaves its mark. An enemy battery is identified – we zoom across but make sure to do some ground-strafing while shelling gun positions. With that over and done with, we focus on some vehicles ahead of us, some of which have come to a dead halt and are obstructing the roads – presumably to mislead us into believing they've been hit – and others which are whizzing ahead at full speed. Our tracers whistle past above their heads. Onward. Somewhere, surely, the emplacements will be located. Aha! Ahead of us, we spot some of the comrades. And there as well! And further on too! Everybody seems to be out and about, off in the direction of Senkovo. Let's have a little look-see. Gracious me, the nest is a beehive. It's time to crank open the bomb bays, fan out and dive while hailing down what we've got onto streets and in between the houses and gardens. Many vehicles are alight, others fragmented by splinters.

A bridge crosses the river and, hanging from it, like clusters of ripe fruit, are Russians. Just you wait! We fling down the last four bombs, letting them have the crushing last word. They detonate, but they weren't exactly the perfectly aimed hit. No time for that. Everything relies on rough estimates. Three bombs burst in the middle of the road … and the fourth one? Hurrah! It struck the bridge full on! That's excellent! Let's keep going. Let's face it, comrades, there's now nowhere for you to go! You've had it! The other Staffel are on their way. As for us, we sweep up into a steep curve, and at full throttle send down one drum after another into the columns, piled up in one huge traffic jam. From time to time we're rudely attacked by twin-MGs, at times even quadruple-barrelled MGs, but those claws of the devil don't manage to get us in their grip. Pity that the dream comes to an end – as our ammunition is at rock bottom. Our crew has chalked up the demolition of some fifteen vehicles and in addition, a heavily damaged bridge. An impressive result! The Staffel has clocked up over fifty vehicles! We know one thing for sure: at our next attack, that bridge down there will be smashed up with nothing left.

The moment we've landed and with the machines filled up and loaded and the drums replenished, the captain comes striding along and hands down the order: there's to be a renewed attack on the town, with a view to us and the other Staffel intensifying the confusion, but also to double up on our onslaught.

We receive the call to board the aircraft, turn on the engine and the wild chase gets off the ground. This time round we take off in separate groups, giving us more opportunity to manoeuvre and be more flexible. Our entire squad takes off.

Our destination is the bridge. And it *must* fall. Richard can barely be contained. Suddenly the crates seem to be extremely sluggish, they barely seem even to move, but obviously it's the feverish tension that's kicked in.

We've arrived at our destination. The dump is on fire, vehicles too are ablaze, others wrecked and still smouldering. Yes, comrades, this is the reality: the Luftwaffe has struck before and we've returned for another round, fully equipped to dish out more blows. Achtung! The 8th Staffel is at it again – here we come – the pick of the bomb throwers!

What follows is a long, drawn-out, but beautifully executed approach flight. At the very beginning already, I've positioned myself 50 metres higher in order to perform my own approach. Two machines posted to our squad are far to my left and hurl their eggs down into the town, right in between the closely packed vehicles.

Light flak takes us on, the little red mice flit past us, but Karl and Pitt fend them off with a barrage of fire. Richard stoops over his bomb sight, makes some tiny course adjustments while I keep the bird completely level, we zoom straight ahead, as flat as is possible under the circumstances.

Bombs come raining down. At very short-spaced intervals the entire load is dumped and we then speed directly on to our destination, the bridge – actually, no, *our* bridge, to be precise.

Suddenly there's screaming and yelling at the back, making it simply impossible to hear anything. Richard turns around, gives me a nod and grins from ear to ear. I don't need to ask any questions, both the fracas in the back and Richard's face tell me all I need to know. At once, the pent-up tension is dissolved. I tear into a steep spiral to have a good long look at the mess of which we are the cause. There! In the middle of the stream I spot a tiny piece of land over which once upon a time there was a bridge. Nothing left of that, only some miserable stumps on each of the riverbanks. Perfect job! Billowing thick smoke tells us that a further stick of bombs – one between the middle of the road and parked or driving motorised vehicles, the second one on the other side of the river, between trucks and field positions – have done their job.

Light flak guns pour their lead into the air as if in revenge for the bridge now destroyed. Hampered by the constant bursts, we bank and sweep into tight curves to disappear swiftly out of the danger zone.

Ammunition depot in an airbase, July 1942
(Source: Atlantic Bilderdienst. PK Doell).

215

On my return flight, I watch as the next squad swoops in, and then, at increasingly longer intervals, one squad after the other departs on their mission. No worries, they'll do the mopping up and blast the remainder of hundreds of vehicles to smithereens – never again to cross the river.

— • —

Night attack follows – as a change of scenery. The Valuiki railway junction is our destination and is the last hub before reaching the Don. Information reports note train concentrations around that area and heavy traffic.

Two squads enlisted to the other groups take off at dawn in order to set fire to the target. They set the train station alight, as well as the surrounding buildings, which allows us to get a better view of the target and then shell it.

Tonight, I'm the last one to depart. Altitude for attack and flight are all prescribed. Preparations are made – we can begin.

Our 'Anton' rapidly climbs up in the crisp air and we reach the front even before the calculated hour. Below us fierce artillery fighting on both sides, shelling and deadly hits. Light flares flood the landscape and help us identify the course of the front line.

From here, it will take us a further three-quarters of an hour to our destination. The prescribed altitude has been reached. Far away, much beyond the horizon we see a bright blotch. A star rising? Our goal? If it's the latter then our comrades must have had perfect aim. It aligns with our course and I'm headed towards it. Gradually, painfully so, the blotch becomes bigger and it's clearly an enormous large-scale fire. Doesn't really require much navigation seeing as our forerunners have practically carved out the landscape with the help of their explosives. Small clusters of searchlights light up the sky. That's it! I just confirm that it's the machine before the last which is now above the target. Light beams roaming around the area try and capture her, but it's nothing more than a good try and we watch the spectacle as the beams, like the arms of an octopus, keep flailing up and down.

For me it's another ten minutes' flight, but time goes by very fast. Only then will it be possible to ascertain the situation down below – what exactly is on fire? The station building and the large storage depot are burning bright, and four trains are also on fire, which is verified by the narrow burn trails streaking through the fields. A large black cumulus cloud soars above it all, mixed with thick oil smoke. Because our vision is obscured by this dense wall of fumes, I'm forced to bank into a wide sweeping curve that allows me to fly with the wind and not be hindered by smoke.

Searchlights appear and nervously flit back and forth. I'm gathering that down below they must be fit to be tied, as every ten minutes or so the area is furiously shelled from above, which only further feeds the fire. Not surprising that there doesn't seem to be rhyme or reason in how these guys are directing the beams of their searchlights. Three sites where flak shells have exploded are identified. Looks like flak has entirely miscalculated their strategy or has recognised that they simply can't measure up to the fierce attacks by the Germanski. Fine by us, as far as I'm concerned.

We've figured out the optimal approach path. The cockpit is lit up brightly, with every detail clearly distinguishable. Bombs are ejected

An He 111 operating for KG55.

217

and our bird, now that much lighter, lurches suddenly upwards. The maze of searchlights has by now gone utterly crazy, and by changing my speed I only add to the confusion, with a sea of lights playing in the sky. I go into a steep nosedive and from the corner of my eye watch as a bomb detonates between the train carriages. Perfect aim. Renewed fires erupt, the train must have been hit. The tracks, for certain, have been disabled.

Satisfied, we fly back to base. On our way, a cluster of searchlights shine up, but they're to our back and quickly go off again. In my rear mirror I still recognise the trouble spot some 100 kilometres in the distance. Gradually I come down, flying above the front line, still confronted with heavy artillery attacks, with houses and entire villages burning. Before too long we spot the lights at the edge of the airbase. We're home.

[27.6.42]

This day will be entered as one of the blackest dates in the annals of the group, starting with the dawn attack on the railway hub of Svoboda on the Don, which was protected by vicious flak and fighter defence.

The order was for two groups to set fire to the transfer point and shunting yard and render them inoperable for future night trains. The commander with his group are in the lead, followed by me with my own group. My aircraft is loaded with incendiaries intended to destroy only large parts of the landscape, while the cargo of the other crews consists of high explosives meant to demolish as much as possible.

Shortly before dawn we're approaching the auxiliary target, hoping to drop our bombs before first light.

There are two groups which steadily climb higher. It's going to be a challenge. Flak gunners are continually banging away with bursts filling the whole sky – I seriously doubt there exists a more skilled flak than this lot; on top of that, fully manned airbases filled with fighter planes are situated in the proximity of the town.

At an altitude of 4,000 metres the unit sets course to the front line. The right-hand wingman, Lieutenant Moldenhauer, a fair-haired pilot from Berlin, lags behind. Looks like something's not quite right with his engine. And this proves to be exactly the case as he goes on to message us that he's experiencing engine problems with the turbocharger. The commander orders him to return, while we continue on. A bit later Moldenhauer radios that his engine is running normally and he intends to rejoin.

We fly a gigantic full circle above the front line in order to pick him up; my left-hand wingman has fallen somewhat behind me, but doesn't fall behind from the unit by more than 50 metres.

Suddenly we get the alarm: 'Fighters!' Far left and level with us, I see three fighters, but can't make out the type. I gently throttle back and pick up my left wingman. It's Feldwebel Hiltner, a good pilot and a fabulous comrade to boot. All MG positions are manned, waiting only for the fighters. I'm puzzled to see Russians so close to the front line.

One appears in front of us. He seems to be aiming at Moldenhauer, who is still lagging behind the unit by some 100 metres but trying to catch up. Everyone is shelling the attacker. We're all framed by tracers, this guy is a deft hand at his game. He makes directly for his victim, who has his undercarriage ripped off along with two gunners dropping to their grave, and the machine goes up in flames. Moldenhauer veers off and vanishes into the depths.

As for us, we've crossed over the front and with full guns blazing we head for Svoboda. The fighter planes launch a renewed attack. Tracers come whizzing by my head, pursuing me unpleasantly close to the cockpit. What's that, for goodness' sake?! It's an Me 109! How did she get here? But a stream of tracers converge on her with bullets slamming into her from all sides. My crew too noticed the Me 109. Russians in a German aircraft? Is this a German attacking his own comrades?

Yes, it's a full-blown attack. It's Hiltner who's being hit time and again. Richard fires off recognition signals, but the He 111 is catching fire, banks, goes into a spin and then, plunging vertically, crashes, engulfed by flames. Karl, Pitt and Toni report sighting a parachute.

Filled with fury at the loss of now two fabulous crews, we continue with our mission. The operation is carried out despite some losing their lives. The fighter doesn't go on a further attack; he's disappeared direction home, that is towards his own territory.

Night is falling. We can still make out the ground, the target lies ahead of us. I've climbed a bit higher than the commander and approach the target solo. The old man is hovering above it, pounded by heavy flak. 'Fresh approach – hold off on bombing!' I hear through the headset. Good man, you're able to approach the target twice, but I can't. I've precisely identified the target and it would be sheer madness if I didn't attack. That's why I push down the talk button and scream: '2nd Wing! Achtung! Bombs! Eject!'

Incendiaries and explosives come hailing down from great heights, exploding down below, while flak is opening up with such intensity and precision that the results are disastrous. Despite the noise in the cockpit I can hear every sound. I have to bank into curves as never before. My trusted wingman follows suit. Jolting forwards, left-hand turn – straight ahead – then right curve and immediately steep upward spiral. This merry-go-round lasts some ten minutes – but they feel like hours. Every shell is more perfect than the previous one. But no matter how hard we pull the trigger, flak seems to come ever closer. We've already been hit several times, some large splinters fly through the machine – but everything comes to an end and so does this frenzied fire waltz. The last shell unleashed one huge splinter whipping through the cockpit, with all of us cowering low. My wingman has fallen behind. I throttle back to allow him to catch up, as I can spot two fighters lurking. Several thumps of fire, they hit nicely, and the brothers clear out. Fine by us!

I'm now able to see the town. Our bombs lie diagonally to the train station and are also carpeting the adjoining town quarters in the north-east. Dusk is falling, starting to be night-time down below, the white gleam of the explosives contrasts especially well with the surrounding darkness. This is precisely the area which the commander's wing is now targeting – which tells me that this is the identified target. Hence, they have finally managed to find it! But, goodness, they've got a lot of shooting to do in order to escape the fireworks. The landscape is sliced in half by a trail of fire, from up here resembling a torch procession. After ten minutes they get away relatively unscathed.

Together with my wingman, I carry on flying until we part ways, each of us returning solo to base with the advantage of a tailwind. I'm the first one to land and give my report to the old man on both our successes and the fate of our two crews. He's completely devastated. The good people of the ground crew are very upset as well. The other machines come in and it's their turn to give an account of their observations. Some of them had identified the Me 109, others didn't. Together with the old man we drive to the command post. The commander congratulates Richard on his successful score and turns to recording the exact details of the attack and officially documenting that an Me 109 had shot down an He 111 which went up in flames and crashed. The other two Me 109s had reportedly kept to the side and away. Only once it was aware of the recognition signals did the fighter bank and it accompanied Moldenhauer part-way down on his vertical dive. It was a crash-landing on his belly in our own territory.[3] From the other one, a lone parachute was sighted. Nobody knows any further details as it all took place so fast.[4]

— • —

A further operation against Svoboda that same night goes ahead nonetheless, with bombs dropping amid fierce flak and under the roving beams of searchlights. We hit the town and its train station, setting fire to several areas.

A few days later the old man informs us that it indeed was an Me 109 which had shot down our crews. One lieutenant with over forty hits. He was sentenced to court martial and one can only hope that he will get what he deserves. We are livid about this guy who couldn't manage to distinguish an He 111 from a Russian bomber plane at a distance of 50–100 metres! A squirt would be able to do this at the drop of a hat. We'd give him no quarter! He'd be well advised to write his last will!

1.7.42
Major Offensive on Voronezh

We're ordered to launch a major attack on the city area of Voronezh. It excites us and boosts our morale. It is anticipated to be a huge Luftwaffe gathering. Our objective is to first demolish the two train stations, and then raze the entire industrial zone. Scorch them. It's precisely here that Russians procure their stock, which immediately

This photo shows how bombs were loaded onto an He 111
(Source: Ron Mackay, *Heinkel He 111* (Ramsbury, 2003), p. 145).

gets processed at numerous ironworks, engine factories, tank and tractor plants, indeed even aircraft companies recycle the scrap. The hope is, as well, that the Russians clear out relatively quickly after their industrial facilities have been reduced to ruins.

Lively activity in the airbase is noted early that afternoon. Bombs of all kinds are delivered and, heaved up by muscular and robust arms, they disappear into the bays or are installed in the ventral racks with the help of special hoists. Fuel tanks move from one machine to the next, pumping the precious juice into their containers. Amazing what such a bird can guzzle up!

Ground mechanics are still busy tinkering with the machines, until they can be cleared for operation. Meanwhile the captain of the squad is briefing the crews on the targets. Our squad is allocated the loading station and the engine factory close by, but other units are also meant to attack these targets. All hell will break loose! Under no circumstances would I want to be in this city doomed to certain death and destruction. The front line is revealed. Hard to believe one's eyes, but our troops have already advanced to 50 kilometres short of the city. And that might already be old news. As of 0200 hours these are now military encampments and our lead tanks may well have rolled a fair distance beyond that point. That means paying attention to the whereabouts of our Landsers.

Another puff on our cigarettes and we make our way to the machines. It's pretty damn hot even at this early hour. Looks like filthy weather is heading our way, judging by the small and large cumuli gathering in the sky. Never mind. Once we've reached the required altitude it'll be time to turn on the heating as some of the young crew members will have their teeth chattering.

A quick glance at the watch and we're boarding. I briefly check around to make sure all is in good order, but it's hardly necessary, seeing as we can rely completely on Toni's workmanship.

The old man is warming up the engines. One machine after the other starts up, slowly rolls down the runway, others follow close up, our goal is to take off in close formation.

We wait for the commander, engines idling, but he's running late. Finally we see him taxiing towards us, he is running his engine at full power; one V-formation after the other takes off, whirling up huge dust clouds. Poor guys working on their birds just 100 metres behind the machines starting up – they must be being choked and blinded.

The group gathers in a circle just above the destination and moves in tight formation towards the target as if on a fly-past at a Reich party rally. It's swelteringly hot. We're tossed about violently. Our group thins out. We climb steadily higher. Soon we've reached the first clouds, which we've penetrated a few seconds later. How calm everything seems to be up here! It feels like swaying on the polar sea with the sun gleaming through the snow-white little clouds. Perhaps commonplace, but beautiful nonetheless …

We set course. Once in a while I touch the stick to regulate the engines. It's what I do practically in my sleep. I keep a watchful eye on the instruments, then glance at the other machines. My 'Anton' lies flat as a plank with the landscape drifting by below us. We almost don't even need to rely on any navigation as we're more than familiar with this countryside which, incidentally, is completely charmless. Vast stretches of fields, monotonous grassland, not a hill in sight, once in a while a village turns up pretty much destroyed by the war. A bit of farmland, very few forests, steppes and arid grassland with extensive areas entirely withered. And it's only 1 July.

Ahead of us the lead aircraft bank into a right-hand turn followed by the rest of the squad. A glance at the watch. What? Two hours passed already? That means that the front line must be very near. We still have a long journey ahead, mostly above our own territory and only some 100 kilometres above enemy land, for our approach and return flight. Small fry.

We reach the point at which our troops have thrust forward, forcing a deep enclave into the area leading to Voronezh.[5] The front line was in complete chaos, and we've returned once again to mobile warfare. Troops and convoys throw up dust from 'streets' and paths, columns winding their way through the landscape in both directions. Most of the vehicles hobble along heading east. Our battle cry is 'off to the Don'. Ivan is barely putting up a fight. He's likely hoping to dig himself in behind the Don. Timoshenko's order is to only put up light, 'flexible' resistance and this serves us well.[6] His troops are thrusting forward, ours hot on their heels, in the process gaining control over vast areas. The enclave reaches far and deep. Finally we can see the spearhead but, other than a few places where shells have exploded, there's nothing more that we can see from this bird's eye view. Now we have to be careful! 25–30 minutes and we'll have reached our target.

Our own fighter planes appear on the scene; they come up quite close, salute-wobbling their wings up and down a bit, and then zoom off.[7] Their remit is to protect the air space above the front line and keep scum away from us.

Far ahead, to the right and left of us, several squads are on course to the industrial city, much like ourselves. German fighters whirr around each and every group to protect and keep them safe.

Towards lunchtime, when high towers of clouds reach up to our altitude, we decide that weather conditions are ideal for an attack. It allows a surprise assault on the city, much like a storm would hit it. But it's equally possible that we'll get a surprise from out of the blue. Our nimble airborne colleagues, however, keep a watchful eye. Won't be easy for Ivan to come close to any of our fat bombs. Happy and relieved, we continue on our path, even venturing a bit higher.

Our target lies behind that enormous cloud. Fires are blazing everywhere you look. Bombers are advancing towards us. They've already jettisoned their cargo. It's our turn now and behind us several more squads are en route. Overwhelming airpower has been deployed. The city appears ahead of us. Despite the dark columns of smoke rising, we can clearly identify each quarter. Bombs of all kinds are hailing down, hurling burning debris and rubble into the air and elsewhere setting places on fire. Our bomb bays open up, the squads fan out, each one zeros in on its defined target. A gentle turn to the left and we sight the railway station on the southern tip of the city, and next to it the engine factory. Just then other squads drop a stick of bombs criss-cross over the large freight-loading station. They converge from all sides and flak is pounding from all angles. I'm not exactly sure who they're meant to be targeting. Looks like a few bullets are aimed at this line, some at another one, then there's an assault on one unit and three, four salvos smash into another one. Everything is in disarray, no coordinated attacks.

Richard releases the bombs. Rockets pass by us but fly much too far left and explode in mid-air. Tracers from down below come up in red-coloured chains. Bomber formations zoom around at all altitudes, their bombs strewn all over the city. It's one hell of a Luftwaffe gathering up here, above Voronezh!

The old man now turns south; we follow. All our pills have crashed into the sections of the railway station, which until now had remained intact. The engine plant, as well, is severely damaged with three out of four buildings hit and one engulfed by flames. Can't be determined who exactly jettisoned those bombs, as they're pouring down like rain. Looks like a volcano has erupted. This one major attack must surely be sufficient to chase those Bolsheviks out of the city for good.

German troops during the capture of Voronezh, July 1942 (source: https://www.bradford-delong.com/2017/06/case-blue-wikipedia.html).

We're now flying the opposite course. Down below fierce air-fighting. A Rata has emerged from the clouds with an Me 109 immediately pouncing on her and … that's it. Our trusted Me sucks the monstrous juggernaut from its trail with a few bursts of fire, just above the large airfield situated in the city's south-west corner … it goes down, a flaming torch now, towards the ground.

Another Rata is on the tail of an He 111 and an Me dives towards it. Once again a Russian plunges vertically, spinning into his muddy tomb. A circus of death is unfolding, wild shelling alternates with a mad circuit of chasing one another. I look on as a 109 hunts down this shrew of an aircraft [JaK-1?] which is trying to escape into the morass. That same moment a few Russians emerge from the clouds only to veer away immediately and disappear again after spotting German fighters. Our seasoned comrades pursue them at great speed.

We've long left the site ravaged by carnage and destruction, but still come across battle units who, like us, have been deployed to this city and continue fighting. We cross over the front line, put our machines in a steep dive and zoom through the clouds. A nosedive such as this is fun if you're in tight formation! We come up close to the lead pilot – and by now the echelons have merged into one solid group. Just above the ground we flare out and continue in low-level flight along the roads on which transport details ferry reinforcements and supply goods to ground forces. And then, low-level flight back to base.

We've all returned. Nobody is missing. Sure, quite a number of crates have been hit by shrapnel in the trunk or the wings, but the damage is not extensive and can soon be repaired. Our control room gets to hear about our attack, our combat theatre in the sky, and they're as pleased as we are about the impressive results. The Wehrmacht report announces that fifty-six planes have been shot down and, three days later, that Voronezh is in German hands.[8]

— • —

After a 200-km flight our troops have reached the Don, and even poured across it at various points. Vicious battles are raging south of Svoboda direction the Don. All roads are clogged with heavy convoys. The routes are thronged with column after column of Russian vehicles, spilling over into the fields. Our Luftwaffe is in hot pursuit, a nightmarish apparition out of the sky for the Bolsheviks. Bullets slam down and bombs explode. Planes climb and circle the area, locating troop sections that have ground to a halt, and then support them with well-aimed drops. Heavy bombers, like birds of prey, cruise higher up, then swoop down, claiming their victim. Fighters and destroyers, alongside Stukas, fly low, skim above and parallel to the road, climb a bit higher, then attack and strafe convoys and spread death and devastation.

We're posted to the crossings over the Don. Scanning a wide area, there's only one bridge we identify. Concentration of motorised vehicles lined up in front. Ferry transports still in full swing at other spots. Looks like the Russians are in a damn hurry to cross that river.

Our target is the bridge over the Don near the insignificant village called Belogorye.

For quite a while already I've had the 'old guy' on board, a senior gentleman, a major and captain of a Staffel. He's not really familiar with heading a squad and that's what we're supposed to train him in – seeing as we're the most senior crew around here.

There's a definite advantage to being the leader of the squad; you're able to select the targets and you're independent, much like, for example, a wingman. You're free to decide which approach flight to choose and how to execute it. No need to add that we're, of course, unbelievably skilled and competent. Surely the 150 enemy operations under our belt count for something.

Long convoys down below roll at full speed towards the Don. Sadly, we must not take any notice of them. Our target remains the bridge, and once it's destroyed, many hundreds of vehicles will be there for the taking, because once they're enclosed on two sides, the

Russians will be pushed to the river. Let's just hope that we'll be able to turn that narrow crossing into a pile of ruins before too long.

Six of our machines cruising at an altitude of 3,000 metres head towards the target. Our approach flight is carried out with utter precision. The two Russian fighter planes intent on foiling this mission don't bother us in the least. Just the opposite. In tight formation, guns blazing, we head for their noses, which brings them to their senses. They choose to disappear, and fast. Richard orders a few changes to our course and at his command both groups jettison their bombs in one coordinated swoop. As such, everyone feels they have scored. Surely something down below must be hit. I keep the machine straight in order to help Karl take pictures of the drop.

All hell has broken loose down below! Our stick of bombs has smashed the bridge in half, with the other bombs punching huge craters into the embankment in front and to the back of the bridge, targeting the columns that have built up – many vehicles bursting into fragments of blazing wreckage. Main thing is that we're now well and truly done with that bridge. The old guy on board is quite elated, in fact; it's his most successful enemy operation to date!

We radio the destruction of the bridge through to our commander, who congratulates us, upon which we return home, to stock up on more bombs and get ready for more attacks.

— • —

Three hours later sees us returning to enemy territory. Roads are jammed with columns of vehicles now reaching back even further. From all sides bombers from our squadron converge, with their ammunition grinding everything below to dust and ashes. Great masses of dirt and mud spurt up, cars rocked by the tremendous explosions burst into flames; disintegrated wreckage whirls around in the air. There're no misses. Even an absolute novice can notch up some direct hits around here. The fragmentation bombs leave complete devastation in their wake. New V-formations come zooming along and once again carpet the area with their bombs, wreaking death and destruction. Some vehicles make feeble attempts to tear away, but before too long they've been hunted down and set ablaze.

Why heavy flak on the other side of the river even makes an effort to respond is beyond me. Nobody cares a jot. Fresh approach flight and another series of massive eggs whistle down. A number of Staffel, having tasted blood, now nosedive while hammering fleeing Russians with their machine guns. By now the landscape has disappeared beneath a veil for all the columns of mud and oil rising into the air. The raging fires and the large mushroom cloud can be seen at a far distance and into the falling night, by which time we're already cruising above our own territory. As the day comes to an end, our crew can record one destroyed bridge and thirty destroyed vehicles. Unfortunately there is no way to determine what else has been damaged or rendered useless by fragments. Our mechanic and the guys in charge of the bombs are pleased as punch. Their work was not in vain after all. But rarely have we found such beautiful targets.

— • —

Troops engaged in combat have moved further south. The aim is to conquer the large industrial zone around Voroshilovgrad. Battles are erupting in the Donbas region. Slowly but surely, our troops line up with Italians and Romanians[9] and advance to this area where a large section is already in our hands. We strafe factory after factory, and one trench after the other is rendered useless by the Bolshevik.They follow their traditional tactics, consisting of working under pressure for as long as possible and then blowing the whole lot up.

In a recent development the Russian is dismantling his tool machinery and loading them onto train carriages, which then rumble in the direction of the Urals, where he's already in the process of setting up industrial plants. Only a limited number of railway lines remain at his disposal, with one of them leading through Millerovo and another from Rostov towards the south to continue from there across Stalingrad to the Urals.

It is these two hubs, Lirkaya and Millerovo, which are our primary targets. During the day, attacks are carried out by other units, while we pick up at night-time, when, with renewed force, our sustained bombardments unleash destruction. Lines are being interrupted at various points. During the beginning of July 1942, night after night we relentlessly target Lirkaya, at times Millerovo as well. Night after night bombs tear apart train tracks and new fires break out in different places. Night after night we enter the sector, eject our high-explosive and incendiary bombs on targets which spew spectacular fireworks into the dark, but at other times we can't even find the targets. Flights are only possible based on navigation transmitted by radio. Flak often gives away the exact position, and recently searchlights installed by the Russians do the same.

There was a day when I came away convinced that we hadn't hit anything. Looked to us that everyone just launched their ammo down at random, hoping to hit flak or searchlights. No fire erupted, no impact. We sorely regretted the waste of bombs, which had clearly all missed their target. But when we get to study the images, we're in for a surprise: over 100 fresh craters had been dug in between the railway tracks and the train station. Not a single track remained intact. That's what one calls *Fliegerglück* [pilot's luck].

The Kramatorsk airbase, summer 1942.

Kramatorsk's industrial zone (to the left is the Kasennyi Torez river)
(Source: *Luftwaffe im Focus*, 23 (2014)).

Gradually our approach flights become too long. Steadily, the front line moves further east. For this reason, we're relocated to Kramatorsk, a narrow and hilly airbase strip in the middle of an industrial zone and on a slight incline. There's only one large barracks still semi-standing, but otherwise destroyed. Our quarters are located some 10 kilometres away, in a workers' estate. Previously labourers from abroad lived here and were employed at the nearby tank manufacturer. Probably that's the reason why the buildings aren't totally neglected. Very likely this must have been something of a model estate. We even have running water and on top of that showers which work, a precious commodity in Russia. What we require to fit out the place is soon sorted out. It's a bit of a business when it comes to the beds. The iron cots which these scruffy-looking rascals offer us in exchange for a few cigarettes prove to be riddled with bugs. No other option than to stuff some bags with straw and kip on the floor.

We're off early the next morning. The order is to attack the Morosovsk train station. Our troops advance from the north. Millerovo has already been captured. All trainlines are clogged with freight trains. The Luftwaffe has cleaned up around here. It was the Stukas above all who selected the trains as their targets. And they scored considerable successes. Along a stretch of some 25 kilometres we note about thirty to forty wrecked trains. Tracks are ripped apart everywhere.

Our aim is to destroy the train station. We've got reports about several freight trains due to arrive, all heading east, towards the Volga, and on to Stalingrad. What's important is to lock the cage before the precious birds slip out. Early that morning our squad flies in tight formation towards its target. We sometimes cross our own territory, sometimes territory occupied by the Russians. Just about everywhere we've managed to drive a deep wedge into the Bolshevik hinterland for the purpose of laying siege to places of particularly strategic importance. Everywhere long columns of trucks and troops choke the roads. At our height it's often difficult to tell who belongs to us and who to the enemy.

Never mind, we don't let up. Any moment now we'll be above our own territory, with another squad just ahead of us. Were they also meant to approach the same target? Oh … looks like he's flying towards us. We travel just below the cloud cover. Before too long the squad turns out to consist of three units of Red attack bombers. We bear down on them, open fire with all guns. The Russians immediately drop their noses and disappear. We fly on, close below the cloud cover.

Far to my right several machines emerge from the morass. Upon setting eyes on us, they vanish. We're talking about eight to ten Red fighters who look like they're trying to escape from the grip of the enemy. But some of them reappear from the clouds and attack the last group. A brisk exchange of fire between the two sides and the 'comrades' seem to have had their fill. They turn round and in tight formation carry on.

Weather conditions improve a bit. The cloud cover rips apart with the blue sky gleaming down, happily also revealing our target. Diving at an acute angle of bank, we converge on the target. The station is not large, but trains are lined up on all tracks. With my Staffel I close in on the sheds housing the locomotives, with several of them stationary in front of it, some of them still spouting steam. We spread out, intending to carpet the entire station.

A military airbase lies south-west of the train station. So far, no dust clouds are detected.

Richard makes a few adjustments to the course and I keep the machine as flat as a pancake. Our approach flight follows in exemplary fashion – nobody can beat us in style. Located in the

Kramatorsk airfield, summer 1942.

centre of the crosshairs several locomotives put out of action are tell-tale signs of previous visitors. We encounter hardly any flak, and when we do, it's badly aimed. Then the bombs drop and flak awakens, shelling us at our altitude. Suddenly trails of black vapour whirl up behind us as we watch a biplane engaging in a vicious dogfight.[10] He's attacking and shelled by his own flak. Skimming low over our heads, tracers come whizzing by, while he does his absolute best to strafe us, turning and spiralling in and out of curves. Meanwhile the boorish Russian troops are firing from below.

In a steep left-hand dive we cut away, which gives me a good view of the results of our bombing. Though I can't quite make out the details, the entire landscape below seems turned into a vast area of rubble, twisted metal and smoke. The train station is one immense heap of ruins. Here and there fires erupt. Buildings, barracks, cargo depots are hit. Freight trains, filled to the brim, are torn apart, direct hits smashing them into hundreds of bits scattered far and wide. The destruction is total. The entire area surrounding the locomotive shed lies in debris, ash and smoke. What a scene this must be down below. This is – as we know – exactly where our extra-large calibre cannons had hit. That's it, then, for Morosovsk. No train will pass through here in the next fortnight. This signifies a successful achievement for each crew of the group and has us flying home very well pleased with ourselves.

— • —

Yet again we're deployed to the train station, ordered to shell anything and everything that might have escaped our first onslaught. Same approach flight as in the morning. Bombs drop yet again, fires erupt, flak opens up as it did previously and, just like before, that odd biplane whizzes around us and in and out of shell smoke clouds.

An inferno rages down below. Huge fires rip through supply barracks, smoke and fire billow up from entire trains, and black clouds of soot and vapour hang over this city of doom. The Luftwaffe has had a field day.

On our return we encounter other units, who're out to grip the Bolsheviks in their clutches, jolting them into action, never granting them a minute's reprieve. With such victories, this is a fun aerial combat – no doubt about it!

Our troops push the Russians further south, towards the Don. Far to the east they've dug in near Rostov, close to where the river flows into the Sea of Azov. Our troop contingents advance at great speed across a distance of hundreds of kilometres along the roads in hot pursuit of escaping Russians but flanked on both the left- and right-hand side by the lurking enemy. One can barely grasp the reality, but such it is, that our own men are being forced to keep to the roads only. Hope is placed on our infantry divisions pulling up from the rear, who're meant to clean up scattered enemy positions and thus enable reinforcements to get through. Vast areas are secured within a few days only, and the advance takes place unhindered.

Probably the Russians are scared of being encircled and therefore keep searching for ways and means to retreat and desperately avoid the slightest possibility of a pocket forming and being trapped by a pincer movement. They've come a long way in mobile warfare and have learned from experience.

Both armies gradually arrive closer to the Don, with the Russians piling up before this broad and threatening river winding its way through the steppe. But where it really gets dangerous is close to Konstantinovsk. It's here that they seek to cross. Reconnaissance has identified heavy concentrations of artillery and massed troop formations, such as we've not encountered previously in this war.

This is where we're deployed. What ensues is a fight against death and annihilation.

We take off at night and before long the target is ahead of us. Heavy traffic in the city, but above all at the ferry crossing. Hundreds of motorcars are assembled and waiting for the transfer. The majority aren't even camouflaged but are lined up, open-topped. We dive-bomb and let the bombs hail down, directing them at the densest spots. Our massive load is a direct hit, boring into vehicles of all kinds. We zoom over the Don, nab trucks on the other riverbank and grind them into scrap. The impact must be enormous, with a ferry also being damaged. Sadly, some bombs just plop into the water.

Diving away, we note the many gorges running vertical to the river and stuffed with vehicles. Dangling like ripe fruit, they seek cover from the storm sweeping across above their heads.

No sooner have we touched down than the machines are refuelled and loaded up again, and we're off for a second round. Same target. We dive-bomb and strafe all gorges and allocate our bombs according to where they are most effective. Great masses of dirt and dust fountains spurt into the air. Many planes hover above the target area, spying out the land for optimal bombing.

We're inspired. Vehicles are ablaze, our hits are perfect or near perfect. What does it matter if it's a bull's eye or not? The splinters manage to turn all vehicles in the vicinity into a heap of iron or at the very least cause heavy damage. Only pity is that we can't carry more bombs. This forces us to turn round and fly home to restock our bellies and refuel. Besides that, we've also got to take care of our grumbling stomachs. Yet another V-formation sets off, the grim reaper. With ever smaller delays, the next machine flies its mission, just as soon as it has been cleared. Suspension of the ferry traffic is to be made as long as possible.

We fly our third operation at the heat of midday. Same target area. It's swelteringly hot in the cockpit and we climb ever higher, otherwise we'll just waste away. Windows are all open and gradually it becomes somewhat bearable, allowing us to clear our minds and make decisions. One can only imagine what it must be like in one of those tanks! The target lies before us. It's quite hectic up above the battle zone. V-formations or Staffel enlisted with other units are coming and going at all times, often circling the area for hours. Today, Ivan doesn't get a moment's rest. There's a gorge ahead of us, it's busy like an anthill and looks like it's barely been strafed. Well, nothing but accurate dive-bombing and then on to strafing

An He 111 operating for Kampfgeschwader 55.

new targets. We don't blanket just anything, seeing as time is on our side and we've become quite picky. Criss-crossing the landscape, we bombard the riverbanks and hail bullets into the gorges until they've been fumigated. Turning into a left curve I can see my wingman sink a well-filled ferry.

There's a fourth operation against the enemy on this oppressively hot day with the same old tactics of dive-bombing and strafing one gorge after the other. Quite a number of vehicles go up in flames to then burn out with a black vapour trail gradually thinning out. For all the smoke and dirt one can hardly count the number of destroyed vehicles. Despite the gleaming sun, and with a thick fog of mud, filth and smoke blanketing the bombed landscape, we press on with bombing the hell out of the Bolsheviks, even though their troops are already much reduced by this time.

At long last, machine and man may rest. The heat was unremittingly hot, but the day is over. We were extremely tense as it is not a simple matter to be hanging in the air for eighteen out of twenty-four hours, with most of it spent hovering above enemy territory. But the success rate is impressive. Both Timoshenko's army troops and their rolling stock have been severely stripped, men killed and supplies cut off. We've made some careful estimates based on the reports of other crews – my own crew alone can record thirty vehicles destroyed and about the same number damaged, putting them out of commission for the foreseeable future – looks like each one of our crews was equally successful. In fact, it turns out that the numbers we report to the command post are probably too low, as nobody can quite determine the damage our bomb shrapnel has caused. It would require us to go into more detail. What we now hope for is more opportunities like this with equally exciting objectives!

— • —

Attack on Rostov!

Seeing as this city is heavily protected by flak, we climb up as high as possible. Flying at standard altitude, we'd manage the approach in forty-five minutes. It forces our unit to perform several circuits, putting huge pressure on our birds as they are carrying massive loads. We need to reach higher.

At long last the unit, encircled by two of our own fighter planes for protection, approaches the objective at an altitude of some 6,000 metres. Cruising along the coast of the Sea of Azov, we reach the Don delta and we bank slightly south in order to avoid flak upon approach. Most of the batteries are positioned at the north-western edge of the city, just where two airbases are located, and also in the south, where two bridges cross the Don. Places such as these are plentifully equipped with flak weapons.

We sight the target. I'm flying as the left wingman to the commander and am instructed, much like the other crews, to stay on the ball at all times and launch our bombs on sight, at the commander's order. Doesn't make sense really as nobody can tell what exactly is being shot at, given such a large expanse for a target area. It would be a completely different story if one could rely on the leader, then each shot is a sure hit, but what with this particular commander who's mucked up plenty already, nobody likes being the wingman.

We set course north heading to the city. Not quite sure what the old man is attacking up there in front, don't know whether he's minded to shell the two bridges or the small railway station located in the southern corner of the city – or what's he up to? It looks like he's en route to the bridge, so we put our nose in that direction. But hey – midway through his approach flight, the old man switches and bears right. Ordered to keep on the ball, I've no choice but to do just that, so I follow him. I lose sight of the bridges, but instead the small station appears. The old man radios for us to eject the bombs and in tight formation we release them. I'm curious about the result. I'm annoyed that the bridges aren't being blown up and Richard is equally incensed about this silly way the old man conducts himself.

Flak opens a perfectly directed fire. We move a bit away from the old man to gain some measure of manoeuvrability and to liberally carpet the dump. Finally our bombs detonate. Our lot zooms across the station, hitting a train, and then goes further. Everything is covered in filth and rubble, but in the port and in the Don, the majority of bombs drop into the water. We can only blame the commander for this nonsense; the entire attack has failed.

A bit later on we're more than just mad, we're totally disgusted and ask ourselves whether the old man is even sane? He doesn't sweep towards the east, but instead climbs up and above the city and airbases and bears west. Little wonder that he comes under concentrated flak fire from batteries banging away with perfect aim and joined by all those fighters who're encamped around this dump. I'm not sure where this will end – in fact, it must surely go wrong at any minute.

Firing from all angles, we try and escape the splinters and zigzag through the sky, determined not to get hit. Shells fly past our ears; as they explode there's a deafening screeching and there's a worrying rattle in the machine as flying splinters fill the cockpit, some embedding themselves in the trunk and wings. A salvo of fire smashes just underneath my plane and like a wild horse this bird of mine rears up and miraculously avoids a mid-air collision. The windshield is shattered, the navigation board perforated, with shredded parts dangling down and of no use. The aiming device, this German miracle of optical and precision craftsmanship, has disappeared, a fuel container has spilled over, but so far, the engines are still running and the crew are alive. At long last we've escaped the thick of the barrage and we can breathe again. Exhausted, but above all furious that this operation is one huge blunder, we return to base. It could have been so different, but the entire mission is butchered without any results. That's what happens when someone's in the lead who has no clue, or only limited knowledge about how to lead a squad and place bombs. Because of his woeful ignorance and ignoring what plainly would be an inferno of flak, he put his entire squad in danger.

Not many planes return from this operation without having suffered serious damage. And so the most experienced and most successful crews are allocated different aircraft and are ordered to depart – in V-formation this time round – into the battle zone north of Rostov. Our actions were to be concentrated mainly on roads, to carry out bombing and strafing runs. But because previous units have already dropped their bombs around that combat zone, the Russians have pre-empted our manoeuvre by moving their vehicles out of the field of vision. We're left scouring the surrounding areas for anything hidden away.

We've only got a few bombs left in our belly when I come across an airbase. I immediately radio through our situation, bank sharply and dive. I make a mental note of a few hunters parked there. The wingmen have caught up and all of us jettison our stuff practically at the same time. Visibility is poor. Large cloud banks obscure part of the airfield. Nonetheless, we manage to place our bombs relatively accurately into the bays where they've tucked away their machines, and huge columns of thick black smoke and dust immediately rise after our drop. Some bombs have punched great big holes either

View of the runway from the cockpit.

next to or in front of the boxes, and I'm guessing that the splinters will have caused a great deal of damage.

There! Three Russian fighter planes are encircling us. Looks like three Yaks, of the I-17 type. A few bursts of fire from our lads, and they scurry off, now keeping a respectful distance. Only once in a while one of them plucks up his courage, pushes forward and starts shelling from a far distance. Doesn't look like this lot will inflict much damage on us. We make a quick circuit of the field and carry on strafing more roads. Seeing as we've now run out of bombs, we just do a mop-up job. We then return to base.

— • —

The third operation that same day is also directed at Rostov. This time our attack is staggered, there are no fighter planes protecting us, but our assault takes place again at great altitude and at dusk. With this kind of twilight no Russian fighter plane dares to fight us. Looks like the gentlemen would have trouble landing.

From a long distance away great columns of smoke are tell-tale signs of the impact from other bombing units. At last we've reached the correct altitude for our attack; we change course and get going. We approach from the west – that is, from where the sun is setting – and then on to the city. Flak only recognises us very late but their shelling is all the fiercer for it, coinciding with us releasing our eggs. Goodness, quite the fireworks going on down there! Blast and fire furnaces glow far into the sky; flak shells crumple, mixed with explosions further below. There's no doubt that our bombs have hit their targets perfectly. New fires erupt and spread to barracks and depots within the surroundings of the railway station. Gently curving right, we withdraw from the combat scene and cut away in a steep dive. We've soon left the cauldron behind and fly towards the sunset.

20.7.42

On 20 July we once again strafe Russian columns of motorised vehicles. The combat zone runs north of Rostov. Some bombs have just been jettisoned when three fighters appear and attack our unit. At about 3,000 metres we're flying between the small and larger cumulus clouds which usually drift through the sky around midday. We see the ground through some holes and note that these three I-17s are a much swifter trio than the birds from the day before. They advance closer, fire, nosedive away and then return. But we're ready, on high alert, and our guns slam bullets against their aircraft like hailstones. The Russians dodge and dive and turn, continually finding dead angles. They don't let go. These must be experts at their craft, and we're clearly no longer dealing with novices. The score stands at 1:1 with everyone called on to prove their mettle and demonstrate who's got the true fighting spirit. We hold back on ammunition as nobody can tell how long this air battle is going to last. These guys are tough. We only fire when it's really worth it and this way we let one of them nose up close at 100 metres. He must have been hit, as he suddenly flips over and dives down into the depths. Through the gaps in the cloud bank I watch him as he disappears, bearing down onto a well-camouflaged field airbase that I hadn't noticed before. We set upon him with Richard stooped over the targeting device and the next minute we drop a stick of bombs right into the direction of the landing machine. The fighter plane disappears behind the sludge and dust churned up. We dive away in order to launch a renewed assault on the base with whatever bombs we've got left – but the fighters have suddenly disappeared. Who the hell knows where they've gone to? Or perhaps they've got a bad conscience seeing as they are unable to protect their airbase from our attacks!

A cloud obscures the airfield, until, at the last minute, I find a hole that I can push through. I swing sharply into a curve and the remainder of our bombs drop in between camouflaged machines.

Stukas over Russia, 1942 (Source: https://www.asisbiz.com/il2/Ju-87/StG2.2/pages/Junkers-Ju-87D3-Stuka-4.StG2-(T6+BM)-over-Russia-1942-04.html).

Four of them are lined up quite close to the fighter planes, which can be registered destroyed or at the very least seriously damaged. In the middle of the field, we spot just by the landing cross the fighter who'd been caught out by our bombs. Sorry, old man, bad luck! Clouds move in again and hide the airfield, with us changing course to the west.

— • —

Concentrated attack on Rostov begins the following day. Our troops thrust forward from the west, the north and the east, advancing onto the city which had been in their possession just a short while back, that past year.

We, the Luftwaffe, are to support the assault from the west by carrying out air attacks on army encampments and all the smaller and larger villages which have become veritable fortifications thanks to the freshly dug Russian trench system. But the impact of our initial attacks is such that these positions are easily overrun at the very first assault. The entire attack moves along swiftly. At the same time our Landsers are pushing down from the north and hardly encounter any resistance. They're supported by Stukas whom we constantly come across as we're heading further east and shelling the Bolsheviks piling up along the Don and attempting to escape south.

This time round we're targeting the area around Kalinin, a small but significant place to both the Russians and ourselves because of its bridge across the Don. The bridge and the columns of rolling material lined up are our destination. Far in the west, huge columns of black smoke rise into the sky. Rostov is on fire.

However, today, unlike several days ago near Konstantinovsk, we don't come across large concentrations of vehicles. Never mind, the few clusters we do find are definitely worth attacking. We dive down to the bridge while the two wingmen are firing away at trucks and lorries. Behind us, more units and Staffel are catching up. Bombs come hailing down. Just prior to our release, we're subjected to artillery fire, not heavy but aimed with precision. We mustn't let this bother us. Bombs are detonating below us. Some land in the river, but the last one demolishes the bridge, with two vehicles plunging in a wide arc into the water. I continue flying straight ahead, then make a full circle, turn round and go on a second attack. Ahead of us a unit is busily shelling away and with a few direct hits manages to silence an artillery position. Tall fountains of mud, smoke and debris gushing forth. Smoke everywhere, which tells us that a number of vehicles have been demolished. Many others, though, are tucked away in the embankment, camouflaged, but visible to our good selves. We don't lose a moment and traverse the second flak position, cross the river and Richard drops the rest of the bombs. While his hits cannot be faulted, he unfortunately doesn't manage to smash the bridge. Nonetheless, we register some fifteen to twenty vehicles destroyed.

— • —

For today Rostov is a taboo subject. Fierce street battles are raging, with gruesome scenes unfolding as large numbers of Bolsheviks thrust across the Don and push towards the south. We're left to concentrate our action on Bataisk from dusk and throughout the night, with extensive areas being set on fire.[11]

Our target for the following few days remains the battle zone south of Rostov, which falls into our hands on 23 July, but not before horrendous fighting in the streets has taken a heavy toll. The remainder of the sorry Russian troops seek to retreat towards the south-west and Azov as well as Koissug, both viciously targeted several times today by our aircraft.[12]

In Azov the piers are being attacked and several streets turned into rubble, molten iron and ash. In Koissug, as could be observed by the other crews, we managed to eliminate several flak emplacements and artillery positions.[13]

After that, it's off to the Tichorezk railway junction. From this hub, the train line leads south from Rostov to Tichorezk; a further line runs along the Caucasus towards the oil-rich Baku area. Yet another line connects Novorossiysk, a large port situated on the Black Sea, with Stalingrad on the Volga, via Tichorezk. In short, the place is indeed a very important railway junction.

There's enough time to rest and listen to the radio.
Kramatorsk airfield, summer 1942.

26.7.42[14]

We attack Tichorezk on 26 July during the night. Bright search-lights throw their beams against a sky already lit up by the moon and navigation becomes a fairly easy task. Wildly the clusters of light begin their play to my far left. Engines run at different revs, intending to confuse the Russians listening in on their earphones. Flak shells come whizzing by but can't stop our bombs. Several small parts of the landscape are ablaze. In the gleam of the moon it is very easy to pick out the glistening train tracks leading into the station.

We embark on our return flight. Once again we fly over the eastern section of the Sea of Azov, the water glistening in the glare of the searchlights. It is this particularly irritating source of light which hindered us on the way here, which is why we now aim to crack it by diving low and hurling a few MG salvos in that direction. But, as if challenged, it obstinately fails to light up despite our crafty approach. Only once we cross over the northern coast is the water behind us once again fully illuminated. Well, we intended to prove to these Russians that it's us who rule the roost, but the lads managed to prove us wrong.[15]

— • —

Tichorezk remains our destination throughout the attacks that follow.[16] We take off at dawn and attack the station with the fading shooting light. Just north of the station is located an airbase, with two runways crossing each other. Ideal to help us orient ourselves in preparation for all future bombings during the night.

And once again our bombs cause widespread damage and disruption, with depots being destroyed. Flak pour their lead into the air – but fail to have any serious impact on us. However, the hoped-for fires don't erupt and that in fact is our primary aim for today. Setting the place ablaze was meant to be our mission, enabling future crews to pinpoint the area more easily during the night and more effectively position their bombs. We're in a bad mood and return to base.

That same night we launch our second attack on Tichorezk. From afar we recognise a brightly lit spot which turns out to be a vast section of land set alight just within our designated target zone. Toni messages through the same results the other crews had transmitted via radio previously: target is on fire, target is burning fiercely.

Looks like the dawn attack was well worth it and the results are satisfactory. It seems that the fire initially was only sort of smouldering and then later grew into a flaming fire, with our crews busily feeding the process.

On approach we clearly recognise two large depots ablaze. We distinctly see the train tracks as they gleam in the bright moonlight, which also lights up the contours of the runways.

Steep dive down to the target. Richard ejects the bombs. Just when I'm throttling back the engines, the thin arms of the searchlights flit back and forth, even though just before they had systematically searched the sky only to my left, trying to catch me.

Flak no longer has any concrete clues as to how to direct the shelling and it thus stops.

One bomb is still resting in its bay, so I continue prowling through the sky. I execute a tight turn and Richard sets course to base. Below us bombs still from the first drop are only now exploding. With some delay, but no less ferociously, the little berries detonate in the middle of the train station and in between the fires, adding to the mad chaos.

On our return, once we're flying deep over enemy territory we spot light signals to our far right. Seems to be an airbase, which Ivan must have used for his take-offs after loading up with bombs, eager to drop them onto our lot in Rostov. We suspected as much during our approach flight. Bombs fall and explode, machine guns and cannons strafe installations, searchlights go on and sweep the sky; the fireworks continue until the whole nightmarish operation is over.

[28–31.7.42][17]

The last days in July see us embark on the most adventurous night-time operation I ever carried out during my deployment as a bomber pilot. In low-level flight, the moon is shining bright, we strafe the ships along the Volga, in the section between Stalingrad and Astrakhan, the city lying on the upper part of the river's delta, a bit away from the Caspian Sea.

At the first absolutely fascinating briefing session with the officer, we learn a fair bit about the shipping industry along this river, the largest in Europe, even though we have gained some knowledge during our previous training. But it is certainly news to us that huge warships of some 5,000 GRT are floating about. What we knew about the Volga was rather based on touristic descriptions, exciting travel reports and descriptions of it as a flat river, with many islands and sandbanks. And now, we have crates of 5,000 GRT!

Well, let's see! With any luck, we'll successfully sink some of those umpteen-ton barges. Those poor fish surely also need something to feed on.

Our combat zone has been subdivided into four large sections, enabling us to manoeuvre freely without getting into each other's way. I, along with my crew, have been charged to hit the southern-most section, north of Astrakhan. Even our Staffel captain, the old man, comes along even though he himself ordinarily doesn't really think much of night flights.

We take off while it's still light. Our flight path is long. It'll take us over four or five hours. Long distances into the hinterland, across the bare expanse of the open steppe. No sign of habitation. It's already dark when we cross the Don, basically the front line, approximately at Kalach. Numerous areas of the steppe, still Russian terrain, have been burned. Dark contours, initially mistaken for forests, are actually scorched patches of arid land. Fires, slithering through the landscape like silver snakes, tell the story of heavy shelling. We simply can't quite figure out why the Russian would have set the steppe on fire. We only understood his logic much later.[18]

We continue on our path. Our bird lies perfectly flat in the air, totally horizontal, and requires practically no adjustments. Finally, having spent many hours cruising along, we pass a series of lakes: salt water, according to the map. Indeed a salt lake straight ahead at the far end reaches from north to south. We have to leave the largest one behind on our left in order to keep on course. And it all goes smoothly. After half an hour we reach the Volga and the naval hunt can commence.

Gradually I dip lower – and eventually we spot a large fire flickering brightly ahead of us. Gleaming in the moonlight, we realise it's the Volga. We join the river at its most northerly point and, turning south, I fly under a clear moonlit sky. The moonlight is so bright and because it is mirrored in the gleaming surface of the river, one can, if looking closely, make out minute details. Nonetheless, long sandbanks breaking the current could easily

250

be mistaken for a steamer or barge. We must have flown quite a distance but haven't spotted a single ship. At long last we recognise a light trail of steam on the right-hand riverbank. Let's head towards that! Emerging from the shadows of the embankments are one large steamer and two even larger cargo ships. The cargo ships are moored at the bay and the steamer has dropped anchor near the shore. These certainly are worthwhile targets and I make a mental note. A small arm in the river and a pointed sandbank are good visual aids for navigation. Keeping straight ahead for just a brief period of time, I then launch into attack, push down and target the ships from a fairly low altitude. What with the moon shining down, visibility is not perfect and it's only at the last minute that a ship appears in front of our eyes. A heavy lump is dropped but misses by 2 metres and smacks into the water. Unperturbed, I cut away to then swiftly whip around and this time circumstances are more favourable. Richard plants a hefty egg onto the stern – not so easy with the moon casting its light onto the water.

We approach for a further attack. This time, we focus on the two cargo ships along the bay. One egg lands a few metres shy, and though certainly not a direct hit, the strong pressure of the waves seriously dents the boards. We zoom down on the other ship. Nothing and nobody budges down below. No defence. The mates must have gone ashore. Now Richard ejects our last two bombs and this time he's successful: one near-hit, the other a direct hit on the last ship. It's already gone under with only the funnel still sticking out of the water. One ship is listing and the other one has been smashed apart. We approach a few more times and, flying low, we pass over our prey, perforating with our MGs and cannons whatever is left. I then pull up high and fly home. It's about time too, according to my fuel levels.

This certainly was a good result for our first mission of this kind. Once again Richard has demonstrated that he is a first-class observer and bombardier. Despite the tricky light of the moon which makes it quite impossible to gauge things with precision, his

251

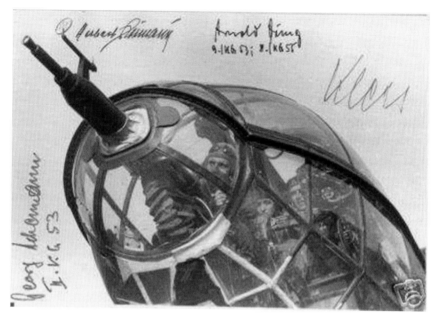

A picture showing a board cannon, mainly used to hit ground targets, signed in 1953 by Döring and other Iron Cross holders.

A picture of an He 111 H6 signed by Döring, among others.

rough guesses with respect to where to drop the bombs were pretty accurate as it turns out.

Gradually I climb to 1,000 metres and meander across the expanse of the steppes. Fires set alight beforehand are convenient points of reference for orientation. The flight is becoming tedious and tiring, one patch of open steppe looking much like the next. Once in a while I feel my eyes closing, but my trimmed crate is holding up nicely, keeping on course and to its altitude with the engines singing their iron song. Aren't these just technological marvels! Powerful and reliable to the nth degree. Without a further hitch, we arrive home. We've put over five hours' flight behind us. When we arrive at the command post we're dead tired, but hand in our reports and registered hits and it's off to bed – we've certainly earned a good night's sleep!

Excerpts from the Diary of Kampfgeschwader 55
5.8.42

On 4.8.42, around midnight, we receive the order to move our group to Samorsk [Crimea] some 30 kilometres north-west of Kerch. To this end the group is ordered to reshuffle. For the time being the 7th Staffel remains in Kramatorsk and hands over to the 8th and 9th Staffel all its fit crews, along with its operational machines, receiving in their stead crews who are ill and machines which haven't been cleared. The 1. FBK [Flughafenbetriebskompanie, in charge of service and repair] also remains behind in Kramtorskaja charged with changing engines and carrying out other repair work.

Early morning the top-flight and technical personnel of the 1. Control Room takes off along with the Abt. Ia, IN and I/TO on the He 111 and a Ju 52. Some parts of the group are sick … along with parts of the Abt. IVa which are also transferred.

Arrival in Samorsk towards lunchtime. All groups are lodged in tents. The camp is directly next to the large bay of the Sea of Azov, some 30 metres above sea level.

Lodgings are shared with KG55 [Chief of Staff, II and III Groups], KG26 (II) and KG100 (I), as well as a reconnaissance Staffel posted to the IV. Fliegerkorps.

The motor transport column departs from Kramatorsk at approx. 14.30 with fifteen trucks and ten passenger vehicles. Leader of column: Reg. Insp. Coldewenz.

One Jeep has been equipped and turned into a repair workshop and follows the column at the rear. The aim is to have all of the vehicles reach the destination. Main target is Sukotovka, north of Stalino. The route leads along the narrow Stary Krim–Feodosia strip of the eastern Crimean peninsula via Stalino–Mariupol–Melitopol to the destination, the port. After a journey of five days, during which a total of 970 kilometres are put behind us, the column arrives in Samorsk. The reason for the amount of time spent en route is because many repairs had to be carried out (springs had broken, equipment had to be installed in one trailer and two field kitchens, engine failures also had to be fixed). Additionally, we had to ensure the supply of fuel. One truck had to be left behind on the road and was towed away to the special truck repair workshop in Melitopol. We reach the destination one day after the column. Unbearable and unusual heat during the journey, causing several trucks to experience engine trouble and difficulties with availability of the coolant. The road conditions, especially between Feodosia and Samorsk, are horrendous.

Several truck drivers fall sick during the journey, forcing soldiers in possession of a driver's licence to drive the vehicles to the destination.

Above all, however, the new camp site at the fabulous location near the Sea of Azov and the prospect of camping out are happy news indeed. There's a brisk wind which eases the discomfort of the broiling heat and does away with those dreadful flies which have plagued us throughout. Also, the proximity to the sea allows for the temperatures between day- and night-time to even out, warm during the day and pleasantly cool nights, which makes camping a safe experience.

Arnold Döring with all his decorations: aircraft and glider pilot,
Iron Cross Second and First Class , Eastern Medal, German Cross in
Gold and Front Flying Clasp in Gold with pennants for three hundred
operational flights flown. The photograph was taken in March 1943 –
after which he would go on to fight more air battles, this time enlisted
to defend the Reich (see Volume 2) (Source: Döring).

Notes

Editor's Foreword

1   The emotional dimension as referred to above is missing in his later writing. Rudolf Graf, one of Döring's comrades in the No. 53 Fighter Wing, chronicles the following: 'I am not embellishing nor exaggerating anything. My subsequent report on our bombing operations only has one mistake: I'm unable to do justice to how we actually experienced and lived through them.' (Kiehl, 1983, p. 162.)

2   *TN: Zahme Sau* (Tame Boar) refers to a nightfighter intercept tactic introduced by the Luftwaffe.

3   This number corresponds to approx. 3,800 flight hours and 800,000 air kilometres, according to Döring's own calculation.

4   Döring and Herrmann both lived in Düsseldorf after the war, where the former served for a long time as the leader of the local section of the Association of Knight's Cross Recipients, of which Herrmann was a member as well.

5   More details are provided in the Appendix to Volume 2.

6   The crew was identified as a so-called *Volksbesatzung*, which indicates the absence of an officer on the aircraft.

7   Though Döring writes the surname Wowarek, the spelling used in the documents of the squadron is Wawareck, which is probably the correct one. Döring's observer was awarded the War Order of the German Cross in Gold on 23 November 1942 and was killed on 17 July 1943 after his aircraft collided with another He 111 just after taking off to attack Soviet positions in Kharkov–Weitschenko.

8   Richard Brösing died on 22 February, a day after he had been wounded when 8./KG55 was bombed by enemy fighters during an attack on Staraja Rotowka. He was posthumously decorated with the War Order of the German Cross in Gold on 28 April. Previously he had suffered a serious head injury during an operation bombing Stalingrad.

9   Karl Krupitza, who on 28 September 1942 was awarded the Ehrenpokal der Luftwaffe – an award established by Reichsmarschall Göring – was killed on 15 October 1943 when his aircraft, operated by Feldwebel Heinz Kirschmeier, was shot down on a flyover to Giessen.

10 Toni Grimmer held the War Order of the German Cross in Gold, awarded to him on 23 November 1942.

11 No further details could be found on Gerhard Eberhardt.

12 This skipping at will is pretty much how Döring dealt with the losses his squadron suffered, with him meticulously listing those at the beginning of his diary, to then omit them entirely when their number increased.

13 Döring's description of Operation 'Gisela', in which he himself participated (contained in Volume 2) is also frequently cited in literature specialising on this period.

14 After Döring's death in April 2001 his manuscripts were acquired by several collectors keen to obtain war memorabilia but then, after several years, by a lucky coincidence, they ended up in the hands of the editor who thus had the opportunity to assemble them. Anybody who may have any knowledge of the whereabouts or presumed existence of diary notes with respect to a fourth part should please contact the publishers.

15 During his deployment with Kriegsgeschwader 55, Döring accomplished several successful nightfighter operations. To this end he had requested that a few machine guns be installed in the cockpit of his He 111 which otherwise was not specifically adapted for nightfighting.

Introduction

1 The Dörings were Catholic, like the majority of the Heilsberg community.

2 On 31 January 1945 the Red Army took Heilsberg. While the town survived the invasion intact, arson attacks a few days later destroyed about 40 per cent of the infrastructure.

3 The equestrian statue created by the sculptor Viktor Seifert commemorates the battle of Heilsberg of 10 June 1807 when the Prittwitz Hussars beat the 55th French line infantry regiment and captured their eagle banner.

4 After 1880 Johann Hermann Ganswindt (1856–1934) developed concepts for a space vehicle propelled by dynamite explosions, on the principle of recoil. He envisioned a two-step approach: the spacecraft was to be towed up by a launcher, and for this purpose Ganswindt designed a helicopter. On 27 May 1893 he introduced his idea in a public lecture at the Berliner Philharmonie. In 1901 the maiden flight of what was very likely the first ever motorised helicopter in history took place in Berlin-Schöneberg (where a bridge was inaugurated in 1976 with his name soldered onto its balustrade). Others, including Ganswindt himself, always maintained that his impact on the development of an aerostatic spacecraft had been exaggerated. Count Zeppelin would later defend his own claims to originality in a handwritten note on 2 March 1908, refuting the claim that he had received precise details from Ganswindt with respect to the measurements required for the Zeppelin construction: 'Yes, indeed, I did receive a letter but it was years after I had submitted the draft for the airship, which at that point already included all the measurements the Zeppelin would have.'

5 Lieutenant Otto Parschau (1890–1916) received his licence on 4 July 1913 and was flying in two-seaters deployed in operations on both the Western and the Eastern Front when he was awarded the Pour le Mérite on 10 July 1916 after successfully shooting down eight aircraft. On 21 July 1916 he was mortally wounded, managed to land his plane behind German lines, but then died on the operating table. Additionally, he was one of two pilots – the other was Kurt Wintgens – who were chosen to fly the prototype of the Fokker Eindecker, a fighter plane fitted with a machine gun synchronised to fire safely through its propeller. He also trained with pioneering field aviation unit No. 62 with the later Aces Oswald Boelke and Max Immelmann.

6 The term 'Alter Adler' refers to the 817 German aviators and flight pioneers who passed the qualification exams to become licensed aircraft pilots in accordance with the Deutscher Luftfahrer-Verband (DLV) prior to the outbreak of the First World War.

7 This information is taken from Döring's *Wehrpass*. *TN:* This was a booklet issued

to all conscripts at the time of registration for the army and then replaced by the *Soldbuch*.

8 Döring obtained his Luftwaffe pilot licence on 25 January 1940, receiving the corresponding badge on 1 March 1940. Eleven days later he passed the more advanced pilot licence exams.

9 On 10 October 1940 Döring obtained the special licences I and II for blind-flying.

10 At the time, Operation 'Adlerangriff' – the German Luftwaffe attempt to force Great Britain's surrender by flying bombing attacks – was already considered to have failed.

11 All dates have been taken from Döring's Luftwaffe pilot licence or, respectively, from his *Wehrpass*.

Part I: With Kampfgeschwader 53 [21 June to 6 October 1941]

1 The 9th Staffel [Unit] des Kampfgeschwaders had been positioned in Radzyn since 18 June. Döring's first entry in his diary and his entry the following day with respect to the attack have previously been reprinted several times and in translation.

2 From 14 April 1943 to 15 March 1945 Fritz Pockrand was the commodore of Kampfgeschwader 53 (KG53) and ended the war in the position of first lieutenant, awarded with the German Cross in Gold on 3 October 1942.

3 The term General Government refers to the area which belonged to the Second Polish Republic until it was invaded then occupied by Nazi Germany from 1939 to 1945. It remained a separate administrative unit and was not annexed or integrated into German territory.

4 The thesis that a preventive war was to be waged against the Soviet Union as circulated by Goebbels and the Wehrmacht are unsubstantiated, and certainly this holds true for 1941. The actual massive movements of Soviet troops along the former eastern border of Poland, the western border of White Russia and the Ukraine were defensive in nature. The controversial issue which still remains is to what extent Stalin seriously considered the possibility of an attack against Germany in 1942.

5 The leaders of the Luftwaffe had gathered twenty-nine fighter squadrons, nine Stuka groups and one battle squadron. Additionally, some seventeen further fighter squadrons with 500 machines were ready to be deployed. This meant that the Luftwaffe mobilised a total of 2,598 machines including Jagdflieger, destroyers, reconnaissance aircraft etc., though on 20 June 1941 only 1,939 were equipped for operation. This number broadly corresponds to the machines in operation in 1940: what had proved insufficient to bring down Great Britain was meant to bring the Soviet Union, many times larger, to its knees by the year's end.

6 The erstwhile air base of Biels-Piliki, situated some 84 km north-west of Brest-Litovsk, was captured by the Soviet Union on 29 September 1939 and was used later on by the German Luftwaffe after repairs had been completed.

7 It might be worth comparing this entry with the memoirs of Herbert Wittman, a comrade of Döring, writing four decades later: 'On 20.5.1941 we all knew it: Germany declares war on Russia! For this kind of war we certainly were the least prepared. We set out to fight an enemy who knew no mercy. Even today, forty years later, I remember well how each one of us tried to come to terms with this fact, trying to do so on one's own or with the support of a comrade or unit. Was it a matter of blind obedience or was it that we had put all our faith in the military and political leadership? We were too young and didn't have the necessary insight, in the end, we were soldiers … that was it.' (Kiehl, 1983, p. 136.)

258

8   It remains unclear whether this Rudi Schwarze is the same as Rudolf Schwarze, first lieutenant of the Sch.Kp/Flugzeugführerschule C 13, who was awarded the German Cross in Gold on 23 November 1943.

9   According to Kurt Braatz, the attack had initially been scheduled for 03.15, but that was changed at the last minute to 03.45.

10 Today Sielce is a part of the city of Warsaw.

11 On the complex question of the role of fighter pilots as escort guards, which had already become acute in the Battle of Britain, Werner Baumbach stated: 'The cardinal question: can the German fighters [at the same time] protect their own bombers and shoot down the enemy fighters? had to be answered with a clear no.' The hunters, by their nature, tended to prefer the second option.

12 The He 111 was equipped with up to seven MG 15 or MG 81 (7.92 mm) whereby the MG in the fuselage would often be replaced by a 20 mm MG FF. It should, however, be noted that crews would quite often install various weaponry specific to their machine.

13 This observation unequivocally negates the thesis of a 'preventive war'.

14 The airfield referred to was likely Bialystok-Dolidy which, however, comprised several satellite sites (Bialystok-Zawady, Bialystok-Mazury, etc.).

15 According to the Heeresgruppe Mitte plan for the campaign the divisions attached to Panzergruppe 2 pushed forward south of Brest-Litovsk towards White Russia, while the divisions belonging to Panzergruppe 3 penetrated the forests on the southern tip of Suwalki, also in the direction of Minsk.

16 A week later Mölders became the highest-scoring fighter pilot in aerial history, having shot down five Soviet aircraft, bringing his tally to eighty-two, beating the legendary Manfred von Richthofen.

17 Extending from the south of White Russia and the north-western area of the Ukraine, with its 90,000 square kilometres this marshland constitutes one of the largest European wetlands, bounding the Pripyat river and surrounding Pinsk; it recalls the sad memory of the Chernobyl nuclear disaster.

18 According to different sources, 528 machines were destroyed on land on the first day alone, while 201 aircraft were shot down in air battle. After the battle of Bialystok-Minsk a further 245 machines were captured. Within the first twenty-four hours of Operation 'Barbarossa' 1,811 Soviet aircraft were destroyed while the losses on the German side purportedly only amounted to 78 machines and 113 flight personnel. Undoubtedly this constituted a major success for the Luftwaffe. As a first step, the prerequisite for a rapid German advance – air superiority – was fulfilled. However, this success only referred to available aircraft, not to the aircraft belonging to the airflight industry, which had been moved by the Russians into the hinterland, where they managed to vastly increase mass production of improved aircraft models in the second half of 1941. The short distance covered by the Ju 88 and He 111, or rather the lack of German long-range planes, began to become an issue. This was due to the decision not to go ahead with the construction of the long-range planes as requested by General Wever in 1935, significantly referred to as the 'Uralbomber'.

19 Conducted by the Wehrmacht's Army Group Centre under Field Marshal Fedor von Bock, large troop contingents led by the Red Army's General Dmitri Grigorjewitsch were liquidated in the battle of Byalistok. However, the destruction of the remaining Soviet troops was delayed until 9 July 1941 due to Stalin's order to capture as many German troops as possible. Some 320,000 Russian soldiers were taken prisoner. Based on Army Group Centre's successes, it was able to penetrate further

towards Moscow and cross the Dnieper. After the final stages of the battle were completed, several divisions which otherwise would have continued to be engaged with the Soviet troops were thus available to undertake further offensive strikes. On Stalin's orders General Pavlov was subsequently accused of failure to perform his duties and was given the death penalty.

20   On 29 June tank units 2 and 3 convened west of Minsk.

21   This reference is somewhat confusing, as Group III had already been transferred to Radzyn on 18 June, according to some sources. One therefore is left wondering whether 9th Staffel was transferred to this location only later on or whether the author is referring to the transfer of Group I to Rogoznica, which took place on 29 June.

22   The battle of Beresina (26–28 November 1812) was Napoleon's last Russian campaign. Only about 40,000 of the 70,000 French soldiers managed to cross over to the west bank.

23   *TN*: The Polikarpov I-16 was the world's first low-wing cantilever monoplane, a diminutive fighter, nicknamed the 'rat' or the 'fly'.

24   This is how the crew was composed: Lieutenant Hans Bauer, observer Max Zink, radio operator Walter Böhme and gunners Lance Corporal Josef Mondel and Manfred Wagner. For more information pertaining to these and other losses, see www.denkmalprojekt.org./Verlustliste.

25   Haster, captain of the 8th Staffel, was killed on 23 October 1941.

26   Along with Lance Corporal and senior pilot Rudolf Nitzsche, the following were part of the crew on that day: Corporal Meister (observer), Corporal Franz Leonards (gunner) and Corporal Richard Wissmüller (gunner).

27   The Stalin Line was the Red Army's line of fortifications constructed along the western border of the Soviet Union as of 1929. Consisting of several concrete bunkers and both heavy and light gun emplacements, stretching across the entire western border, from the Baltic Sea to the Black Sea, the line passed Witebsk, Mogilev, Gomel and Schitomir and along the Dnjestr river up to Odessa.

28   The crew consisted of the following: Sergeant Josef Niggemann (pilot), Private Erwin Zabel (observer), Corporal Paul Weck (radio operator) as well as gunner Corporal Heinz Haase.

29   Also spelt Schlobin or Shlobin. The text uses names used by Döring unless the modern names are very familiar.

30   Stuka is the abbreviation for Sturzkampfflugzeug (dive-bomber).

31   According to Russian custom, its air force's machines were identified by the first initial of the type of machine, e.g. I = Istrebitel (fighter plane). The Luftwaffe identified its aircraft by the first initials of their manufacturer, e.g. Ju = Junkers.

32   On 13 July the 21st Soviet Army, by then under the command of General Kusnezow, crossed the Dnieper on pontoon bridges and recaptured Rahachow an Zhlobin, then took a bridgehead on the Berezina river.

33   This was in preparation for Nazi Germany's offensive against Roslavl, Rogachev and Gomel.

34   III/KG53 began its transfer to Orsha on 4 August.

35   *TN*: Landsturmleute, different from Volkssturm, were military units considered of inferior quality, mostly veterans of the First World War.

36   Legion Condor was a unit composed of Wehrmacht military personnel and in the Spanish Civil War supported Franco's troops (the Nationalists).

37   It should be noted that generally the head of the Luftwaffe employed a 'needlepoint tactic' whereby single bombers or very small units attacked railway targets.

38 *TN:* A German idiom referring to the Prussian count Graf von Blücher, who fought valiantly in the Napoleonic Wars and was known for his forceful style.

39 Against the will of his generals, Hitler forced the battle of Kiev on his army as he was keen to obtain the fertile Ukraine and only thereafter did he turn his attention to Moscow (which was made impossible, at least in part, by Stalin's 'scorched earth' policy). Hence the attack on Moscow was delayed by two decisive months. Hitler had recognised as early as August that his eastern campaign could not be fully carried out by the end of the year. This enabled Stalin, in the knowledge that Japan did not plan an attack against the Soviet Union – something he had learned from the spy Richard Sorge – to withdraw the divisions from Siberia and deploy them against the German troops.

40 On 1 October 1941 Group III relocated to the Schatalowka-East airfield. Ernst Ebeling, decorated with the Knight's Cross in a later year, wrote the following on this subject: 'Unlike Orschka, here the barracks at Schatalowka-East, situated further towards the front line, were better equipped and we had proper beds. However, there was no running water, no heat and no toilets, which made it necessary to build latrines out in the open and heat remained a rare commodity in the ensuing months. Even once some iron stoves were delivered, it was difficult to avail oneself of heating material.' (Kiehl, 1983, p. 166.)

41 The Russians had a surprising ability to repair destroyed railway stations as well as the disrupted railway network. According to official Soviet sources, the average duration of suspended traffic following each attack lasted a mere five hours and forty-eight minutes.

Part II: With Kampfgeschwader 53 (continuation) [11 October to 16 December 1941]

1 On 7 October the 3rd and 4th Panzer Armies encircled Soviet troops.

2 In September 1941 the Soviet leadership set up partisan training schools in locations behind the front line. Towards the end some 2,000 groups of partisans were in force with a total of 90,000 men; however, they received little support from local citizens at that time. In August their strength dwindled to 12,000 men.

3 Kalinin, indeed, had been conquered two days prior, on 14 October.

4 The period when the rivers burst their banks brought great difficulty, with roads and paths sinking into the mud, which in turn reduced the supply to the army divisions drastically from 900 tons per day to 20 tons per day. With the German attacks coming to a halt, Soviet troops took advantage and used the time to improve their defensive systems and installations.

5 Commander Heinrich Eberbach of the 4th Tank Brigade.

6 A total loss of four crews posted to III Group has been recorded for 23 October.

7 The isolated bomb attacks already carried out in July and August remained largely unsuccessful, but had revealed confusion on the part of Germans at the Eastern Front.

8 Situated 80 kilometres north-east of Minsk and north of Borisow.

9 For those days the only reported crewmember missing is FW Franz Grave, who in fact was deployed to the 8th Staffel, to which the following sergeants were also posted : Theo Markgraf, Werner Groppler, Friedrich Schmid and Lance Corporal Josef Hanisch. Grave and Groppler were the only ones to return, the other three ended up in Russian captivity. Here is the report of the events:

   '[Grave and Goppler] crash-landed in a forest clearing. They rolled up their parachutes, hid them underneath heaps of collected leaves and then crawled into brushwood some 20 metres away – each one individually. The minute they were thus concealed Russians emerged from a wood path armed with their carbines and folded bayonets. Obviously, they had been searching for them. The radio operator reported that the Ivans were still some 15 metres away from the aerial gunner's hiding-place when the latter lost his nerve and started shooting with his 08 pistol. Two Russians sank to their knees and then fell to the ground while the rest of them randomly hailed bullets around the forest, still not knowing from where they had been attacked. Soon after that a truck arrived bringing reinforcement. Then this mate of ours starts banging away again. Now the Russians finally identify his hide-out. When they started shooting, he climbed out of his hiding place and raised his arms into the air. Livid by now, the Russians started beating and kicking him while piercing him with their bayonets. He let out some awful screams. They threw him onto the truck and drove away. Our operator kept still and waited for night to fall. Then he ran towards the west, in the direction of the main front line as from there reverberated the cannon thunder and the explosions – hard to miss. Cleverly, he made his way through unoccupied fields, swam across two ice-cold rivers and chanced upon German infantry units the following day. After being granted special leave of four weeks to return to his home in Schatalowka, he was deployed to the Kunzmann crew. He never returned from his first operation with them. Their machine caught fire during low flying, targeted by superbly skilled Russian flak and exploded while still in the air. One of his wingmen observed the entire incident.' (Kiehl, 1983, p. 169.)

10 Even prior to the actual Operation 'Taifun', KG53 attacked military encampments in the greater area of Moscow during the night of 1 October. Due to flak defence, attacks on the Russian capital could not be carried out during daytime.

11 Apart from the weather conditions that day, it is also worth noting that the Luftwaffe leadership seriously underestimated Moscow as a strategic target, particularly in terms of its central importance as a transport hub. Thus, of a total of seventy-six night sorties flown during 1941 targeting the Russian capital, fifty-nine were carried out by only three to ten fighter planes.

12 The QGH procedure is a ground-based landing procedure in bad weather conditions based on radio information to the pilot; it was used in the German Reich from 1920 until the end of the Second World War. It was followed in instances where visibility of the ground was only possible at very low altitude, but when the cloud base was still above 60 to 80 metres.

13 Cross-winds blow the aircraft off course. If the pilot directs his aircraft towards a specific point, keeping the aircraft directed to that point either by sight or by radio or radar, the path is not a straight line, but a narrowing curve/target curve called a *Hundekurve*, or homing curve.

14 It is not clear in the original whether it says 20 or 50.

15 Ansbach was the normal peacetime location of I Group, Kampfgeschwader 53 (Legion Condor 53). During their stay at Anbach, the staffing and structure of the group was changed.

16 Between 1936 and 1937 this location was turned into an airbase for the Luftwaffe. Throughout its existence it was the training site for various Luftwaffe departments, including different pilot education centres, navigation programmes and a military school (later on it was renamed as I. Gruppe der Kampfschulgeschwader 1). The airbase, which covered an extensive area, was bombed and levelled to the ground in 1945.

17 There, among other activities, test flights were carried out on aircraft fitted out with the bombsight Lofte D 7.
18 The III./KG53 was first transferred to France for the invasion of England before being moved to the Eastern Front in mid-August.
1 Döring was awarded the cup for exemplary achievement in air battle on 25 February 1942.

Part III: With Kampfgeschwader 55 [Legion Condor] [22 May to 5 August 1942]

1 First Lieutenant Hermann Josef Freiherr von dem Bongart (1897–1952) was appointed commander of III./KG55 on 2 September.
2 This was one of the crucial mistakes made during the Eastern operation. In principle, it would have been more important to carry out attacks in the far rear hinterland, which would have resulted in a serious delay to military production and transport.
3 Two members of the Moldenhauer crew lost their lives when the He 111 crash-landed at Woltschansk: Lance Corporal Leopold Horchy (radio operator) and Corporal Konrad Skraitzke (mechanic). Lieutenant Heinz Moldenhauer and his observer Lance Corporal Josef Schams were injured. Moldenhauer was killed on 5 January 1943 above Nowotscherkask.
4 Sergeant Karl Hiltner (pilot) and his observer, Sergeant Arthur Höcker, were taken prisoner. Sergeant Herbert Stenkel (radio operator) was injured. Mechanic Corporal Johann Febish and his gunner Sergeant Albert Schwarz both lost their lives.
5 The German summer offensive under the name 'Fall Blau' commenced on 28 June. The 4th Panzer Army together with the 2nd Army started its main drive along the front line towards Voronezh, a stretch measuring some 100 kilometres wide, situated between Orel and Kupyansk. The aim was to reach the Don. The 40th Russian Army withdrew from practically everywhere as the Soviet army command had expected the German summer offensive to be launched near Moscow, where it had stationed some 50 per cent of its troops. After the German army thrust forward some 70 kilometres, it began crossing the Oskol section on 1 July and reached the Don, between Voronezh and Korotojak, by 5 July. The spearhead of the 4th Panzer Army advanced to Voronezh and became embroiled in capturing the city, though units engaged in this success should have been deployed further south where they were needed.
6 Marshal Semyon Timoshenko (1895–1970) was the People's Commissar of Defence, Chairman of the Soviet Forces High Command, a role taken over by Stalin in 1941.
7 This probably refers to 3. Jagdgeschwader 'Udet'.
8 Voronezh was captured on 6 July.
9 Soldiers of the 3rd Romanian and the 8th Italian Army, as well as the 2nd Hungarian Army were engaged on the German side in Army Group B.
10 Probably a Polikarpov I-15.
11 Diary No. 7 III of Kampfgeschwader 55, kept by First Lieutenant Werner Schmidt, has the following entry for 24.7.42: 355th Operation. Mission to attack Bataisk. Number of machines:16 He 111H-6. Start time: 15.58–16.00. Landing: 17.50–18.00. Time of attack: 17.04–17.10. Altitude of attack: 4,300 metres. Result: All bombs hit the city boundaries, stretching from the west to its eastern boundary. About twelve smaller to larger fires erupted, several explosions.
12 The diarist notes the following: 356th Operation: Mission to attack Koissug. Num-

ber of machines: 17 He 111H-6. Start: 06.30–06.47. Landing: 08.20–08.51. Time of attack: 07.25–07.48. Altitude of attack: 3,500–3,600 metres. Result: All bombs recorded perfect hits in the west, east and in the middle of the target area. Several explosions, many fires and extensive demolition.

13   Again from the the the diary of KG55: 357th Operation. Mission: To attack the city of Asov. Number of machines: 17 He 111H-6. Start time: 17.00–19.10 [sic.]. Landing: 18.40–18.57. Duration of attack: 17.40–17.55. Altitude of attack: 3,500–3,700 metres. Result: 17 aircraft attacked the designated target. Majority of bombs dropped in the city centre. 4–5 explosions. 1 large and 1 small fire. Smaller fires in the eastern and western sector. At the southern edge of the city 3 light flak batteries wiped out – all direct hits.

14   From the same diary: 358th Operation. Mission: To attack the railway station and the city of Tichorezk/Tichoreck: Number of machines: 7 He 111H-6. Start: 17.49–23.40. Landing: 20.45–02.00. Duration of attack: 19.33–00.57. Altitude of attack: 4,500–5,200 metres. Result: 27 aircraft attacked the target as per order. 1 major explosion followed by a bright fire raging in the station. Tracks in the southern section hit. 8 larger and smaller fires in the entire area targeted.

15   In the diary this event is followed by a day of rest. It notes on 27.7.42: Rest for the entire group. It is the first day of rest after recapturing the peninsula Kerch and is greeted by all the soldiers with delight, as the many operations have taken a both physical and emotional toll on both the ground- and air crews.

16   Excerpt from the diary dated 28.7.42: 359th Operation. Mission: Attack on train station and city of Tichorezk. Number of machines: 29 He H111H-6. Start time: 17.47–23.25. Landing: 20.23–01.55. Duration of attack: 19.31–00.45. Altitude of attack: 3,500–5,100 metres. Result: 28 aircraft drop bombs onto station and city. 4 large and several smaller fires are observed. 1 aircraft at 13.32 and at an altitude of 3,500 metres drops bombs on Retowskij Pl 9715 due to failure of pumping system. Result: No observation possible.

17   The following are excerpts from the diary covering these days:

28.7.42
360th Operation. Mission: To attack ships on the Volga, via Astrakhan heading to Stalingrad. Number of machines: 15 He H111H-6. Start: 17.50–19.04. Landing: 22.55–00.38. Duration of attack: 20.45–22.15. Altitude of attack: 10–400 metres. Result: 14 aircraft attacked the targets as per order. 1 freight vessel of approx. 1,500 GRT sunk by 2 direct hits..2 barges of approx. 500–800 GRT seriously damaged (Pl 78791). 1 freight vessel of approx. 1,200 GRT listed, bombs penetrated ship's hull. 1 freight vessel also listed, hit suffered close to the stern. One direct hit by a 250-kg bomb into freight vessel of 1,000 GRT and bomb holes 5 metres away from the hull. Unidentified results. A 500-kg bomb hit a freight vessel of 1,500 GRT 10 metres shy of the ship's hull. Results not observed. 2 hauling ships set alight by incendiaries, one of them listed. 1 freight vessel loaded with wooden barrels attacked by MGs. Structures caught fire. 4 bombs dropped close to a barge towing 3 boats. Results not observed. 500-kg and 250-kg bombs dropped in between 2 vessels (800 GRT) about 15 metres apart from each other, close to their stern. Results not recorded. 2 barges (500 GRT) hit by bombs, 3 metres shy of the hull, damage was likely caused. 500-kg bomb hit 1 freight vessel of 1,000 GRT. On the right side of the stern. Vessel stopped – no further results observed. 2 x 250 kg bombs hit 1 freight vessel of 1,000 GRT, 10 metres shy of the hull , results not observed. 1 aircraft loaded with bombs landed at airbase having suffered engine damage.

29.7.42

361st Operation. Mission: Armoured reconnaissance in the Rytschov area–
Alimovo–Popovo–Rubeshnj west of Kalac-na-Donu. Number of machines: 13 He
111 H-6. Start: 10.50–11.20. Landing: 13.55–14.20. Duration of attack: 12.35–12.55.
Altitude of attack: 3,200–3,500 metres. Result: Direct hits achieved by 13 aircraft
attacking large truck convoys and transport columns massed at the western
bridgehead near Kalach. A total of 32 trucks destroyed or damaged.

362nd Operation. Mission: to attack vessels along the Volga river by travelling from Astrakhan to Stalingrad. Number of machines: 13 He 111H-6. Start:
20.00–22.10. Landing: 01.25–02.20. Duration of attack: 22.32–00.30. Altitude of
attack: 30–300 metres. Result: 9 aircraft attacked main target. 1 tankship of some
1,500 GRT. 2 x 250-kg bombs dropped close to the hull. Observation of fires
erupting. One passenger ship with high structures of approx. 1,500 GRT hit by 3
bombs of 250 kg. Ship listed, stern lowering then sinking observed. Freight ship
of 1,500–2,000 GRT suffered midship direct hit by 250-kg bomb, immediately
followed by explosion and fire erupting, columns of smoke and flames rising into
the air, followed by further explosions. Ship most certainly destroyed. Freight
ship of 1,500 GRT suffered hit at bow, results not recorded. Freight ship of some
1,500 GRT hit midship and immediately destroyed. Barge of 600 GRT hit in
hull by 500-kg bomb. Results not recorded. Bombs penetrated hull of barge of
some 500–700 GRT. Results not recorded. 4 freight ships of 500 GRT damaged
by direct bomb hit punching holes into the hull. 3 aircraft headed to secondary
targets. Bombs dropped on Karagali station buildings and trains under steam.
One building ablaze, one locomotive destroyed by 500-kg bomb. One locomotive damaged by bombs. Some 10–15 wagons demolished. A larger explosion of
a train recorded, probably with ammunition cargo. Tracks running north of the
Tschaptschatschi railway station interrupted by 5 bomb hits. Flight of 1 aircraft
suspended due to crew falling ill.

30.7.42

363rd Operation. Mission: To attack ships travelling on the Volga from Astrakhan
to Stalingrad. Secondary target: Railway Astrakhan–Werch, Poskintschak. Number
of machines: 10 He 111H-6. Start: 20.00–21.40. Landing: 01.07–03.00. Duration
of attack: 22.10–01.00. Altitude of attack: 20–50 metres. Result: 7 aircraft targeted
ships on the Volga. 1 tanker of 800–1,000 GRT suffered direct hit, jets of flame and
clouds of black smoke rising, sunk later on. 1 barge of 600 GRT sunk after hit by
bomb. 1 barge of 500 GRT on its side after hit by bombs. 1 barge of 800 GRT on
its side after hit by bombs. 1 ship including superstructures of approx. 1,000–1,500
GRT sank after 3 bomb attacks hitting the hull. 1 freight ship of 1,200–1,500 GRT
directly hit by 2 bombs, the ship is burning with black smoke columns developing.
1 freight ship of some 1,000 GRT hit in the hull, no results recorded. 3 barges of
some 800 GRT damaged in the hull. 2 aircraft attacked the Karagali railway station.
5 trains under steam attacked. Bombs dropped onto trains and tracks. 1 barracks
set on fire. 1 aircraft jettisons bomb onto Poskintschak. After drop, fires erupt.

31.7.42

364th Operation. Mission: To attack ships heading from Astrakhan to Stalingrad.
Secondary target: Train line Werch to Poskintschak. Number of machines: 10 He
111H-6. Start: 20.40–22.00. Landing: 01.20–04.10. Duration of attack: 23.30–01.00.
Altitude of attack: 10–60 metres. Result: 5 aircraft attack ships in the target area.

1 freight ship of 800 GRT sunk as a result of direct hit. Fires erupt with dark smoke. 1 barge of 500 GRT hit by incendiary – ablaze. 2 freight ships damaged. 1 barge demolished by fire. 2 aircraft attack secondary target. Bombs ejected onto Werbljuschja train station and on tracks leading into the station. 1 aircraft returned to base due to bad weather, no bombs ejected. 2 aircraft did not return from enemy operation.

18   On 17 November 1941 Stalin had issued the so-called 'torchmen order', essentially ordering his units to destroy and set fire to all villages, towns and other settlements where German troops had taken up quarters in a depth of 40 to 60 kilometres behind the main line of combat – the 'scorched earth' tactic.

Bibliography

Aders, Gebhard, and Werner Held, *Jagdgeschwader 51: 'Mölders'* (Stuttgart, 1985).

Baumbach, Werner, *Zu spät* (Buenos Aires, 1949).

Bekker, Cajus, *Angriffshöhe 4000: Ein Kriegstagebuch der Luftwaffe* (Stuttgart, 1964).

von Below, Nicolaus, *Als Hitlers Adjutant 1937–1945* (Mainz, 1980).

Braatz, Kurt, *Werner Mölders: Die Biographie* (Moosburg, 2008).

Bronnenkant, Lance J., *The Blue Max Airmen Volume 3: German Airmen Awarded the Pour le Mérite* (Reno, CA, 2013).

Cescotti, Roderich, *Langstreckenflug: Erinnerungen 1919-2012*, ed. Kurt Braatz (Moosburg, 2012).

de Zeng, Henry, *Bomber Units of the Luftwaffe, Volume 1: 1933–1945* (Hinckley, 2007).

de Zeng IV, Henry L., *Luftwaffe Airfields 1935-45* (online, 2020).

Deumling, Klaus, *41 Sekunden bis zum Einschlag: Als Bomberpilot im Kampfgeschwader 100 Wiking mit der geheimen Fernlenkbombe Fritz X* (2008).

Dietrich, Wolfgang, *Kampfgeschwader 55 'Greif': Eine Chronik aus Dokumenten und Berichten 1937–1945* (Stuttgart, 1975).

'Fotos mit Geschichte: Angriffsziel "Panzerwerk Kramatorskaja", KG 55 – 1941', *Luftwaffe im Fokus*, 23 (2014).

Galland, Adolf, *Die Ersten und die Letzten* (Darmstadt, 1953).

Gartmann, Heinz, *Träumer, Forscher Konstrukteure: Das Abenteuer der Weltraumfahrt* (Düsseldorf, 1955).

Griehl, Manfred, *Heinkel He 111, Kampfflugzeug – Torpedobomber – Transporter* (Stuttgart, 1997).

Guderian, Heinz, *Erinnerungen eines Soldaten* (Stuttgart, 1951).

Häberlen, Klaus, *Erzählungen eines Lebens in drei Epochen* (Ulm, 1998).

Haupt, Werner, *Sturm auf Moskau: Der Angriff, Die Schlacht, Der Rückschlag, 1941* (Friedberg, 1986).

Held, Werner, *Die deutschen Jagdgeschwader im Russlandfeldzug* (Friedberg, 1986).

Held, Werner, and Holger Neuroth, *Die deutsche Nachtjagd* (Stuttgart, 1982).

Herrmann, Hajo, *Bewegtes Leben: Kampf- und Jagdflieger 1935–1945* (Stuttgart, 1984).

Hesse, Erich, *Der sowjetrussische Partisanenkrieg 1941 bis 1944 im Spiegel deutscher Kampfanweisungen und Befehle* (Göttingen, 1993).

Heuer, G., 'Arnold Döring', *Der Landser-Grossband*, 1057 (April 2001), pp. 61–5.

Kellerhoff, Sven Felix, 'Wer Hitlers Präventativkrieg gegen Stalin erfand', *Welt*, 22 June 2016.

Kesselring, Albert, *Soldat bis zum letzten Tag* (Berlin, 1953).

Kiehl, Heinz, *Kampfgeschwader Legion Condor 53 – Eine Chronik: Berichte, Erlebnisse, Dokumente 1936–1945* (Stuttgart, 1983).

Luther, Craig W.H., *The First Day on the Eastern Front: Germany Invades the Soviet Union, June 22 1941* (Guildford, 2019).

Mackay, Ron, *Heinkel He 111* (Ramsbury, 2003).

Mackay, Ron, *Junkers Ju 88* (Ramsbury, 2001).

Metcalf, William A., *Junkers Ju 88, Volume 1: From Schnellbomber to Multi-Mission* (Manchester, 2013).

Metcalf, William A., *Junkers Ju 88, Volume 2: The Bomber at War* (Manchester, 2014).

Musial, Bogdan, *Sowjetische Partisanen 1941–1944* (Schoeningh, 2009).

Nowarra, Heinz J., *Die Ju 88 und ihre Folgemuster* (Stuttgart, 1978).

Nowarra, Heinz J., *Henkel He 111: A Documentary History* (London, 1980).

Obermaier, Ernst, *Die Ritterkreuzträger der Luftwaffe, Band 1: Jagdflieger* (Mainz, 1989).

Obermaier, Ernst, and Werner Held, *Jagdflieger Oberst Werner Mölders* (Stuttgart, 1982).

Philippi, Alfred, and Ferdinand Heim, *Der Feldzug gegen Sowjetrussland* (Stuttgart, 1962).

Prien, Jochen, et al., *Die Jagdfliegerverbände der Deutschen Luftwaffe 1945 bis 1945* (Eutin, 2000).

Stahl, P.W., *Kampfflieger zwischen Eismeer und Sahara in meinem Fall Ju 88* (Stuttgart, 1974).

von Tippelskirch, Kurt, *Geschichte des Zweiten Weltkriegs* (Bonn, 1951).

Unmack, Hans, *Fernkampfflieger: Als Kommandant im Kampfgeschwader Greif mit der Heinkel 111* (Aachen, 2003).

Weal, John, *He 111 Kampfgeschwader on the Russian Front* (Hinckley, 2013).

Weeks, Albert L., *Stalin's Other War: Soviet Grand Strategy, 1939–1941* (Lanham, MD, 2002).

Wetzig, Sonia, *Die Stalin-Linie 1941: Bollwerk aus Beton und Stahl* (Eggolsheim, 2005).